Lecture Notes of the Institute for Computer Sciences, Social Informatics and Telecommunications Engineering 555

The LNICST series publishes ICST's conferences, symposia and workshops.

LNICST reports state-of-the-art results in areas related to the scope of the Institute. The type of material published includes

- Proceedings (published in time for the respective event)
- Other edited monographs (such as project reports or invited volumes)

LNICST topics span the following areas:

- General Computer Science
- E-Economy
- E-Medicine
- Knowledge Management
- Multimedia
- Operations, Management and Policy
- Social Informatics
- Systems

Zhiyuan Tan · Yulei Wu · Min Xu
Editors

Big Data Technologies and Applications

13th EAI International Conference, BDTA 2023
Edinburgh, UK, August 23–24, 2023
Proceedings

 Springer

Editors
Zhiyuan Tan (iD)
Edinburgh Napier University
Edinburgh, UK

Yulei Wu (iD)
University of Bristol
Bristol, UK

Min Xu (iD)
University of Technology Sydney
Sydney, NSW, Australia

ISSN 1867-8211 ISSN 1867-822X (electronic)
Lecture Notes of the Institute for Computer Sciences, Social Informatics
and Telecommunications Engineering
ISBN 978-3-031-52264-2 ISBN 978-3-031-52265-9 (eBook)
https://doi.org/10.1007/978-3-031-52265-9

This Springer imprint is published by the registered company Springer Nature Switzerland AG
The registered company address is: Gewerbestrasse 11, 6330 Cham, Switzerland

Paper in this product is recyclable.

Preface

We are thrilled to present the proceedings of the thirteenth edition of the European Alliance for Innovation (EAI) International Conference on Big Data Technologies and Applications (BDTA 2023). This conference served as a premier platform for showcasing new advances and research findings in the field of big data technologies and applications. The conference brought together eminent researchers and scientists from around the globe who are working in this field of interest.

The BDTA 2023 technical program had 12 papers, including 9 Regular and 3 Short papers presented in oral sessions at the main conference track, PhD Track, and technical workshops. The conference's overarching theme revolved around transforming Big Data into valuable knowledge and creating innovative, intelligent systems. The PhD Track was designed to give PhD students the opportunity to present their ongoing work and interact with experienced senior researchers for constructive feedback and advice. The workshop, SECSOC 2023, aimed to build a secure smart society in the next-generation networking paradigm and solicited novel schemes to enhance the reliability, robustness, and privacy of the smart society built upon Cyber-Physical Systems (CPS). The technical program also featured two keynote speeches from Jungong Han from the University of Sheffield, UK and Huiyu Zhou from the University of Leicester, UK.

The success of the conference was made possible through the coordination with the steering chair, Imrich Chlamtac, and the general co-chair, Huiyu Zhou, whose constant support and guidance we sincerely appreciate. We also had the pleasure of working with an excellent organizing committee team who worked hard to organize and support the conference. The Technical Program Committee, led by our TPC Co-Chairs, Yulei Zhou, Min Xu, Wenwu Wang, and Ashkan Sami, completed the peer-review process of technical papers to create a high-quality technical program. We are grateful to Conference Managers Kristina Havlickova and Sara Csicsayova for their support and to all the authors who submitted their papers to the BDTA 2023 conference and the joint workshop.

We firmly believe that the BDTA conference offers a valuable platform for researchers, developers, and practitioners to discuss various science and technology aspects that are pertinent to big data technologies and applications. Moreover, we anticipate that future BDTA conferences will be just as successful and thought-provoking as evidenced by the contributions presented in this volume.

Zhiyuan Tan
Yulei Wu
Min Xu

Organization

Steering Committee

Imrich Chlamtac   University of Trento, Italy

Organizing Committee

General Chair

Zhiyuan Tan   Edinburgh Napier University, UK

General Co-chair

Huiyu Zhou   University of Leicester, UK

TPC Chair and Co-chairs

Min Xu   University of Technology Sydney, Australia
Yulei Wu   University of Bristol, UK
Wenwu Wang   University of Surrey, UK
Ashkan Sami   Edinburgh Napier University, UK

Sponsorship and Exhibit Chair

Nour Moustafa   University of New South Wales (UNSW)
                                                Canberra, Australia

Local Chair

Kehinde Babaagba   Edinburgh Napier University, UK

Workshops Chair

Xingjie Wei   University of Leeds, UK

Publicity and Social Media Chair

Yanchao Yu   Edinburgh Napier University, UK

Publications Chair

Amin Beheshti   Macquarie University, Australia

Web Chair

Yanfei Zhu   Edinburgh Napier University, UK

Technical Program Committee

Abd El-Aziz Ahmed	Cairo University, Egypt
Abdulwahab Qureshi	Saudi Electronic University, Kingdom of Saudi Arabia
Adrian Byrne	University College Dublin, Ireland
Aniello Castinglione	University of Salerno, Italy
Bin Liang	University of Technology Sydney, Australia
Bujar Raufi	Hibernia College, Ireland
Daniel Gibert	University College Dublin, Ireland
Di Wu	Norwegian University of Science and Technology, Norway
Fangwei Wang	Hebei Normal University, China
Geng Yang	Zhejiang University, China
Hamidreza Rabiei-Dastjerdi	University College Dublin, Ireland
Heye Zhang	Sun Yat-sen University, China
Hongtao Xing	Department of Environment and Science, Queensland, Australia
Hongyu Yang	Civil Aviation University of China, China
Ihsan Ullah	University of Galway, Ireland
Jabar Yousif	Sohar University, Oman
Jean-Pierre Corriveau	Carleton University, Canada
Jianhua Li	Deakin University, Australia
Junbin Gao	University of Sydney, Australia
Kehua Guo	Central South University, China
Kuo-Hui Yeh	National Dong Hwa University, Taiwan
Liang Zhao	Shenyang Aerospace University, China
Liangfu Lu	Tianjin University, China
Lihong Zheng	Charles Sturt University, Australia

Contents

SECSOC Workshop

Main Track – Regular Papers

CTL-I: Infrared Few-Shot Learning via Omnidirectional Compatible Class-Incremental

Biwen Yang[1], Ruiheng Zhang[1(✉)], Yumeng Liu[2], Guanyu Liu[1], Zhe Cao[1], Zhidong Yang[1], Heng Yu[1], and Lixin Xu[1]

[1] Beijing Institute of Technology, No.5 Yard, Zhong Guan Cun South Street Haidian District, Beijing, China
`ruiheng.zhang@bit.edu.cn`
[2] Beijing Key Laboratory of Human-Computer Interaction, Institute of Software, Chinese Academy of Sciences, Beijing, China
`yumeng@iscas.ac.cn`

Abstract. Accommodating infrared novel class in deep learning models without sacrificing prior knowledge of base class is a challenging task , especially when the available data for the novel class is limited. Existing infrared few-shot learning methods mainly focus on measuring similarity between novel and base embedding spaces or transferring novel class features to base class feature spaces. To address this issue, we propose Infrared (omnidirectional) Compatibility Training Learning (CTL-I). We suggest building a virtual infrared prototype in the basic model to preserve feature space for potential new classes in advance. We use a method of coupling virtual and real data to gradually update these virtual prototypes as predictions for potential new categories, resulting in a more powerful classifier that can effectively adapt to new categories while retaining knowledge about general infrared features learned from the base class. Our empirical results demonstrate that our approach outperforms existing few-shot incremental learning methods on various benchmark datasets, even with extremely limited instances per class. Our work offers a promising direction for addressing the challenges of few-shot incremental learning in infrared image.

Keywords: Infrared · Few-shot Learning · Class-incremental Learning

1 Introduction

In recent years, significant breakthroughs have been made using various neural network architectures [1]. These achievements hinge on extensive datasets with well-balanced class distribution. However, the challenge emerges when dealing with infrared image data, which often arrives as a continuous stream [2], introducing novel classes [3] in open-world scenarios, such as newly discovered frog species in rainforests. This necessitates flexible methods for incorporating novel

Z. Tan et al. (Eds.): BDTA 2023, LNICST 555, pp. 3–17, 2024.
https://doi.org/10.1007/978-3-031-52265-9_1

class knowledge, termed Class-Incremental Learning (CIL). Yet, training models with new class data triggers catastrophic forgetting [4], where accuracy on old classes sharply declines post-update. CIL mitigates this, but designing compatible CIL algorithms remains challenging due to limited access to high-quality infrared data [11,13].

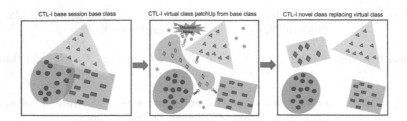

Fig. 1. The left figure represents the occupancy of base class data in the feature space. The middle represents the association between virtual class instances generated through collaboration between base class instances and random Gaussian noise, which exceeds the range of the base class due to the latter. The right shows that the new class data inherits a portion of the feature space of the virtual class and the resolution ability from the base class.

For the practical application of CIL, amassing sufficient new class instances is often unrealistic, particularly in scenarios like infrared scenes where factors like noise and ambient light limit data collection. This gives rise to incremental learning with few shots (FSCIL), where models learn new classes with limited instances, risking overfitting to new classes and forgetting old ones. To address overfitting, algorithms [5,14] have been proposed for less-shot learning.

In FSCIL, models learning new class data must retain distinctiveness for base classes, akin to retaining knowledge of solid geometry after learning calculus. This is termed backward compatibility [6]. The CIL method attempts to increase backward compatibility by reducing the distinguishability of old classes, while the FSCIL method achieves this by abandoning the update of old classifiers and adding novel class classifiers.

Currently, the main focus of research is on backward compatibility patterns, leaving the task of learning novel classes to subsequent models. Some work has shown that if the previous model is not well learned, the latter model will also degrade on this basis. This is indeed a potential issue to encounter, but it is not the focus of the current issue discussion. The fundamental problem with backward compatibility mode is that in the incremental stage, the data participating in learning is all novel classes, competing with the old class data, thus completely occupying the feature space of the old class data. In addition, there is a forward compatible method [15] that, although it solves the problem of accepting novel classes, lacks protection for the base class. In contrast, a better solution is to consider future additions and retention of growth space in the base class model. Therefore, another type of compatibility, omnidirectional compatibility, is more suitable for FSCIL, which is both backward and forward compatible.

Fig. 2. This figure shows the visualization of the results, which are categorized into base class instances, virtual instances of base class patchUp and novel class instances. The classification ability on the base class instance can be transferred to the virtual instance with random Gaussian noise through the patchUp operation, and ultimately successfully transferred to the novel class instance.

Building upon Zhou's framework [15], we introduce Infrared (Omnidirectional) Compatibility Training Learning (CTL-I) for Infrared FSCIL. CTL-I establishes a model structure that ensures compatibility between new and existing classes. To facilitate seamless model updates, we pre-construct virtual prototypes, aligning with the count of newly introduced categories in the feature space. These virtual prototypes are derived from existing class prototypes. Through optimization, we not only condense the space occupied by same-class data, thus reserving more room for updated novel classes as depicted in Fig. 1, but also generate virtual instances corresponding to the virtual prototypes using the patchUp technique [7]. During the foundational training, the feature space of the virtual prototype is solely populated by virtual instances. Leveraging these instances, the model progressively learns classifiers effective for both new and base classes.

The main contributions of our CTL-I method can be concluded as follows:

1) We propose a new virtual prototype generation method that is compatible with base class and new class features in incremental learning models for few shot infrared classes, improving the classification accuracy of new classes and base classes.
2) We design a new Loss function, which can infer virtual prototype and improve the performance of incremental learning of infrared class with few lenses.
3) Our method has wide adaptability and excellent performance for various types of infrared images.

The rest of this article is organized as follows. The second section briefly introduces the few shot learning and class incremental learning in infrared images. In the third section, we provide a detailed description of the proposed CTL-I method. The fourth section introduces the comprehensive experiments on our infrared dataset. Finally, the fifth section provides the conclusion of this article.

2   Related Work

In this section, we first describe the specific methods of the few shot learning and class incremental learning in infrared images.

2.1   Few Shot Learning

Few-shot learning algorithms can be broadly categorized into three groups: data augmentation-based methods, fine-tuning-based methods, and meta-learning-based methods. Data augmentation-based approaches aim to generate additional data for novel classes, while fine-tuning-based methods focus on achieving rapid backward compatibility. On the other hand, meta-learning-based algorithms leverage extensive data to pre-train the backbone and employ suitable metrics to compute the distance between support and query sets [8]. These methods are collectively referred to as backward-compatible few-shot learning strategies.

Prototypical Network: The sample sizes of the base class and the novel class may differ, but they can be transformed into functional expressions, ensuring that each sample type has an equal number of specific metrics. ProtoNet [16] employs cross-entropy loss to train on base class data and subsequently adapts the same network for novel class data. This involves constructing embeddings using distinct depth feature sets $\phi(\cdot)$, resulting in the computation of average prototypes for each class. Notably, both novel and base classes adhere to the same $\phi(\cdot)$ parameters, thereby maintaining uniformity in parameter quantity and formulation.

$$p_i = \frac{1}{K} \sum_{j=1}^{|\mathcal{D}^b|} \mathbb{I}\left(y_j = i\right) \phi\left(\mathbf{x}_j\right) \tag{1}$$

$\mathbb{I}(\cdot)$ is the indicator function. The average embedding represents a classifier that stores the differences in the features of each class, i.e. $\mathcal{W}_i = \mathcal{P}_i$, which does not mean that the average embedding truly distinguishes between new and old classes, as well as different novel classes. The average embedding layer is nearly frozen throughout the entire novel class learning stage in order to maintain backward compatibility between new and old models. Therefore, it can be seen that the updated part is actually the backbone part, and the classifier is not significantly updated. This is a relatively conservative learning mode that prioritizes sacrificing the ability to learn novel classes. Knowledge Distillation and Prototypical Network approach backward compatibility from distinct angles. The Prototypical Network preserves the distinctiveness of old classes by aligning the new model with the established one, whereas Knowledge Distillation partially freezes the embedding layer to hinder excessive updates and replacements to the embedding layer associated with old classes. Both methodologies approach class incremental learning through the lens of backward compatibility. To elaborate further, their primary objective is to minimize alterations to the old class model while introducing new classes, ensuring stability and continuity throughout the update process.

However, these approaches did not account for the inherent trade-off between ensuring backward compatibility and preserving adaptability for new classes. This trade-off is evident when considering both base class accuracy and novel class accuracy.

Forward compatibility presents a fresh perspective to address this challenge. It involves preparing the model during the current training session to accommodate potential future updates.

2.2 Class Incremental Learning in Infrared Images

This novel perspective aims to address the challenge of learning from novel classes without forgetting old ones [9] within the context of infrared images. The currently available Class-Incremental Learning (CIL) algorithms can be broadly categorized into two groups. The first group focuses on assessing crucial parameters and safeguarding them against adverse updates [10,11]. The second group leverages techniques like knowledge distillation or meta-learning, blending novel and base class data to mitigate forgetting [12,13]. Notably, CEC [14] employs additional graph models to propagate contextual information among classifiers for adaptation. In the realm of CIL, compatibility learning was introduced [9] to enhance the model's backward compatibility, while FACT [15] represents the pioneering effort to address the forward compatibility challenge in the CIL model.

FACT: Inspired by the promise of forward compatibility, FACT endeavors to integrate forward compatibility techniques into the framework of Few-Shot Class-Incremental Learning (FSCIL) [15]. In essence, FACT adopts a dual-classifier approach involving two pre-constructed classifiers with identical structures but distinct update sequences. This configuration is reminiscent of the prototype method. During the foundational learning phase, the classifier's posterior probability is optimized to yield a bimodal distribution. Subsequently, a virtual prototype is formulated by amalgamating prototypes from the base class. The virtual prototype is then augmented by generating virtual data through instance mixing with base class data, facilitating virtual prototype updates. This augmented virtual prototype reserves a designated feature space to accommodate potential new classes.

$$\mathcal{L}_v(\mathbf{x}, y) = \underbrace{\ell\left(f_v(\mathbf{x}), y\right)}_{\mathcal{L}_1} + \gamma \underbrace{\ell\left(\text{Mask}\left(f_v(\mathbf{x}), y\right), \hat{y}\right)}_{\mathcal{L}_2} \qquad (2)$$

$$\text{Mask}\left(f_v(\mathbf{x}), y\right) = f_v(\mathbf{x}) \otimes \left(\mathbf{1} - \text{OneHot}(y)\right),$$

Forward compatibility methods operate under the premise that the base class shares a certain level of resemblance with the novel class, exhibiting either explicit or implicit similarities in their features. An analogy can be drawn from the similarity in deep features between kittens and puppies. When examined through the lens of feature space theory, the virtual prototype's feature representation for the base class is an approximation. Similarly, the features of the novel class must bear resemblance to the virtual prototype to facilitate a seamless transition from the old model trained on the base class to the updated new model enriched with novel class data. This ensures the retention of base class knowledge while facilitating the acquisition of novel class knowledge.

However, it's worth noting that forward compatibility has its limitations. If the disparity between the features of the novel class and the base class is substantial, it can result in a pronounced difference between the novel class and the virtual prototype. This disparity can subsequently constrain the learning potential of the novel class to some extent.

3   Proposed Method

3.1   Preliminary

Few shot incremental learning has two stages: base training session and incremental training session.

Base Training Session: In first stage, a model with random parameter initialization accepts a session 0 training set $D_{train}^{session=0} = \{(x_i, y_i)\}_{i=1}^{N_0, class_0}$ with sufficient base class instances firstly, and then evaluates it using the base class data testing set $D_{test}^{session=0} = \{(x_j, y_j)\}_{j=1}^{M_0, class_0}$. $D^{session=0}$ is called the base session. $x_i \in R^D$ is one of training data in class $y_i \in Y_0$. Y_0, which is the label set of session 0. Although x_i has a large amount of data, in order to maintain the compatibility of the model before and after the training session, it is necessary to maintain the same quantity of instances for each class. $x_j \in R^D$ is a testing instance of class $y_j \in Y_0$. Each type of test set and training set instance is divided by 7/3.The algorithm fits a model $f(x)$ to minimize the empirical risk over testing set.

$$\sum_{(\mathbf{x}_i, y_i) \in \mathcal{D}_{train}^{session=0}} \ell\left(f\left(\mathbf{x}_j\right), y_j\right) \tag{3}$$

where $\ell(\cdot, \cdot)$ represents the difference between the prediction and the ground-truth label, and the cross entropy loss function is used here. The output layer of the model is a Linear classifier and an embedding weight matrix: $f(x) = W^T \phi(x)$, where $\phi(\cdot) : R^D \longrightarrow R^d$. Both $\phi(x)$ and W^T are learnable parameters.

Incremental Session: In practical situations, novel classes usually surface incrementally with a limited number of instances. These instances are presented as a sequence of datasets $D^1, \cdots, D^B$, following a specific order. The practical approach of arranging the training categories' order is viable. We posit that access to a given dataset D^b is only possible during the training session corresponding to b. Alternatively, if the available number of new class categories falls short of the specified count, we can supplement the training data for that session with old class data. This mimics the chronological emergence of data and supports the intended order.

Each dataset contains a set of instances represented as $D^b = (x_i, y_i)_{i=1}^{NK}$, where $y_i \in Y_b$ belongs to the label space of the corresponding session b. The label spaces of different tasks are linearly independent, which means that if $b \neq b', Y_b \cap Y_{b'} = \emptyset$.

In order to handle limited instances, the dataset is structured in N-way K-shot format to avoid imbalanced sample sizes between new classes. Each dataset has N classes, and each class has K instances, which is also a commonly used small sample learning training setting.When using a new dataset, the model must effectively learn the new class while preserving its performance on the old class. The optimization goal of the model during the training process is to minimize the empirical risk of all training datasets.

$$\sum_{(\mathbf{x}_j, y_j) \in \mathcal{D}_t^0 \cup \cdots \mathcal{D}_t^b} \ell\left(f\left(\mathbf{x}_j\right), y_j\right) \tag{4}$$

3.2 Model of CTL-I

Through the lens of backward compatibility, the focus lies in safeguarding the integrity of base class information. However, the vantage point shifts when examining incremental learning from a forward compatibility standpoint-anticipating and accommodating future updates. Essentially, the learning process of base classes should remain 'unperturbed by what lies ahead.' By allocating embedding space for potential novel classes and projecting their potential patterns, the incurred costs of adaptation can be substantially minimized.

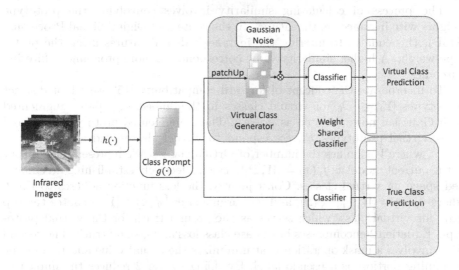

Fig. 3. CTL-I model Network architecture. The base class prediction is presented by green vector, base classifier. The virtual class prediction in Session 0 is presented by the orange vector, extending classifier. The novel prediction after Session 0 is presented by the orange vector. During the learning process, the base classifier and the extended classifier will be updated separately. (Color figure online)

Inspired by both two theories, our novel omnidirectional compatibility model, CTL-I, synergistically harnesses the benefits of both forward and backward compatibility. This model bifurcates the learning process for the base class and the novel class into two distinct and independent stages, as depicted in Fig. 3. This design ensures not only the preservation of the base class but also the effective acquisition of knowledge pertaining to the novel class. Consequently, a seamless transition through the update phase is facilitated, reducing the costs associated with adaptation and enhancing the processing capabilities for infrared images.

Initially, we introduce the approach of amalgamating virtual and real prototypes. Subsequently, we elucidate the process of utilizing these prototypes for logical inference.

3.3   Virtual Prototypes Assignment with Loss

In Session 0, we introduce the concept of metrics to gauge the resemblance between instance embedding and prototypes of the base class, denoted as $p(y \mid x) \propto sim \langle \omega_y, \phi(x) \rangle$. This similarity score reflects the likelihood that instance x belongs to class y, with a higher score indicating a stronger association. By employing prototypes, we can project K instances of novel classes into the deep feature space and aggregate them into a unified class representation. Similarly, base class instances are also aggregated, resulting in an equivalent number of clustering centers for novel and base classes. This approach effectively mitigates data imbalance concerns.

The process of calculating similarity involves convolving the prototype weights with instance depth features. In the context of Digital Signal Processing (DSP), this equates to filtering the instance's depth features using the prototype weight. A higher similarity value corresponds to more pronounced filtering outcomes.

To incorporate the concept of forward compatibility [15], we adopt distinct prototypes $|Y_0| \in D_0$ for virtual classes in the embedding space, augmented with Gaussian noise denoted as $noise_G$. These augmented prototypes, referred to as virtual prototypes P_v, correspond to virtual classes and are defined in $R^{d \times V}$, where V signifies the number of virtual classes. We represent the output of the current model as $f_v(x) = [W, P_v]^\top \phi(x)$, effectively establishing an embedded space for virtual classes. Consequently, the loss function adheres to Eq. 2, where $f_v(x) = [W, P_v]^\top \phi(x)$, and $\hat{y} = \operatorname{argmax} v \boldsymbol{p} v^\top \phi(\mathbf{x}) + |Y_0|$ denotes the top logit for virtual class, which serves as the ground truth for the virtual prototype. Equation 2 encompasses both base class loss and ground truth. The second term involves a mask operation that minimizes the actual value and retains the remaining portion as a pseudo-label. By doing so, Eq. 2 reduces the impact of actual values on virtual classes while accentuating the influence of virtual labels.

Furthermore, to facilitate the update of the virtual prototype and enable its integration of novel knowledge, we introduce a fusion of base class instances into virtual instances, thereby enhancing the virtual prototype's capacity to assimilate new insights. Given that interpolation between base classes often lies far from the center of the two categories within the feature space, discerning the original classes can prove challenging. To address this, we employ the "patchUp" technique, segmenting the intermediate hidden layer output into blocks and interchanging them to meld the two instances.

The embedding layer $\phi(\cdot)$ is bifurcated into two components, $\phi(\cdot) = g\,(h\,(\cdot))$. To bolster the virtual prototypes' adaptability to arbitrary novel classes, we introduce standard Gaussian noise, emulating the randomness inherent to novel classes:

$$z = g\left[\lambda h\,(\mathbf{x}_i) + (1 - \lambda)h\,(\mathbf{x}_j) + noise_G\right] \tag{5}$$

where λ denotes the hyperparameter governing the feature mixing ratio employed in patchUp. When combining n instance features to compose the features of a virtual prototype, the resulting representation of the virtual prototype can be expressed as follows:

$$z = g\left[\left\|\sum_{i=1}^{n}\lambda_i h\,(\mathbf{x}_i)\right\|_2 + noise_G\right], \lambda = \{\lambda_1, \ldots, \lambda_n \mid \lambda_n \in (0,1)\} \tag{6}$$

where $\|\cdot\|_2$ signifies the utilization of 2-norm normalization for two-dimensional vectors. This normalization technique is employed to mitigate potential instability stemming from excessively large or minute random parameters. Its purpose is to strike a balance between the virtual prototype and the random noise, preventing one from overpowering the other. Given the low resolution of infrared images and the pronounced similarity across different categories, training models to emphasize the learning of more akin category features leads to improved testing outcomes.

We can build a loss function for virtual instance z to reserve embedded space:

$$\mathcal{L}_f(\mathbf{x}, y) = \underbrace{\ell\left(\mathrm{Mask}\,(f_v(\mathbf{z}), \hat{y}), \hat{\hat{y}}\right)}_{\mathcal{L}_3} \tag{7}$$

Equation 7 serves to strike a balance between mixed instances from known classes and the introduction of randomness through virtual classes. This equilibrium is crucial to avoid known classes from unduly constraining the adaptability of virtual classes to novel ones, effectively mitigating the risk of overfitting. The final loss formulation combines the contributions from Eq. 2 and Eq. 7, yielding $\mathcal{L} = \mathcal{L}_v + \mathcal{L}_f$. By introducing heightened randomness to virtual classes, the model gains a more efficient capability to simulate future instances, thereby enhancing the implementation of forward compatibility compared to the approach presented in [15].

To encompass the representation of both virtual and known classes within the model, we expand the classifier as follows: $C = [C_{base}; C_{novel}], novel = N * B]$. Here, C_{base} signifies the classifier dedicated to base classes, while C_{novel} pertains to the classifier tailored for novel classes. During Session 0, the update of C_{novel} is driven by virtual class data, while C_{base} is refined through real data from D^0.

3.4   Compatibility Update

We have elucidated the process of generating virtual prototypes and their impact on the model's grasp of base classes. Now, let's delve into the strategy for substituting acquired virtual data with data from new classes in subsequent updates.

During the acquisition of each batch of novel class data, we adhere to Eq. 1 for extracting class prototypes and populating the extended classifiers. To be specific, in Session 1, we utilize D^1 to update $C_{novel}(1, N)$, while concurrently maintaining the immutability of the C_{base} branch. Subsequent sessions follow a similar update procedure.

Freezing the base class classifier during the update with novel class data is a characteristic trait of backward compatibility methodologies. This approach serves to preserve the base class's discriminative capability. To harness the benefits of backward compatibility, we will introduce novel class classifiers alongside the ongoing training sessions. In a novel class session, both the base class classifier and embedding layer will coexist, effectively maintaining their frozen state. Leveraging the inclusion of virtual classes in the base class training phase allows us to attain a more comprehensive information distribution for $\phi(x)$, thus aiding the model in assimilating a greater volume of information during the incremental phase. This proposition is corroborated through testing.

Our approach capitalizes on the strengths of both backward compatibility and forward compatibility techniques, intelligently circumventing their individual limitations. In doing so, we strike a harmonious equilibrium between the precision of acquiring novel class knowledge and safeguarding the integrity of base classes.

4   Experiments

In this section, we present a comprehensive comparison of CTL-I with state-of-the-art methods on our infrared Few-Shot Class-Incremental Learning (FSCIL) dataset. Through extensive experimentation, we validate the efficacy of omnidirectional compatibility training and provide visual insights into the incremental process of CTL-I. Moreover, we introduce novel evaluation metrics for incremental learning, encompassing base accuracy and novel accuracy. These metrics offer a more nuanced perspective compared to the conventional full class accuracy, as they better capture the learning dynamics of both novel and base classes.

4.1   Implementation Details

Dataset: After benchmark setting [19], we evaluated the performance on our infrared street view dataset. Our infrared dataset contains 22000 images from 40 classes.

Dataset Split: For our infrared dataset, 40 classes are divided into 10 base classes and 30 novel classes. The base class is divided into 10-way 30-shot tasks, while the novel class is designated as four 5-way 5-shot incremental tasks. For fair comparison, we use the same training segmentation for each comparison method [19] (including basic and incremental sessions). The test set is sampled from the current training category, and the same session uses the same test set for overall evaluation.

Compared Methods: We first compared the classic CIL methods iCaRL [17]. In addition, we also compared the current SOTA FSCIL algorithms: SPPR [5], CEC [14], method[15]. The baseline method we reported is 'fine-tuning' by fine-tuning the model with a few instances of shots.

Training Details: All models are deployed using PyTorch [18]. We use the same backbone [19] for all comparison methods. For all datasets, we use ResNet18. The model is trained with a batch size of 256 for 600 epochs and optimized using SGD with driving capacity. The learning rate starts at 0.1 and decays with cosine annealing.

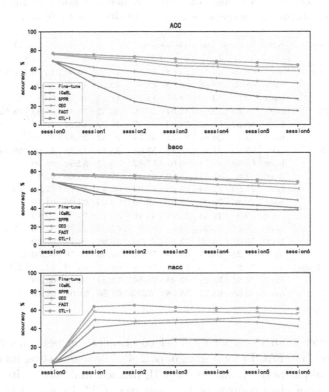

Fig. 4. Top-1 accuracy, bacc and nacc of each incremental session. We have shown the legend in (a) and annotated the performance gap between CTL-I and the runner up method after the last session at the end of each curve. The specific values are shown in Table 1 and the supplementary table.

Evaluation Protocol: After [19], we represent the Top-1 accuracy after the i-th session as A_i. We set the base class accuracy (bacc) and the novel class accuracy (nacc) to evaluate them separately. We also quantitatively measured the forgetting phenomenon using performance drop rate (bPD), which is $bPD = bA_0 - bA_B$, where bA_0 represents the accuracy after the basic session and bA_B represents the accuracy after the last session,visualized in Fig. 2. We calculated bPD for the base class.

4.2 Benchmark Comparison

We report the performance curves on the benchmark dataset [19] (i.e. our infrared dataset) in Fig. 4 and Table 1.

Table 1. The acc, bacc, and nacc of each incremental session on the our infrared dataset. The results of the comparison method are cited from [19] and [14].

Method	Acc	Accuracy in each session (%)							bPD ↓
		0	1	2	3	4	5	6	
Fine-tune	acc	68.69	43.71	25.08	17.80	17.56	16.96	15.10	30.71
	bacc	68.69	58.66	48.73	44.15	40.26	38.24	37.98	
	nacc	2.7	13.73	14.65	12.30	11.98	10.55	9.78	
iCaRL	acc	68.69	52.65	48.61	44.16	36.52	30.46	27.83	28.55
	bacc	68.69	55.32	52.82	48.87	45.22	43.21	40.14	
	nacc	3.1	24.45	25.21	27.74	27.34	26.84	25.94	
SPPR	acc	68.69	61.85	57.43	52.68	50.19	46.88	44.65	20.19
	bacc	68.69	63.71	60.09	57.82	55.51	52.64	48.50	
	nacc	1.8	41.17	45.20	46.18	47.50	46.69	42.14	
CEC	acc	75.86	71.54	68.48	63.52	62.45	58.29	57.80	14.76
	bacc	75.86	74.33	72.08	69.10	65.56	63.96	61.10	
	nacc	5.3	49.51	48.02	49.16	50.16	51.98	50.16	
FACT	acc	76.0	73.26	70.9	66.7	65.42	62.10	61.78	10.20
	bacc	76.0	74.89	73.02	71.80	70.86	66.97	65.80	
	nacc	4.28	57.71	56.05	57.60	57.46	56.76	55.50	
CTL-I(our)	acc	76.9	75.25	73.2	70.98	68.23	66.79	64.21	**8.34**
	bacc	76.9	**76.31**	**75.28**	**73.60**	**71.24**	**70.60**	**68.56**	
	nacc	3.65	**63.71**	**65.08**	**62.80**	**61.56**	**61.96**	**61.10**	

We can infer from Fig. 4 that CTL-I consistently outperforms the current SOTA method (i.e. FACT) by a margin of 2–4%, demonstrating its clear superiority. The subpar performance of the CIL method underscores its limitations in handling novel class compatibility. Moreover, CTL-I's superiority over the FSCIL approach reinforces the significance of considering forward compatibility for improved results.

Moreover, CTL-I surpasses the forward compatibility method, which leans towards compatibility with virtual novel classes. This underscores that omnidirectional compatibility is better aligned with FSCIL requirements. Furthermore, CTL-I outperforms FACT, which approaches forward compatibility from a different angle. Collectively, our training strategy is better suited for FSCIL. Detailed results for our infrared dataset are presented in Table. 1. Notably, CTL-I demonstrates minimal degradation in bPD metrics for both visible and infrared data. This highlights the effectiveness of omnidirectional compatibility training in combating base class forgetting during FSCIL, all the while mastering novel classes with high precision.

In summary, CTL-I always handles small-scale FSCIL tasks with SOTA performance.

4.3 Further Analysis

The performance metrics encompass precision evaluations spanning both old and novel classes. To delve into novel class learning and the resilience against base class forgetting, we present base class and novel class accuracies across sessions, along with their harmonic mean, for our infrared dataset. These measurements adhere to the identical benchmark testing conditions. It is evident that CTL-I exhibits superior performance in novel class learning, thereby validating the efficacy of omnidirectional compatibility training and its adeptness in effectively mastering infrared data.

5 Conclusion

FSCIL capability stands as the initial stride into open-world learning in Infrared images, demanding models to grasp new classes with limited data while retaining knowledge of old classes. This article emphasized the significance of developing an FSCIL omnidirectional compatible model. We devised a virtual prototype incorporating random noise for forthcoming new classes within the classifier, harmonizing the feature space between new and old classes from dual perspectives. This approach, which preserves the attributes of old classes, promotes a balanced growth between novel and old classes, consequently mitigating performance deterioration during updates. Surprisingly, virtual prototypes integrated into the embedding space unexpectedly enhance FSCIL's learning performance for base classes and effectively curtail overfitting concerns. CTL-I effectively integrates new knowledge into old models and achieves SOTA performance.

Acknowledgments. This work was funded by the STI 2030-Major Projects under grant 2022ZD0209600, the National Natural Science Foundation of China under grant 62201058, the Beijing Institute of Technology Research Fund Program for Young Scholars under grant 6120210047, and the China Postdoctoral Science Foundation under grant 2021M700399.

References

1. Deng, J., Dong, W., Socher, R., Li, L.J., Li, K., Fei-Fei, L.: ImageNet: a large-scale hierarchical image database. In: 2009 IEEE Conference on Computer Vision and Pattern Recognition, pp. 248–255 (2009). https://doi.org/10.1109/CVPR.2009.5206848
2. Gomes, H.M., Barddal, J.P., Enembreck, F., Bifet, A.: A survey on ensemble learning for data stream classification. ACM Comput. Surv. **50**, 23:1–23:36 (2017). https://doi.org/10.1145/3054925

3. Chou, Y.Y., Lin, H.T., Liu, T.L.: Adaptive and generative zero-shot learning. In: International Conference on Learning Representations (2021). https://openreview. net/forum?id=ahAUv8TI2Mz
4. French, R.M.: Catastrophic forgetting in connectionist networks. Trends Cogn. Sci. **3**(4), 128–135 (1999). https://doi.org/10.1016/S1364-6613(99)01294-2, https:// www.sciencedirect.com/science/article/pii/S1364661399012942
5. Zhu, K., Cao, Y., Zhai, W., Cheng, J., Zha, Z.J.: Self-promoted prototype refinement for few-shot class-incremental learning. In: 2021 IEEE/CVF Conference on Computer Vision and Pattern Recognition (CVPR), pp. 6797–6806 (2021). https:// doi.org/10.1109/CVPR46437.2021.00673
6. Nagarakatte, S., Bb, A., Martin, M., Zdancewic, S.: SoftBound: highly compatible and complete spatial memory safety for c. ACM SIGPLAN Notices **44**, 245 (2009). https://doi.org/10.1145/1543135.1542504
7. Faramarzi, M., Amini, M., Badrinaaraayanan, A., Verma, V., Chandar, S.: PatchUp: a feature-space block-level regularization technique for convolutional neural networks. arXiv e-prints arXiv:2006.07794 (2020). https://doi.org/10. 48550/arXiv.2006.07794
8. Liu, B., et al.: Negative margin matters: understanding margin in few-shot classification. arXiv e-prints arXiv:2003.12060 (2020). https://doi.org/10.48550/arXiv. 2003.12060
9. Bansal, G., Nushi, B., Kamar, E., Weld, D.S., Lasecki, W.S., Horvitz, E.: Updates in human-AI teams: understanding and addressing the performance/compatibility tradeoff. In: Proceedings of the AAAI Conference on Artificial Intelligence **33**(01), 2429–2437 (2019). https://doi.org/10.1609/aaai.v33i01.33012429, https://ojs.aaai. org/index.php/AAAI/article/view/4087
10. Aljundi, R., Babiloni, F., Elhoseiny, M., Rohrbach, M., Tuytelaars, T.: Memory aware synapses: learning what (not) to forget. arXiv e-prints arXiv:1711.09601 (2017). https://doi.org/10.48550/arXiv.1711.09601
11. Kirkpatrick, J., et al.: Overcoming catastrophic forgetting in neural networks. CoRR abs/1612.00796 (2016). http://arxiv.org/abs/1612.00796
12. Hinton, G., Vinyals, O., Dean, J.: Distilling the knowledge in a neural network. arXiv e-prints arXiv:1503.02531 (2015). https://doi.org/10.48550/arXiv. 1503.02531
13. Li, Z., Hoiem, D.: Learning without forgetting. IEEE Trans. Pattern Anal. Mach. Intell. **40**(12), 2935–2947 (2018). https://doi.org/10.1109/TPAMI.2017.2773081
14. Zhang, C., Song, N., Lin, G., Zheng, Y., Pan, P., Xu, Y.: Few-shot incremental learning with continually evolved classifiers. In: 2021 IEEE/CVF Conference on Computer Vision and Pattern Recognition (CVPR), pp. 12450–12459 (2021). https://doi.org/10.1109/CVPR46437.2021.01227
15. Zhou, D.W., Wang, F.Y., Ye, H.J., Ma, L., Pu, S., Zhan, D.C.: Forward compatible few-shot class-incremental learning. In: 2022 IEEE/CVF Conference on Computer Vision and Pattern Recognition (CVPR), pp. 9036–9046 (2022). https://doi.org/ 10.1109/CVPR52688.2022.00884
16. Snell, J., Swersky, K., Zemel, R.S.: Prototypical networks for few-shot learning. arXiv e-prints arXiv:1703.05175 (2017). https://doi.org/10.48550/arXiv.1703. 05175
17. Rebuffi, S.A., Kolesnikov, A., Sperl, G., Lampert, C.H.: iCaRL: incremental classifier and representation learning. In: 2017 IEEE Conference on Computer Vision and Pattern Recognition (CVPR), pp. 5533–5542 (2017). https://doi.org/10.1109/ CVPR.2017.587

18. Paszke, A., et al.: PyTorch: an imperative style, high-performance deep learning library. arXiv e-prints arXiv:1912.01703 (2019). https://doi.org/10.48550/arXiv.1912.01703
19. Tao, X., Hong, X., Chang, X., Dong, S., Wei, X., Gong, Y.: Few-shot class-incremental learning. In: 2020 IEEE/CVF Conference on Computer Vision and Pattern Recognition (CVPR), pp. 12180–12189 (2020). https://doi.org/10.1109/CVPR42600.2020.01220

Can Federated Models Be Rectified Through Learning Negative Gradients?

Ahsen Tahir, Zhiyuan Tan$^{(\boxtimes)}$, and Kehinde O. Babaagba

School of Computing, Engineering and the Built Environment, Edinburgh Napier
University, Edinburgh EH10 5DT, UK
{A.Tahir,Z.Tan,K.Babaagba}@napier.ac.uk

Abstract. Federated Learning (FL) is a method to train machine learning (ML) models in a decentralised manner, while preserving the privacy of data from multiple clients. However, FL is vulnerable to malicious attacks, such as poisoning attacks, and is challenged by the GDPR's "right to be forgotten". This paper introduces a negative gradient-based machine learning technique to address these issues. Experiments on the MNIST dataset show that subtracting local model parameters can remove the influence of the respective training data on the global model and consequently "unlearn" the model in the FL paradigm. Although the performance of the resulting global model decreases, the proposed technique maintains the validation accuracy of the model above 90%. This impact on performance is acceptable for an FL model. It is important to note that the experimental work carried out demonstrates that in application areas where data deletion in ML is a necessity, this approach represents a significant advancement in the development of secure and robust FL systems.

Keywords: Federated Learning · Machine Unlearning · Negative Gradients · Model Rectification

1 Introduction

The use of traditional Artificial Intelligence (AI) systems requires large amounts of data to be collected and stored on a central server or cloud storage. However, this can be difficult due to the various obstacles that can arise when transferring, collecting, and integrating data. In reality, data is often collected from edge devices such as smartphones and exists in isolated pieces. For example, health records are typically kept in separate, disconnected entities that are unable or unwilling to share data due to the privacy and security risks associated with sharing personal information.

Federated Learning (FL) introduced by Google [18,19,27], allows the training of Machine Learning (ML) models locally and the sharing of computations or model parameters to build a federated global model. FL enables a large number

Z. Tan et al. (Eds.): BDTA 2023, LNICST 555, pp. 18–32, 2024.
https://doi.org/10.1007/978-3-031-52265-9_2

of participants to develop joint ML models without sharing their data and sacrificing their data privacy. However, recent work in FL revealed that poisoning attacks [1, 2, 11] significantly temper the security of the federated global model. New data regulations, such as the General Data Protection Regulation (GDPR) and the California Consumer Privacy Act (CCPA), cast further challenges on data transactions. These new regulations emphasise on the user's right to be forgotten in light of current data regulations [14]. They raise the requirements for data deletion to restore the poisoned model or delete user data due to privacy regulations [3, 10, 15, 16, 21]. Although the problem can be solved trivially by retraining the model with the absence of the designated data from scratch, model retraining is not always sustainable and computationally feasible, especially in the current popularity of large models.

This leads to the emergence of machine unlearning, a set of strategies to eliminate the impact of training data on an ML model and its parameters in particular. Training data may need to be removed in order to fix a model that has been deliberately corrupted by a malicious user, or may need to be taken away by a user for privacy purposes. Removing this data and its effects from the ML model does not significantly reduce performance and is more computationally efficient than retraining the model from scratch. The ideal outcome is that the unlearned model is the same as or similar to the re-trained model.

In this paper, we introduce a machine learning technique based on negative gradients to reduce the effect of the selected subset of training data on a federated global model. We use the Federated Averaging (FedAvg) algorithm [27] to construct the global model in the context of this study. Additionally, we seek to answer two research questions.

1) To what extent does subtracting local model parameters serve to reduce the influence of the associated training data on the model to facilitate unlearning?
2) What impact does federated unlearning have on the performance of models?

The remainder of the paper is structured as follows. Section 2 provides a review of related work. Section 3 describes the methodology of our research. Section 4 presents and discusses the experimental results and analysis. Section 5 draws the conclusions of the investigation and the direction for future research.

2 Related Work

Federated models are created by combining updates from all participant models. The model aggregator carries out secure aggregation and does not have access to the updates given by individual models or their training data. The aggregation process makes federated models vulnerable to model poisoning attacks. Machine unlearning can be used when the model is contaminated/poisoned or a data deletion request is made by a client due to their right to be forgotten under current privacy laws.

2.1   Model Poisoning and Defending Mechanisms

In order to comprehend the process of unlearning in FL systems, it is essential to recognise the origins of model contamination. Model poisoning attacks can be classified into label-flipping attacks and backdoor attacks. Model poisoning incorporates data poisoning. Figure 1 portrays the poisoning attack comprising of the poisoner objective, the genuine objective, and the element space which incorporates the attack target.

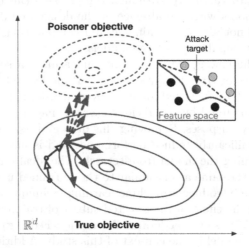

Fig. 1. Poisoning attack in Stochastic Gradient Descent (SGD). The red dotted vectors represent contributions from malicious clients (*Fung et al.* (Color figure online) [11])

Recent literature has explored poisoning attacks against FL. Sybil-based poisoning attack is studied in [11], which illustrates that a malicious client can increase the effectiveness of attacks by exploiting Sybils [9] and presents a defence strategy based on contribution similarity. The authors believed that a group of Sybils could potentially provide updates with a similar objective resulting in a lack of diversity amongst the malicious client updates.

The research, documented in [2], demonstrates a single malicious client-based model poisoning attacks against FL, where the updates from the malicious client were boosted to overwhelm the effect of benign clients. Furthermore, a strategy was introduced to keep malicious updates undetected by alternately optimising for the attack objective and training loss. The strategy keeps the validation accuracy of the resulting global model above a specified threshold and the pairwise distance between updates below a specific value to avoid attack detection.

In addition, backdoor attacks with a replacement model for FL are explored in [1]. The work proposed a constraint and scale technique for model replacement attacks, which uses the attacker's loss function during training to stay undetected.

2.2 Detection of Poisoned Models

Detecting a poisoned model in a federated setting is essential and has received increasing research interest [6,7,13,23,24,32,33]. Wang et al. [33] proposed the 'Neural Cleanse' model to identify and detect backdoor attacks in deep neural networks. An optimisation scheme is used to determine the minimal trigger required to cause misclassification of all samples from other labels into the target label. The size of each trigger is measured by the number of pixels it contains and an outlier detection algorithm is applied to identify any significantly smaller triggers, which represent real triggers for the backdoor attack.

In a similar fashion, [6] presents DeepInspect, a pioneering black-box backdoor detection and mitigation technique, which does not assume benign samples or require full access to the model being tested, unlike Neural Cleanse. Instead, it uses model inversion to create a substitution training set and a conditional Generative Adversarial Network (cGAN) to recover potential triggers used by the adversary for each output class. [24] proposes Artificial Brain Stimulation (ABS), a model-level backdoor detection method.

2.3 Formulation of Machine Unlearning

Machine unlearning is a process that focusses on the removal of certain subsets of training data to make it more efficient than the traditional retraining approach. This is especially useful when adapting an ML model to a changing environment, where a data subject may choose to exercise their right to be forgotten. By using this method, information from the data subset can be effectively removed from the trained model [36].

Recent studies are attempting to develop algorithms that can "exactly" or "approximately" remove the details of a particular subset of training data from a given ML model. In the context of machine unlearning, "Deletion" and "Efficiently Deletable" can be mathematically described as the following problems.

Definition of Deletion. Let D be a dataset and A be a learning algorithm, such that

$$D \in \mathbb{R}^{n \times d} \tag{1}$$

$$A : D \to A(D) \in \mathcal{H} \tag{2}$$

where $\mathcal{H}$ refers to a hypothesis space (i.e., a model space or classifier space), such as linear regression models, and the function $A(D)$ returns model parameters or weights. If a data point i is deleted from the dataset D, then the remaining dataset can be represented as D_{-i}. Consequently, a model trained on the dataset D_{-i} can be represented as $A(D_{-i})$. The deletion operation R is another mapping in the hypothesis space.

$$R : (D, A(D), i) \to \mathcal{H} \tag{3}$$

$$\text{s. t. } R(D, A(D), i) = A(D-i) \tag{4}$$

where $R(D, A(D), i)$ returns a model that belongs to the space $\mathcal{H}$, defined by Eq. (3). The deletion operation, $R(D, A(D), i)$, defined in Eq. (4), results in a new model that is identical to that trained using the dataset D_{-i}. Equation (4) implies that the learning algorithm is deterministic. If the learning algorithm is randomised, then Eq. (4) is then redefined as Eq. (5), which means that the two resulting models are equal in distribution.

$$R(D, A(D), i) \overset{d}{=} A(D_{-i}) \tag{5}$$

Definition of Efficiently Deletable. In this work, we define *Efficiently Deleta-ble* for the sequential learning algorithm A, which runs in time $\Omega(n)$. Ideally, the deletion operation, $R(D, A(D), i)$, is independent of the size of the dataset or, in other words, constant in time and is part of efficiently deletable. However, for the worst case, the algorithm is sublinear in time, which implies that an asymptotic lower bound for n data points and m deletion operations should be $\Omega(\frac{n}{m})$.

2.4 Unlearning Federated Learning

Studies have sought to create a generic unlearning process for various learning algorithms and ML models. Bourtoule et al. [3] proposed the well-known model-agnostic SISA framework, which divides the data into shards and slices. Each shard has a single model, and the final result is a combination of the various models in these shards. A model checkpoint is saved for each slice of a shard during training so that a new model can be re-trained from the interim state [3].

It may be difficult to create a model-agnostic unlearning framework due to the complexity of ML algorithms and the training process in the federated setting, where global weights are calculated using aggregation rather than simple gradients and multiple clients are involved [12]. Therefore, the early unlearning approaches cannot be simply transferred to the federated setting. In addition, clients may have some data that overlap, making it hard to determine the effect of each training item on model weights [25]. Applying conventional unlearning methods, such as gradient manipulation, can lead to a decrease in accuracy or extra privacy risks [20].

Data that need to be erased are assumed to belong to a single client in current research on federated unlearning [20,25,31,34]. This assumption makes it easy to keep track of and delete the contributions a certain client has made to the global model training.

The gradients obtained from the client's data can be used to reverse the effects on the global model [21]. However, the unlearning hypothesis may not be the same as that initially learnt from the data. Removing the previous parameter adjustments could still damage the overall model. To address this issue, there are several potential solutions:

- Liu et al. [20] proposed calibration training to differentiate the individual contributions of clients as much as possible. However, this technique does not work well for deep neural networks apart from basic architectures such as a 2-layer CNN or 2 fully connected layers. Additionally, there is a compromise between scalability and accuracy due to the cost of storing historical data on the federated server.

- Wu et al. [35] proposed a knowledge distillation strategy that uses a primary global model to train the unlearned model on the remaining data. However, since the server is unable to view the client's data, it is necessary to sample some unlabelled (fake) data that reflect the distribution of the entire dataset. This requires additional rounds of communication between the client and the server, which makes the process costly and approximate. Furthermore, if the data is non-IID [22], the results may be further distorted.
- In a different area of the field, Liu et al. developed a smart retraining approach for federated unlearning without communication protocols [22]. This approach approximated the L-BFGS technique by using historical parameter changes to retrain the entire model. Unfortunately, this strategy is only suitable for models with fewer than 10,000 parameters and requires the storage of previous model snapshots, which contain past gradients and parameters that could potentially breach privacy.

2.5 Challenges to Federated Unlearning

Many ML algorithms are stochastic, which means they incorporate randomness in their optimisation or learning processes. This stochasticity is a fundamental concept in ML and must be understood to accurately interpret the behaviour of numerous predictive models. However, the randomness of ML algorithms presents additional difficulties for federated unlearning [21]. To make the unlearning hypothesis valid both mathematically and practically, the model to be unlearnt must start from the same state or with the same random weights as the original model. Additionally, randomness during optimisation could lead to different hypotheses that may correspond to different local minima in the optimisation space.

Furthermore, the probability of violating privacy and security increases with unlearning. This can take the form of:

- Information leakage [28]: The potential for unintentionally possessing confidential information can arise if a model is created using a mixture of confidential and non-confidential data.
- Reconstructing training data [5]: Malicious parties attempt to reconstruct the data used to train a model.
- Model inversion attacks [37]: A well-known privacy violation attempts to infer sensitive information from the training dataset, which leads to serious privacy issues.

Other serious implications can arise from adversarial exploitation [29], and systemic bias [17] among others. These can be addressed using a multifaceted approach that includes federated learning.

3   Methodology

A rudimentary approach to Federated Unlearning could involve retraining the model without the client's data, however, this is highly inefficient. Efficiently deleting data from ML models is a computational problem. Furthermore, it is important to formulate whether the data are "exactly" or "approximately" deletable.

To answer the questions raised in Sect. 1, we have introduced a technique that uses a negative gradient approach to unlearning the model. This method can be implemented on the client side without the need for sharing the client's data. The gradients obtained from the model trained on the client's data locally are used to subtract from the main global model. We reduce the impact of stochasticity by beginning with the same initial parameters and eliminating randomness in the training process.

The implementation of the proposed machine-unlearning solution involves the preparation of non-IID data for FL and the subsequent unlearning process. To achieve this, the unlearning hypothesis should be able to replicate the user data in a manner similar to how it is represented in the original model. This is because multiple hypotheses that follow different learning paths can be derived from the same data.

3.1   Experimental Data

Non-IID input data are generated from MNIST data [8], a large database of handwritten digits regularly used to train a variety of image processing systems systems, for Federated Learning (FL). Pre-processing of MNIST is performed using Leaf[1] [4], so that the data can be keyed by the original writer of the MNIST digits, because of the unique style of each writer, this dataset becomes the kind of non-IID data required for federated datasets.

The original 28×28 sized images are flattened into 784-element 1-D arrays, which are shuffled and organised in batches. The features are renamed from pixels and labelled input x and output y for use with PyTorch. The output y is multiclass with 10 output classes.

3.2   Network Implementation

A 5-layer deep neural network model with 3 fully connected hidden Rectified Linear Unit (ReLU) layers is employed to train the MNIST images in PyTorch 1.7.1 [30] with torchvision 0.7.0 [26]. The Federated Averaging (FedAvg) algorithm is implemented in PyTorch to add gradients and merge the local user models into a federated main model. The FedAvg algorithm uses two optimisers: a client side and a server optimiser. The client optimiser computes updates to the local model, while the server optimiser averages the updates in the global model. The process is tested with regular Stochastic Gradient Descent (SGD).

The implemented model ran with the following parameters:

---

[1] https://github.com/TalwalkarLab/leaf.

* Learning rate, $\eta = 0.01$.
* SGD learning algorithm, Momentum $= 0.9$.
* Number of Epochs, $\epsilon = 10$.
* Batch size $= 32$.
* The loss function, CrossEntropyLoss(), is applied.

Five local client models were used to build the federated main model. Each of the client models was trained on 10,000 samples, validated on 1,000, and was also tested on 1,000 samples.

4 Experimental Results and Discussion

Two deep learning-based image recognition models are compared by training them (1) centrally on all data and (2) with FL which trains five local client models on their respective selected subsets of data, then merges them into a main model using the FedAvg algorithm. Experimental results are depicted in Figs. 2 and 3.

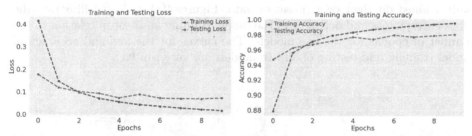

(a) The training and test loss rates of the centrally trained model.

(b) The training and test accuracy rates of the centrally trained model.

Fig. 2. Preliminary experimental results of the centrally trained model.

- The model that was trained centrally achieved the highest training accuracy of 99.54% and the highest test accuracy of 98.04%, as illustrated in Fig. 2(b). Further details of the cross-entropy loss function and the training/test accuracy with the number of epochs can be seen in Figs. 2(a) and 2(b).
- The federated main model performs remarkably well, attaining a test accuracy of 98. 01% across the entire dataset, as seen in Fig. 3(b). It should be noted that the federated main model begins with a much lower loss and a much higher accuracy than the main model did in its initial run, as demonstrated in Figs. 3(a) and 3(b).

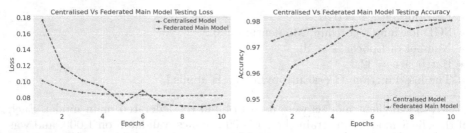

(a) The comparison of the test loss rates of the centrally trained model and the federated main model.

(b) The comparison of the test accuracy rates of the centrally trained model and the federated main model.

Fig. 3. The comparison of the preliminary experimental results of the centrally trained model and the federated main model.

4.1 Federated Main Model

In this section, we provide a comprehensive analysis of the federated main model, which is established by averaging the five local models that have been individually trained on their own subset of data. Figures 4(a) and 4(b) illustrate the cross-entropy loss and accuracy of the model training and test in relation to the number of epochs for the five models. The curves for the loss and accuracy of model training and testing of all five models are very similar.

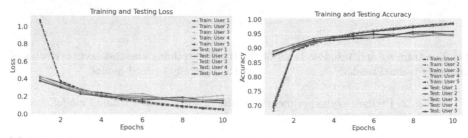

(a) The training and test loss rates of the five local client models.

(b) The training and test accuracy rates of the five local client models.

Fig. 4. Experimental results of the five local client models.

The detailed performance of the local client models on their respective partitioned datasets is given in Table 1. The local models of the five client/users provide good accuracy rates of 94.28%, 95.39%, 94.44%, 94.83% and 96.04%, respectively. The removal of each of the local models from the federated main model reduces the accuracy of the main model in the respective partitions, as illustrated in Table 1. The results show that

Table 1. Merged federated main model vs local models on their respective data before and after model removal

Dataset Partition	Local Client Model (%)	Federated Main Model (%)	Federated Main Model with Local Client Model 1 Removed (%)	Federated Main Model with Local Client Model 2 Removed (%)	Federated Main Model with Local Client Model 3 Removed (%)	Federated Main Model with Local Client Model 4 Removed (%)	Federated Main Model with Local Client Model 5 Removed (%)
1	0.9428	0.9567	0.9183	0.9306	0.9067	0.8639	0.7183
2	0.9539	0.9617	0.9261	0.9444	0.9156	0.8717	0.7267
3	0.9444	0.9572	0.9089	0.92	0.89	0.85	0.7228
4	0.9483	0.9589	0.9167	0.9239	0.9117	0.8678	0.7167
5	0.9604	0.9665	0.918	0.9291	0.909	0.8638	0.7166

- Removing any of the local model parameters from the main model will cause a decrease in the resulting federated main model's performance on all partitions of the dataset,
- The resulting federated main model may not show lower accuracy on the data that was removed from the original federated main model than on the other partitions of the dataset,
- No relationship exists between the accuracy of the local model and that of the resulting federated main model when the parameters of the local model are removed from the original federated main model,
- The accuracy of the federated main model is reduced from 96.17% to 94.44%, when the Local Client Model 2 with an accuracy of 95.39% is subtracted from the main model,
- The accuracy of the federated main model is reduced to 91.83% when Local Client Model 1 with an accuracy of 94.28% is subtracted from the main model.
- Subtraction of Local Client Model 2 with accuracy 95.39% produces the least reduction in the accuracy of the federated main model and subtraction of Local Client Model 5 with accuracy 96.04% results in the largest reduction in the accuracy of the performance of the federated main model.

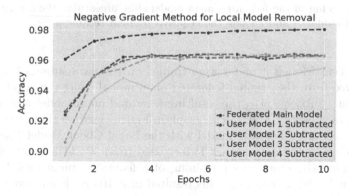

Fig. 5. The performance of the federated main model after client model subtraction

The implementation of the negative gradient method results in the subtraction of the parameters of the local client model from the federated main model at each epoch, illustrating a graph of the lower performance testing accuracy across the entire dataset in Fig. 5. The figure illustrates that different local models can potentially have different effects on the accuracy of the federated main model.

4.2 Retraining of Federated Main Model

Once the parameters of each local client model have been taken away from the original federated main model one at a time, the various resulting federated main models are re-trained using the data from the models that were taken away directly. The FedAvg algorithm is no longer involved; instead, local retraining is used to update the federated model. This experiment demonstrates that after unlearning the federated main model can be used to learn the same or new data on the server or by a new user. Then, it can reach the same performance levels as before. The retraining of the federated main model was then carried out using data subsets 1 and 2. Figure 6 shows the retraining of the federated main model with data subsets 1 and 2.

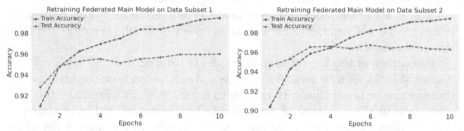

(a) Retraining of federated main model on data subset 1

(b) Retraining of federated main model on data subset 2

Fig. 6. Re-training of the federated main model after unlearning the contributions of Local Client Models 1 and 2 using the negative gradient technique.

Local Client Models 1 and 2 were trained on the data subsets 1 and 2 and then removed from the original federated main model using the negative gradient technique. Subsequently, the resulting federated main model was re-trained with the data subsets 1 and 2. The graph in Fig. 6(a) shows that the test accuracy of the federated learning model with the Local Client Model 1 subtracted (corresponding to the data subset 1) increased from 93. 44% to 96. 06% in 10 epochs. Figure 6(b) shows the retraining of a federated main model with the Local Client Model 2 removed. This resulted in a 10-epoch improvement from 94.61% to 96.33%.

The retraining of the federated main model was then performed on the data subsets 3 and 4. The negative gradient method was used to remove Local Client Models 3 and 4 from the federated main model. Subsequently, the federated main model was re-trained using data subsets 3 and 4, as shown in Fig. 7. Figures 7(a)

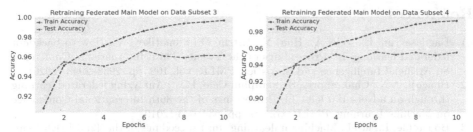

(a) Retraining of federated model on data subset 3

(b) Retraining of federated model on data subset 4

Fig. 7. Retraining of federated main model after removal of user models 3 and 4 through negative gradient technique.

and 7(b) show that the accuracy of the federated learning model with the Local Client Models 3 and 4 subtracted, respectively, increased from 92.5% and 92.83% to 95.94% and 95.50% respectively, over the course of 10 epochs.

5 Conclusion

Federated unlearning has been shown to be a viable solution to the issues caused by data deletion in Federated Learning (FL). This approach involves the removal of unwanted updates from a selection of clients, which can help reduce the negative impact of data deletion on the accuracy and dependability of federated learning models.

This paper has introduced a technique for machine unlearning by using negative gradients of local models to erase their effect on the main model based on FL. The results showed that subtracting local model parameters can be used to eliminate the influence of the corresponding training data on the model and unlearn it for the FL paradigm. Although there was a decrease in the model's performance on the data due to deletion, the performance of the model on the overall data remained above 90%. It is important to note that the experimental work conducted demonstrates that in application areas where data deletion in machine learning is necessary, such as when a client may need to remove their data from the model, potentially exercising the right to be forgotten, the model performance will not be significantly affected.

Despite the fact that there are still difficulties to be solved in the implementation of federated unlearning, such as the possibility of privacy infringements and the necessity of efficient detection of poisoning assaults, this method represents a major advance in the formation of secure and reliable federated learning systems.

Acknowledge. This work was supported by ENU Development Trust Ref. LH Oct19.

References

1. Bagdasaryan, E., Veit, A., Hua, Y., Estrin, D., Shmatikov, V.: How to backdoor federated learning. In: Proceedings of the Twenty Third International Conference on Artificial Intelligence and Statistics, PMLR. vol. 108, pp. 2938–2948 (2020)
2. Bhagoji, A.N., Chakraborty, S., Seraphin Calo, P.M.: Analyzing federated learning through an adversarial lens. In: Proceedings of the 36th International Conference on Machine Learning, PMLR. vol. 97, pp. 634–643 (2019)
3. Bourtoule, L., et al.: Machine unlearning. In: Proceedings of the 42nd IEEE Symposium on Security and Privacy (2021)
4. Caldas, S., et al.: Leaf: A benchmark for federated settings. In: Workshop on Federated Learning for Data Privacy and Confidentiality (2019)
5. Chai, X., Tang, G., Wang, S., Peng, R., Chen, W., Li, J.: Deep learning for regularly missing data reconstruction. IEEE Trans. Geosci. Remote Sens. **58**(6), 4406–4423 (2020). https://doi.org/10.1109/TGRS.2020.2963928
6. Chen, H., Fu, C., Zhao, J., Koushanfar, F.: DeepInspect: a black-box trojan detection and mitigation framework for deep neural networks. In: Proceedings of the Twenty-Eighth International Joint Conference on Artificial Intelligence, IJCAI-19, pp. 4658–4664. International Joint Conferences on Artificial Intelligence Organization (2019). https://doi.org/10.24963/ijcai.2019/647
7. Chen, H., Fu, C., Zhao, J., Koushanfar, F.: DeepInspect: a black-box trojan detection and mitigation framework for deep neural networks. In: Proceedings of the Twenty-Eighth International Joint Conference on Artificial Intelligence (IJCAI), pp. 4658–4664 (2019)
8. Deng, L.: The MNIST database of handwritten digit images for machine learning research [best of the web]. IEEE Signal Process. Mag. **29**(6), 141–142 (2012)
9. Douceur, J.R.: The Sybil attack. In: Druschel, P., Kaashoek, F., Rowstron, A. (eds.) IPTPS 2002. LNCS, vol. 2429, pp. 251–260. Springer, Heidelberg (2002). https://doi.org/10.1007/3-540-45748-8_24
10. Fu, S., He, F., Xu, Y., Tao, D.: Bayesian inference forgetting. arXiv preprint arXiv:2101.06417 (2021)
11. Fung, C., Yoon, C.J., Beschastnikh, I.: Mitigating Sybils in federated learning poisoning. arXiv abs/1808.04866 (2018)
12. Gao, X., et al.: VeriFi: Towards verifiable federated unlearning (2022). arXiv preprint arXiv:2205.12709
13. Gao, Y., Xu, C., Wang, D., Chen, S., Ranasinghe, D.C., Nepal, S.: STRIP: a defence against trojan attacks on deep neural networks. In: Proceedings of the 35th Annual Computer Security Applications Conference, pp. 113–125 (2019)
14. Garg, S., Goldwasser, S., Vasudevan, P.N.: Formalizing data deletion in the context of the right to be forgotten. In: Canteaut, A., Ishai, Y. (eds.) EUROCRYPT 2020. LNCS, vol. 12106, pp. 373–402. Springer, Cham (2020). https://doi.org/10.1007/978-3-030-45724-2_13
15. Ginart, A., Guan, M.Y., Valiant, G., Zou, J.: Making AI forget you: Data deletion in machine learning (2019). arXiv preprint arXiv:1907.05012
16. Golatkar, A., Achille, A., Soatto, S.: Eternal sunshine of the spotless net: selective forgetting in deep networks. In: Proceedings of the IEEE/CVF Conference on Computer Vision and Pattern Recognition, pp. 9304–9312 (2020)
17. Huang, X., Zhu, D., Zhang, F., Liu, T., Li, X., Zou, L.: Sensing population distribution from satellite imagery via deep learning: model selection, neighboring effects, and systematic biases. IEEE J. Sel. Top. Appl. Earth Observations Remote Sens. **14**, 5137–5151 (2021). https://doi.org/10.1109/JSTARS.2021.3076630

18. Konečný, J., McMahan, H.B., Ramage, D., Richtárik, P.: Federated optimization: Distributed machine learning for on-device intelligence (2016). arXiv preprint arXiv:1610.02527
19. Konečný, J., McMahan, H.B., Yu, F.X., Richtárik, P., Suresh, A.T., Bacon, D.: Federated learning: Strategies for improving communication efficiency (2016). arXiv preprint arXiv:1610.05492
20. Liu, G., Ma, X., Yang, Y., Wang, C., Liu, J.: FedEraser: enabling efficient client-level data removal from federated learning models. In: 2021 IEEE/ACM 29th International Symposium on Quality of Service (IWQOS), pp. 1–10 (2021). https://doi.org/10.1109/IWQOS52092.2021.9521274
21. Liu, Y., Ma, Z., Liu, X., Ma, J.: Learn to forget: User-level memorization elimination in federated learning (2020). arXiv preprint arXiv:2003.10933
22. Liu, Y., Xu, L., Yuan, X., Wang, C., Li, B.: The right to be forgotten in federated learning: An efficient realization with rapid retraining. In: IEEE INFOCOM 2022 - IEEE Conference on Computer Communications, pp. 1749–1758 (2022). https://doi.org/10.1109/INFOCOM48880.2022.9796721
23. Liu, Y., Lee, W.C., Tao, G., Ma, S., Aafer, Y., Zhang, X.: ABS: scanning neural networks for back-doors by artificial brain stimulation. In: Proceedings of the 2019 ACM SIGSAC Conference on Computer and Communications Security, pp. 1265–1282 (2019)
24. Liu, Y., Lee, W.C., Tao, G., Ma, S., Aafer, Y., Zhang, X.: ABS: scanning neural networks for back-doors by artificial brain stimulation. In: Proceedings of the 2019 ACM SIGSAC Conference on Computer and Communications Security, pp. 1265–1282. CCS 2019, Association for Computing Machinery, New York, NY, USA (2019). https://doi.org/10.1145/3319535.3363216
25. Ma, Z., Liu, Y., Liu, X., Liu, J., Ma, J., Ren, K.: Learn to forget: machine unlearning via neuron masking. IEEE Trans. Dependable Secure Comput. **20**(4), 3194–3207 (2023). https://doi.org/10.1109/TDSC.2022.3194884
26. Marcel, S., Rodriguez, Y.: Torchvision the machine-vision package of torch. In: Proceedings of the 18th ACM International Conference on Multimedia, pp. 1485–1488 (2010)
27. McMahan, H.B., Moore, E., Ramage, D., y Arcas, B.A.: Federated learning of deep networks using model averaging (2016). arXiv preprint arXiv:1602.05629
28. Milburn, A., Van Der Kouwe, E., Giuffrida, C.: Mitigating information leakage vulnerabilities with type-based data isolation. In: 2022 IEEE Symposium on Security and Privacy (SP), pp. 1049–1065 (2022). https://doi.org/10.1109/SP46214.2022.9833675
29. Oosthoek, K., Doerr, C.: Cyber security threats to bitcoin exchanges: adversary exploitation and laundering techniques. IEEE Trans. Netw. Serv. Manage. **18**(2), 1616–1628 (2021). https://doi.org/10.1109/TNSM.2020.3046145
30. Paszke, A., et al.: PyTorch: an imperative style, high-performance deep learning library. In: 33rd Conference on Neural Information Processing Systems (NeurIPS2019) (2019)
31. Thudi, A., Deza, G., Chandrasekaran, V., Papernot, N.: Unrolling SGD: understanding factors influencing machine unlearning. In: 2022 IEEE 7th European Symposium on Security and Privacy (EuroS&P), pp. 303–319 (2022). https://doi.org/10.1109/EuroSP53844.2022.00027
32. Veldanda, A.K., et al.: NNoculation: Broad spectrum and targeted treatment of backdoored DNNs (2020). arXiv preprint arXiv:2002.08313

33. Wang, B., et al.: Neural cleanse: identifying and mitigating backdoor attacks in neural networks. In: 2019 IEEE Symposium on Security and Privacy (SP), pp. 707–723. IEEE (2019)

34. Wang, J., Guo, S., Xie, X., Qi, H.: Federated unlearning via class-discriminative pruning. In: Proceedings of the ACM Web Conference 2022. p. 622–632. WWW 2022, Association for Computing Machinery, New York, NY, USA (2022). https:// doi.org/10.1145/3485447.3512222

35. Wu, C., Zhu, S., Mitra, P.: Federated unlearning with knowledge distillation (2022). arXiv preprint arXiv:2201.09441

36. Xu, H., Zhu*, T., Zhang, L., Zhou, W., Yu, P.S.: Machine unlearning: a survey. ACM Comput. Surv. 56(1), 1–36 (2023). https://doi.org/10.1145/3603620

37. Zhang, Z., Liu, Q., Huang, Z., Wang, H., Lee, C.K., Chen, E.: Model inversion attacks against graph neural networks. IEEE Trans. Knowl. Data Eng. 35(9), 8729–8741 (2022). https://doi.org/10.1109/TKDE.2022.3207915

BigText-QA: Question Answering over a Large-Scale Hybrid Knowledge Graph

Jingjing Xu[1]([⊠]) [iD], Maria Biryukov[1] [iD], Martin Theobald[1] [iD],
and Vinu Ellampallil Venugopal[2] [iD]

[1] University of Luxembourg, 4365 Esch-sur-Alzette, Luxembourg
{jingjing.xu,maria.biryukov,martin.theobald}@uni.lu
[2] International Institute of Information Technology (IIIT), Bangalore, India
vinu.ev@iiitb.ac.in

Abstract. Answering complex questions over textual resources remains a challenge, particularly when dealing with nuanced relationships between multiple entities expressed within natural-language sentences. To this end, curated knowledge bases (KBs) like YAGO, DBpedia, Freebase, and Wikidata have been widely used and gained great acceptance for question-answering (QA) applications in the past decade. While these KBs offer a structured knowledge representation, they lack the contextual diversity found in natural-language sources. To address this limitation, BigText-QA introduces an integrated QA approach, which is able to answer questions based on a more redundant form of a knowledge graph (KG) that organizes both structured and unstructured (i.e., "hybrid") knowledge in a unified graphical representation. Thereby, BigText-QA is able to combine the best of both worlds—a *canonical set of named entities*, mapped to a structured background KB (such as YAGO or Wikidata), as well as an *open set of textual clauses* providing highly diversified relational paraphrases with rich context information. Our experimental results demonstrate that BigText-QA outperforms DrQA, a neural-network-based QA system, and achieves competitive results to QUEST, a graph-based unsupervised QA system.

Keywords: Question Answering · Large-Scale Graph · Hybrid Knowledge Graph · Natural Language Processing

1 Introduction

Information extraction (IE) has made strides in extracting structured data ("facts") from unstructured resources like text and semistructured components (e.g., tables and infoboxes) [49]. Established knowledge bases (KBs) such as YAGO [44], DBpedia [2], Freebase [6] or Wikidata [47] use IE techniques to store numerous facts. However, KBs are mostly limited to triple-based representations of knowledge, capturing semantic relationships between real-world objects (entities and concepts) but lacking contextual information about the facts' origins. On the other hand, information retrieval (IR) efficiently

Supported by Luxembourg National Research Fund (FNR).

Z. Tan et al. (Eds.): BDTA 2023, LNICST 555, pp. 33–48, 2024.
https://doi.org/10.1007/978-3-031-52265-9_3

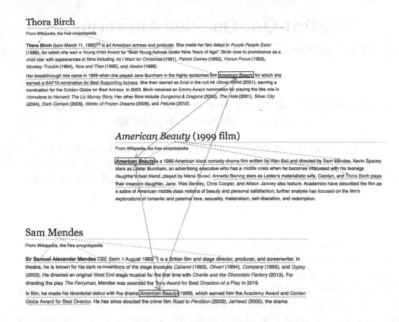

Fig. 1. A snapshot of the BigText graph viewed as a corpus of interconnected documents.

operates on large document collections using context-based statistics like term frequencies and co-occurrences [34]. Yet, classical IR approaches often rely on a simplified "bag of words" representation, overlooking the documents' internal structure.

Our BigText approach aims to combine the strengths of information extraction (IE) and information retrieval (IR) without simplifying their concepts. It represents a document collection as a redundant (hybrid) knowledge graph (KG), preserving the original document structure, domains, hyperlinks, and metadata. The graph includes substructures like sentences, clauses, lists, and tables, along with mentions of named entities and their syntactic and semantic dependencies. By linking mentions to a canonical set of real-world entities, additional links between entities and their contexts across document boundaries are established. Figure 1 illustrates this approach using snapshots of Wikipedia articles about actors and movies[1], where the articles are interconnected through jointly mentioned entities like "American Beauty".

From a syntactic point of view, the grammatical structures of the sentences are represented by hierarchically connected document substructures which become vertices in our BigText-KG. Specifically, *interlinked documents* form the basic entry points to our knowledge graph. These are decomposed into *sentences* which, in turn, consist of *clauses* (i.e., units of coherent information, each with an obligatory subject and a verbal or nominal predicate, and several optional (in)direct object(s), complement(s) and

---

[1] We use Wikipedia articles here to keep aligned with the experiments described in this paper. Note however that the choice of the document collection is not limited to any particular document type and can also combine heterogeneous natural-language resources, such as books, news, social networks, etc.

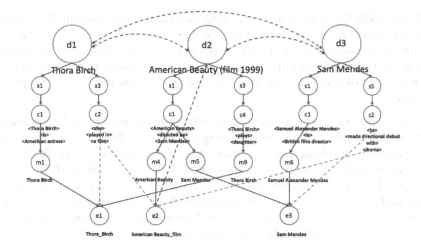

Fig. 2. Internal representation of the BigText graph of Fig. 1 as a property graph. The graph distinguishes five types of *vertices*: *documents* (*d*), *sentences* (*s*), *clauses* (*c*), *mentions* (*m*), and *entities* (*e*). The blue edges connect document's structural components. Red edges connect mentions to entities due to the named entity disambiguation and linking to real-life objects and, as a result, interlink the documents; green edges are "implicit" connections, linking mentions to entities due to syntactic dependencies and co-reference resolution.

adverbials that further contextualize the two mandatory components). Clauses further contain *mentions* of *named entities* (NEs) within their narrow clause contexts which then finally also capture the *relationships* among two or more such entities.

In natural language, entities are often referred to in various ways, requiring resolution and disambiguation before mapping them to a canonical set of real-world named entities (NEs) in a background KB like YAGO or Wikidata. This process establishes reliable links within and across documents' boundaries. Syntactic dependencies are crucial for disambiguation as they expand the fixed list of vocabulary variations to dynamically occurring local contexts. For instance, consider the sentence "*she* played Jane Burnham in the highly acclaimed *film American Beauty*." The apposition between "*film*" and "*American Beauty*" helps to link "*she*" directly to the real-world entity "*American Beauty*" instead of the generic concept "*film*". Similarly, in the sentence "he made his directorial debut with the *drama American Beauty* (1999)," the apposition between "*drama*" and "*American Beauty*" enriches the entity with a semantic attribute describing its genre, which may be useful for sentiment analysis or further profiling of Sam Mendes' movie portfolio. Figure 2 shows a small subset of explicit and implicit relations that can be established between the entities Thora Birch, Sam Mendes and American Beauty using the structural representations of the respective documents from Fig. 1. Additionally, the analysis reveals different functions attributed to Thora Birch and Sam Mendes in American Beauty: Thora Birch *plays in* "American Beauty" while Sam Mendes *directs* "American Beauty" (an inverse relation obtained from a passive sentence "American Beauty is a 1999 American black comedy-drama film written by Alan Ball and *directed by* Sam Mendes.").

By incorporating more entities, exploring the syntactic and semantic dependencies between them and connecting the mentions to their real-world concepts, BigText incrementally builds a large-scale hybrid KG of highly interlinked and semantically enriched documents. This BigText-KG is designed to serve as a generic basis for a variety of text-analytical tasks such as searching and ranking, relation extraction, and question answering.

In this paper, we present a case study in which BigText is employed as an underlying knowledge graph of a *question answering* (QA) system, BigText-QA. When evaluated on questions involving multiple entities and relations between them, BigText-QA achieves competitive results with state-of-the-art QA systems like QUEST [32] and DrQA [8]. The rest of the paper is organized ass follows: Sect. 2 provides a survey of related work; Sect. 3 formally presents the BigText knowledge graph; Sect. 4 introduces the BigText question-answering system; Sect. 5 presents the experimental setup; Sect. 6 discusses the experimental results; and Sect. 7 finally concludes the paper.

2 Background and Related Work

In this section, we take a closer into the main QA approaches, which we broadly categorize based on their foundations: TextQA, KGQA (knowledge graph-based QA), and HybridQA (such as our BigText-QA), which seeks to integrate both textual and structured knowledge resources.

TextQA. TextQA approaches typically retrieve answers from raw unstructured text by extracting and aggregating information from relevant documents. Early systems like START [27] are representative of such approaches, while more recent ones like DrQA, DocumentQA [9], and R3 [48] employ neural-network techniques to enhance the matching capabilities. They leverage vast amounts of textual data and benefit from identifying semantic similarities but may struggle with complex queries calling for a concise structural representation.

KGQA. Traditionally, KG-based QA approaches transform a Natural Language (NL) input question into a logical representation by mapping NL phrases to various structured templates (e.g., in SPARQL). These templates can be executed against a query engine (e.g., by indexing RDF data) [4,12]. Recent KGQA techniques have improved upon this approach in two main ways: (1) incorporation of information retrieval (IR)-style relaxation on the templates to allow for selection and ranking of the relevant KG subgraphs in response to the input [7,14,20,51]; and (2) application of Neural Semantic Parsing (NSP) that converts the input question into a logical representation which, in turn, is translated into an actual query language understood by the KG [13,17,29,33,57]. While KG-based QA systems are strong in handling the logical structure of the question, the KG is inherently condensed and largely oblivious to the question's context which may weaken the system's performance.

HybridQA. Hybrid QA systems have been proposed for the sake of overcoming the limitations of the TextQA and KGQA paradigms while capitalizing on their respective strengths. A hybrid approach suggested in IBM seminal work [16] followed by [3], obtains candidate answers from separate structured and unstructured resources. Among the systems that adopted such an integrated approach are [42], that combines external textual data and SPARQL-based templates for answering questions; [11] and [38,45] that employ neural networks to merge knowledge graphs (KGs) and textual resources into a common space using a universal-schema representation [41,46]. More recent research has explored the integration of KGs into large pre-trained language models (LLMs) and their application for open-domain question answering [26,38,52,53,56]. For example, UniK-QA [38] utilized the T5 model [39], a powerful LLM, to answer open-domain questions by leveraging heterogeneous sources.

Current state-of-the-art QA approaches achieve impressive results but also require vast amounts of data and significant time for training. Furthermore, they often need to dynamically integrate data retrieved from various external sources with KGs, adding to the systems' complexity. In contrast, BigText-QA circumvents the need for extensive training by building a unified property graph. This graph incorporates structured knowledge from disambiguated entities, while also preserving the original NL phrases that provide context and express relationships between the entities. This approach makes hybrid knowledge readily available for the QA process, thus reducing question-processing time. Furthermore, BigText-QA employs a Spark-based distributed architecture, enabling easy scalability and efficient handling of very large graphs.

3 BigText Knowledge Graph

Our BigText project is driven by the strong belief that natural-language text itself is the most comprehensive knowledge base we can possibly have; it just needs to be made machine-accessible for further processing and analytics.

Design and Implementation. BigText aims at processing large collections, consisting of millions of text documents. We currently employ Apache Spark [54] and its integrated distributed graph engine, GraphX [50], which allows us to model the entire collection as a unified property graph that can also be distributed across multiple compute nodes or be deployed on top of any of the common cloud architectures, if desired.

Property Graph. As depicted in Fig. 2, our BigText graph distinguishes five types of *vertices*: *documents* (d), *sentences* (s), *clauses* (c), *mentions* (m), and *entities* (e). Spark's GraphX allows us to associate an extensible list of properties for each vertex type, such that the (ordered) vertices are able to losslessly (and partly even redundantly) capture all the extracted information from a preconfigured Natural Language Processing (NLP) pipeline together with the original text sources. Figure 4 shows an internal representation of the property graph. For example, a document property stores the corresponding title and other relevant metadata, such as timestamp and source URL, while a mention vertex is augmented with morphological data, such as part-of-speech (POS) and lemma, the syntactic role within the sentence, as well as entity-type information, where applicable. Entity vertex property carries on the result of the mention disambiguation to a canonicalised entity.

Sentences, clauses and mentions form hierarchical substructures of documents, while links among different mentions (possibly from different clauses or sentences, or

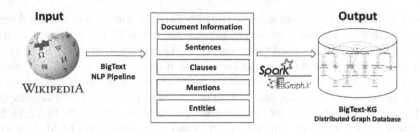

Fig. 3. High-level construction of the BigText knowledge graph.

```
class VertexProperty()

case class DocumentProperty(val
title: String, val timestamp,
val URL, val sentences:
Array[String]) extends
VertexPropert

case class SentenceProperty(val
content: String, val clauses:
Array[String]) extends
VertexProperty

case class ClauseProperty(val
content: String, val mentions:
Array[String]) extends
VertexProperty
```

```
case class
MentionProperty(val content:
String, val entities: String)
extends VertexProperty

case class EntityProperty(val
content: String) extends
VertexProperty

class EdgeProperty(val
source: String, val
destination: String)

var graph:
Graph[VertexProperty,
EdgeProperty](vertices,
edges)
```

Fig. 4. Case classes (in Scala) capturing the BigText-KG as a property graph in Spark's GraphX APIs.

even from different documents) to a same entity vertex in the background KB express additional coreferences. Recovered implicit relations resulting from appositions (e.g., "drama", and "film" with respect to "American Beauty") and co-reference resolution ("she" and "he" with respect to Thora Birch and Sam Mendes, respectively) are shown as green thin dashed lines in Fig. 2. Furthermore, the presence of *clause* vertices in combination with the disambiguated entity mentions, allows for dynamic extraction of the facts' subgraphs, containing mentions as vertices and the clauses' predicates as labeled edges.

NLP Pipeline. Before populating the property graph, documents in the collection are passed through a preconfigured and extensible NLP pipeline which decomposes the input into documents, sentences and clauses. Clauses are generated from sentences with an Open Information Extraction (OIE) technique. While each clause represents a semantically coherent block of entity mentions linked by a predicate, mentions first appear in their original lexical form without further linking to typed entities (such as PER, ORG, LOC) or unique knowledge base identifiers, for example WikiData IDs. Therefore, our pipeline also incorporates the steps of Named Entity Recognition (NER) and Named Entity Disambiguation (NED) as they are available from recent IE tools. Since clauses may have pronouns as their subject and/or object constituents, Coreference Resolution (CR) has been added to the NLP pipeline to increase the coverage of downstream analytical tasks. For example, linking *she* in "... she played Jane Burnham in the highly acclaimed film American Beauty" to *Thora Birch* establishes a connection between the two real-world entities, "American Beauty" and "Thora Birch", which can then further be explored.

Table 1. Annotators and background KBs used in the BigText NLP pipeline.

Annotation type	Tools
HTML parser	**Jsoup**[a]
Tokenization	Spacy
OpenIE	**ClausIE** [10], OpenIE5[b], OpenIE6 [28]
NER	**StanfordNLP**, Flair [43]
NED	**AIDA-Light** [37], REL [23], ELQ [31]
CR	SpanBERT:2018 [30], SpanBERT:2020 [24]
Background KB	**YAGO**, WikiData[c]

[a] https://jsoup.org/
[b] https://github.com/dair-iitd/OpenIE-standalone
[c] https://www.wikidata.org/

Projects which involve the stage of text (pre-)processing typically apply either an entire end-to-end suite of annotation tools, such as NLTK [5], StanfordNLP [35], SpaCy[2], or a specific component from it (which can also be substituted with a stand-alone or equivalent tool). Conversely, our text annotation pipeline does not limit the choice of annotators. We intend to use state-of-the-art target-specific components to minimise the risk of error propagation. This strategy allows us to adapt the selection of tools to the type of documents being processed (e.g., long documents corresponding to full-text Wikipedia articles versus short ones, such as Wikipedia articles' abstracts or news). Our implementation also allows for integrating outputs provided by different tools with the same annotation goal. In that way, the pipeline can be configured with further rules that prioritize either precision or recall (e.g., by considering either the intersection or the union of annotations). Table 1 depicts the annotation tools that have been integrated into the BigText NLP pipeline so far. Figure 3 depicts the entire construction process of the BigText knowledge graph (BigText-KG).

Table 2. BigText-KG statistics (in millions) for Wikipedia.

Documents	Sentences	Clauses	Mentions	Entities
5.3	97	190	283	2

Applications. In the following part of this paper, we focus on *question answering* (QA) as our main target application which relies on the BigText-KG as its underlying knowl-

[2] https://spacy.io/.

edge graph. We use full-text articles of an entire Wikipedia dump from 2019[3]. Statistics are shown in Table 2. Tools that have been used to process the version discussed here and used for the experiments are shown in Table 1 in bold font.

4   BigText Question Answering

The design of BigText-QA is based on QUEST, a graph-based question-answering system that specifically targets complex questions with multiple entities and relations. QUEST constructs a so-called *quasi-graph* by "googling" for relevant documents in response to an NL input question and by applying a proximity-based decomposition of sentences into $< \texttt{sub} >, < \texttt{pred} >, < \texttt{obj} >$ triplets (SPO). Similarly to our BigText-KG, leaf nodes of the quasi-graph are *mentions* (vertex labels in BigText), *relations* (edge properties in BigText) and *type* nodes (vertex properties in BigText). In QUEST, the latter are the result of a semantic expansion of mentions via the application of Hearst patterns [21] and/or lookups in an explicit mention-entity dictionary. In BigText, both the structural decomposition of the documents and their annotations have been provided by the preconfigured NLP pipeline.

Since our instance of the BigText-KG is built using Wikipedia as the text resource, our system consequently retrieves relevant Wikipedia documents by using Lucene as underlying search engine[4]. The top-10 of the retrieved documents then serve as pivots for the respective subgraph that is selected from the entire BigText-KG upon each incoming NL question. In summary, we translate such a BigText subgraph to a structure equivalent to QUEST's quasi-graph (depicted in Fig. 5) as follows:

Vertex Translation. Mention ("m") and entity ("e") vertices are directly translated from the BigText subgraph to the QUEST quasi-graph. These can be the subject and/or object of a clause. Type vertices ("t") are added based on the syntactic and semantic properties of the vertices, augmented with the application of Hearst patterns, following the QUEST approach. Predicate vertices ("p") are created out of the verbal component of a clause, while synonymous relation nodes are added using word/phrase embeddings (Sect. 4.1).

Edge Translation. Edges between predicates, mentions and disambiguated entities are directly translated from the BigText subgraph into the QUEST quasi-graph. Similarly to QUEST, we additionally introduce *type* and *alignment* edges from the respective vertex and edge properties in BigText. Type edges connect mention nodes with type nodes. For example, an organge edge between the mention node "Thora Birch" and type node "American actress" on the Fig. 5 is one such edge. It expresses the relation of type NP_1 is NP_2 captured by Hearst pattern. Alignment edges connect potentially synonymous mention nodes resolved to the same entity (thick blue edges between, for example, m_5 "Sam Mendes" and m_6 "Samuel Alexander Mendes", connected via e_3 to the entity "Sam_Mendes"), and potentially synonymous relation nodes such as "made directional debut" and "directed by"(dashed blues edges) in the same figure.

---

[3] https://dumps.wikimedia.org/enwiki/latest/.

[4] https://lucene.apache.org/core/.

4.1   Question-Answering Pipeline

In more detail, our QA pipeline processes an incoming NL question (or clue) as follows.

(1) The NL input question serves as a keyword query to Lucene which then retrieves the top-10 most relevant documents from the Wikipedia corpus. These documents are used as entry points to the BigText-KG to select a relevant subgraph that captures the questions' context; this subgraph includes all the documents' hierarchical substructures plus their links to the background KB.

(2) A syntactic parser (similar to QUEST) is applied to the question in order to identify its subject, predicate and object, which we refer to as the *question terms*.

(3) The subgraph is translated into QUEST's quasi-graph (see below for details).

(4) Vertices in the quasi-graph, which have high similarity with the question terms, become terminals (so-called "cornerstones" in QUEST). For example, "Thora Birch", "played in" and "plays" are examples of cornerstones, corresponding to question terms "Thora Birch" and "starred" (orange nodes in Fig. 5), respectively.

(5) Together with the quasi-graph and its weighted edges (see below), cornerstones constitute the input to QUEST's Group Steiner Tree (GST) algorithm [18] which is used to compute an answer set. A final ranking among the matching vertices in the answer set provides the ranked answers to the input question.

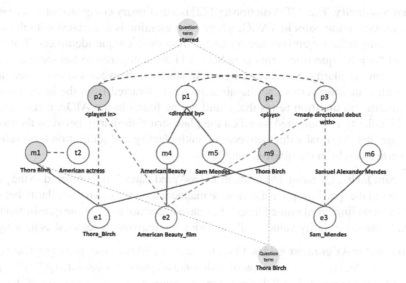

Fig. 5. QUEST quasi-graph for the question *"Which British stage director is best known for his feature-film directing debut, which starred Kevin Spacey, Annette Bening, and Thora Birch?"*. It results from the translation of the BigText (sub)graph in Fig. 2.

4.2   Weighting Schemes

Before we can proceed with the application of the GST algorithm and its answer-set calculation, both vertices and edges in QUEST's quasi-graph have to be assigned with weights, which (in our case) are derived from the relevant BigText subgraph.

- **Vertex weights** are defined by the similarity between the question terms and the vertices in the quasi-graph. Specifically, we adopt the two weighting schemes suggested in [32] and discuss their application.
- **Edge weights** are calculated depending on the edge type. The weight of an edge between a mention and a predicate vertex is the inverse of the distance between the two vertices in the BigText subgraph. Formally, this is defined as the number of words between a mention (i.e., subject and object) and a predicate of a clause vertex in the BigText subgraph. If two vertices are directly connected via multiple edges, the highest such weight is selected. Weights of alignment edges are calculated based on the semantic similarity between the vertices they connect (see Subsect. 4.3).

4.3   Similarities and Thresholds

Question terms are compared to the vertices in the quasi-graph according to their syntactic type as follows.

Jaccard Similarity. The AIDA dictionary [22] is a dictionary composed of a large number of entity-mention pairs in YAGO, where each mention is associated with the set of entities it may refer to; entities are represented by their unique identifiers. The "subject" and "object" question terms (see Sect. 4.1) are compared to the mention nodes using Jaccard similarity. Similarly, Jaccard similarity is between the entity sets associated with a mention vertex and the question term extracted from the input question. For mentions and question terms that could not be found in the AIDA dictionary, the Jaccard similarity is computed based on the plain string similarity between the two. In either case, the maximal value between a mention/entity and a question term selected as the vertex weight in the quasi-graph.

Cosine Similarity. Question terms identified as "predicates" are compared to the *predicate nodes* of the quasi-graph in a pair-wise manner using the Cosine similarity between their corresponding word embeddings[5]. For each predicate node in the quasi-graph, the maximal cosine similarity value of all pair-wise comparisons is selected as its weight.

Similarities for Alignment Edges. Once the node weights of the quasi-graph are computed, we can decide on the insertion of additional *alignment edges* into QUEST's quasi graph to further support the GST algorithm. An alignment edge is inserted if the similarity between two candidate vertices of the same type exceeds a pre-defined threshold. The similarity value then becomes the weight of the corresponding edge. Similarities between two mention vertices are again computed using Jaccard similarity (otherwise it is set to 1 if the two mentions are linked to the same entity), while the ones between predicate and type vertices are calculated using Cosine similarity.

---

[5] We use the default word2vec model [36] trained on Google news.

After the quasi-graph has been constructed, it is its largest connected component, together with the cornerstones, which is used as an input to the GST-algorithm.

Thresholds. All thresholds (calculated either by Jaccard or Cosine similarities) are set to 0.25 except the ones for the *predicate alignment edges* where we experiment with a range of values: 0.25, 0.375, 0.5, 0.6, 0.75 (see Table 3). We remark that our threshold policy is different from the one applied by QUEST, where all thresholds are the same and set to 0.5.

After the quasi-graph construction, we proceed with the answer-set computation, ranking and filtering. These steps are performed exactly as in the QUEST framework.

5   Experiments

All experiments reported in this paper are conducted on a single large Intel Xeon Platinum server with 2.4 GHz, 192 virtual cores and 1.2 TB of RAM, holding the entire BigText-KG in main memory. All translation steps are performed using PySpark 2.4.1 [55] for transforming Spark's GraphX RDDs into the relevant BigText subgraph via parallel processing. The BigText subgraph is translated into QUEST's quasi-graph by a second Python library, NetworkX 2.8 [19].

We use two benchmark datasets for the evaluation: CQ-W [1] and TriviaQA [25]. Regarding CQ-W, we remove questions whose answers are not present in the Wikipedia-based BigText subgraph, which is the case for about 25% of the questions[6]. The remaining 75% of the questions are used for the comparative evaluation. As for TriviaQA, we randomly select 79 questions from the development set (wikipedia-dev.json). CQ-W is a curated dataset of question-and-answer pairs, which consists of 150 complex questions from Wiki-Answers [15]. TriviaQA is a large-scale dataset made of complex and compositional questions and corresponding gold answers.

To run the experiments, we feed the top-10 documents selected from Wikipedia by Lucene both to the original QUEST engine and to BigText-QA in order to ensure a fair comparison. We also quote the results achieved by DrQA on the CQ-W dataset as a further baseline. As opposed to QUEST and BigText-QA, DrQA is a neural-network-based QA system, and thus represents another class of QA systems. DrQA is trained on the SQuAD [40] question-and-answer set which is also based on a subset of Wikipedia articles.

6   Result and Discussion

The main scoring metric for evaluating the QA systems is Mean Reciprocal Rank (MRR), calculated as $MRR = \frac{1}{Q}\sum_{i=1}^{Q}\frac{1}{rank_i}$, where Q is the number of questions and $rank_i$ is the rank of the first correct answer for the i-th question. Other important metrics include Precision@1 (P@1) and Hit@5. P@1 represents the precision of the

---

[6] This decision was motivated by the fact that, for those questions, none of the top-10 documents returned by Lucene actually contained the answer.

Table 3. Comparison between BigText-QA, QUEST and DrQA on the CQ-W and TriviaQA datasets.

Dataset	System	Cosine	#Vertices	#Edges (10^5)	MRR	P@1	Hit@5
CQ-W	BigText-QA	0.250	1,276	7.234	0.387	0.324	0.441
		0.375	1,276	7.234	0.387	0.324	0.441
		0.500	**1,268**	**6.727**	**0.398**	**0.342**	**0.423**
		0.600	**579**	**0.510**	**0.264**	**0.198**	**0.297**
		0.750	210	0.030	0.140	0.081	0.189
	QUEST	0.500	2,385	13.580	0.464	0.423	0.495
		0.600	**1,267**	**0.609**	**0.329**	**0.279**	**0.369**
		0.750	**642**	0.032	0.181	0.099	0.279
	DrQA	-	-	-	0.120	0.171	0.315
Trivia-QA	BigText-QA	0.375	840	2.073	0.412	0.342	0.494
		0.500	**838**	**1.968**	**0.412**	**0.342**	**0.468**
		0.600	**365**	**0.163**	**0.258**	**0.190**	**0.316**
		0.750	121	0.007	0.130	0.063	0.190
	QUEST	0.500	1,710	4.025	0.425	0.380	0.468
		0.600	**968**	**0.241**	**0.285**	**0.215**	**0.329**
		0.750	**490**	0.025	0.198	0.139	0.241

top-ranked document retrieved, while Hit@5 is 1 if one of the top 5 results includes the correct answer. These metrics offer valuable insights into the system's performance. A higher score indicates better performance for the QA system. The results are shown in Table 3 and Table 4. In these tables, *Cosine* refers to the edge threshold which is used to select *predicate alignment edges*; *#vertices* and *#edges* refer to the largest connected component of the quasi-graph which is used as input to the GST-algorithm. *MRR*, *P@1*, *Hit@5* (as well as the number of nodes and edges in the respective quasi-graphs) are averaged across all questions.

Table 3 shows that BigText-QA achieves very competitive results, usually generating more compact yet denser graphs compared to QUEST. This compactness positively impacts the results, as it involves fewer answer candidates. QUEST slightly outperforms BigText-QA when its quasi-graph has nearly twice as many nodes. However, in cases where both systems generate quasi-graphs of comparable order (BigText-QA with $Cosine = 0.5$, QUEST with $Cosine = 0.6$, and BigText-QA with $Cosine = 0.6$, QUEST with $Cosine = 0.75$, shown in bold font in Table 3), BigText-QA outperforms QUEST on both question sets, CQ-W, and TriviaQA.

Table 3 indicates two ways of achieving close results using the GST algorithm: either by having sufficient, even "poorly" connected vertices (QUEST), or by having fewer but better connected vertices (BigText-QA). Different quasi-graph configurations in both systems arise from distinct underlying NLP pre-processing of input documents, particularly in the decomposition of sentences into clauses. BigText-QA yields fewer but more accurate vertices, facilitating the generation of dense graphs even with the increasing threshold values for edge insertion, which positively affects the performance.

Note, that the effect of changing the edge threshold below 0.5 is negligible (first two rows in the Table 3). However, raising it from 0.5 to 0.6 significantly decreases the number of edges. This may be due to the word2vec model itself, as a low similarity

Table 4. Comparison of QUEST and BigText-QA over different categories of questions in CQ-W.

Type	System	Cosine	#Vertices	#Edges(10^5)	MRR	P@1	Hit@5
People	BigText-QA	**0.500**	**1,375**	9.451	**0.388**	**0.333**	**0.407**
		0.600	**654**	0.667	**0.273**	**0.185**	**0.333**
		0.750	250	0.035	0.173	0.111	0.204
	QUEST	0.500	2,600	19.396	0.448	0.389	0.500
		0.600	**1,384**	0.793	0.304	0.259	0.333
		0.750	**741**	0.037	0.159	0.074	0.259
Movie	BigText-QA	**0.500**	**1,428**	4.843	0.353	0.333	0.333
		0.600	**657**	0.507	0.242	0.200	0.233
		0.750	185	0.029	0.074	0.033	0.100
	QUEST	0.500	2,636	9.279	0.504	0.500	0.500
		0.600	**1,381**	0.496	**0.441**	**0.433**	**0.433**
		0.750	**589**	0.027	**0.094**	**0.067**	**0.067**
Place	BigText-QA	**0.500**	**756**	2.059	**0.580**	**0.444**	**0.722**
		0.600	254	0.107	0.293	0.167	0.389
		0.750	129	0.006	0.108	0.056	0.222
	QUEST	0.500	1,393	3.126	0.498	0.444	0.556
		0.600	**729**	0.168	0.315	0.167	0.500
		0.750	414	0.013	0.359	0.222	0.500

threshold results in numerous "weak" alignment edges. A change from 0.5 to 0.6 is typically where the model becomes more discriminative, leading to a smaller number of synonymous edges. This trend continues with a further increase in the threshold to 0.75.

When compared to DrQA, both QUEST and BigText-QA outperform it, as they are designed to handle complex questions and incorporate evidence from multiple documents. In contrast, DrQA embodies an IR-based approach to QA, expecting the answer to a question to be narrowed down to a specific text span within a single document that closely matches the question.

To gain a more detailed understanding of the performance of BigText-QA versus QUEST, we divided the CQ-W set into six question categories: *People, Movie, Place, Others, Language, Music*. However, the last three categories turned out too small to be representative (containing only 4, 2 and 3 questions, respectively). We therefore focus on the first three categories (*People, Movie, Place*) in Table 4. Here again we highlight in boldface the lines which show the results obtained by both the systems on the quasi-graphs of comparable order. Consistent with the overall results, BigText-QA and QUEST demonstrate similar performance patterns in *People*- and *Place*-related questions as we discussed previously. However, BigText-QA does not compare favorably in *Movie*-related questions. We leave an in-depth investigation of this result as a future work.

7 Conclusion

In this paper, we have presented BigText-QA—a question answering system that uses a large-scale hybrid knowledge graph as its knowledge base. To this end, BigText-QA outperforms DrQA, a state-of-the-art neural-network-based QA system, and achieves competitive results with QUEST, a graph-based unsupervised QA system that inspired the design of BigText-QA. We see these results as a proof-of-concept for our hybrid knowledge representation which captures both textual and structured components in a unified manner in our BigText-KG approach.

Acknowledgments. This work was funded by FNR (Grant ID: 15748747). We thank Rishiraj Saha Roy and his group at the Max Planck Institute for Informatics for their helpful discussions and their support on integrating QUEST with our BigText graph.

References

1. Abujabal, A., Yahya, M., Riedewald, M., Weikum, G.: Automated template generation for question answering over knowledge graphs. In: WWW (2017)
2. Auer, S., Bizer, C., Kobilarov, G., Lehmann, J., Cyganiak, R., Ives, Z.: DBpedia: a nucleus for a web of open data. In: ISWC (2007)
3. Baudiš, P., Šedivỳ, J.: Modeling of the question answering task in the yodaqa system. In: CLEF (2015)
4. Berant, J., Chou, A., Frostig, R., Liang, P.: Semantic parsing on freebase from question-answer pairs. In: EMNLP (2013)
5. Bird, S., Klein, E., Loper, E.: Natural language processing with Python: analyzing text with the natural language toolkit. O'Reilly Media, Inc. (2009)
6. Bollacker, K., Evans, C., Paritosh, P., Sturge, T., Taylor, J.: Freebase: a collaboratively created graph database for structuring human knowledge. In: SIGMOD (2008)
7. Bordes, A., Chopra, S., Weston, J.: Question answering with subgraph embeddings. arXiv preprint arXiv:1406.3676 (2014)
8. Chen, D., Fisch, A., Weston, J., Bordes, A.: Reading wikipedia to answer open-domain questions. arXiv preprint arXiv:1704.00051 (2017)
9. Clark, C., Gardner, M.: Simple and effective multi-paragraph reading comprehension. arXiv preprint arXiv:1710.10723 (2017)
10. Corro, L.D., Gemulla, R.: Clausie: clause-based open information extraction. In: WWW (2013)
11. Das, R., Zaheer, M., Reddy, S., McCallum, A.: Question answering on knowledge bases and text using universal schema and memory networks. arXiv preprint arXiv:1704.08384 (2017)
12. Diefenbach, D., Lopez, V., Singh, K., Maret, P.: Core techniques of question answering systems over knowledge bases: a survey. KAIS (2018)
13. Dong, L., Lapata, M.: Language to logical form with neural attention. arXiv preprint arXiv:1601.01280 (2016)
14. Dong, L., Wei, F., Zhou, M., Xu, K.: Question answering over freebase with multi-column convolutional neural networks. In: ACL-IJCNLP (2015)
15. Fader, A., Zettlemoyer, L., Etzioni, O.: Paraphrase-driven learning for open question answering. In: ACL (2013)
16. Ferrucci, D., et al.: Building watson: an overview of the deepqa project. AI Mag. (2010)
17. Fu, B., Qiu, Y., Tang, C., Li, Y., Yu, H., Sun, J.: A survey on complex question answering over knowledge base: recent advances and challenges. arXiv preprint arXiv:2007.13069 (2020)

18. Garg, N., Konjevod, G., Ravi, R.: A polylogarithmic approximation algorithm for the group steiner tree problem. J. Algorithms (2000)
19. Hagberg, A., Swart, P., S Chult, D.: Exploring network structure, dynamics, and function using networkx. Technical report, Los Alamos National Lab. (LANL) (2008)
20. Hao, Y., et al.: An end-to-end model for question answering over knowledge base with cross-attention combining global knowledge. In: ACL (2017)
21. Hearst, M.A.: Automatic acquisition of hyponyms from large text corpora. In: COLING (1992)
22. Hoffart, J., et al.: Robust disambiguation of named entities in text. In: EMNLP (2011)
23. van Hulst, J.M., Hasibi, F., Dercksen, K., Balog, K., de Vries, A.P.: REL: an entity linker standing on the shoulders of giants. In: SIGIR (2020)
24. Joshi, M., Chen, D., Liu, Y., Weld, D.S., Zettlemoyer, L., Levy, O.: Spanbert: improving pre-training by representing and predicting spans. Trans. Assoc. Comput. Linguistics (2020)
25. Joshi, M., Choi, E., Weld, D.S., Zettlemoyer, L.: Triviaqa: a large scale distantly supervised challenge dataset for reading comprehension. arXiv preprint arXiv:1705.03551 (2017)
26. Ju, M., Yu, W., Zhao, T., Zhang, C., Ye, Y.: Grape: knowledge graph enhanced passage reader for open-domain question answering. arXiv preprint arXiv:2210.02933 (2022)
27. Katz, B., Felshin, S., Lin, J.J., Marton, G.: Viewing the web as a virtual database for question answering. In: New Directions in Question Answering (2004)
28. Kolluru, K., Adlakha, V., Aggarwal, S., Mausam, Chakrabarti, S.: OpenIE6: iterative grid labeling and coordination analysis for open information extraction. In: EMNLP (2020)
29. Lan, Y., Jiang, J.: Query graph generation for answering multi-hop complex questions from knowledge bases. In: ACL (2020)
30. Lee, K., He, L., Zettlemoyer, L.: Higher-order coreference resolution with coarse-to-fine inference. CoRR (2018)
31. Li, B.Z., Min, S., Iyer, S., Mehdad, Y., Yih, W.: Efficient one-pass end-to-end entity linking for questions. In: EMNLP (2020)
32. Lu, X., Pramanik, S., Saha Roy, R., Abujabal, A., Wang, Y., Weikum, G.: Answering complex questions by joining multi-document evidence with quasi knowledge graphs. In: SIGIR (2019)
33. Luo, K., Lin, F., Luo, X., Zhu, K.: Knowledge base question answering via encoding of complex query graphs. In: EMNLP (2018)
34. Manning, C.D.: An introduction to information retrieval. Cambridge University Press (2009)
35. Manning, C.D., Surdeanu, M., Bauer, J., Finkel, J.R., Bethard, S., McClosky, D.: The stanford corenlp natural language processing toolkit. In: ACL (2014)
36. Mikolov, T., Sutskever, I., Chen, K., Corrado, G.S., Dean, J.: Distributed representations of words and phrases and their compositionality. In: NIPS (2013)
37. Nguyen, D.B., Hoffart, J., Theobald, M., Weikum, G.: AIDA-light: high-throughput named-entity disambiguation. In: LDOW (2014)
38. Oguz, B., et al.: Unik-qa: unified representations of structured and unstructured knowledge for open-domain question answering. arXiv preprint arXiv:2012.14610 (2020)
39. Raffel, C., et al.: Exploring the limits of transfer learning with a unified text-to-text transformer. JMLR (2020)
40. Rajpurkar, P., Zhang, J., Lopyrev, K., Liang, P.: Squad: 100,000+ questions for machine comprehension of text. arXiv preprint arXiv:1606.05250 (2016)
41. Riedel, S., Yao, L., McCallum, A., Marlin, B.M.: Relation extraction with matrix factorization and universal schemas. In: NAACL-HLT (2013)
42. Savenkov, D., Agichtein, E.: When a knowledge base is not enough: question answering over knowledge bases with external text data. In: SIGIR (2016)
43. Schweter, S., Akbik, A.: FLERT: document-level features for named entity recognition. CoRR (2020)

44. Suchanek, F.M., Kasneci, G., Weikum, G.: Yago: a core of semantic knowledge. In: WWW (2007)
45. Sun, H., Bedrax-Weiss, T., Cohen, W.W.: Pullnet: open domain question answering with iterative retrieval on knowledge bases and text. arXiv preprint arXiv:1904.09537 (2019)
46. Verga, P., Belanger, D., Strubell, E., Roth, B., McCallum, A.: Multilingual relation extraction using compositional universal schema. arXiv preprint arXiv:1511.06396 (2015)
47. Vrandečić, D., Krötzsch, M.: Wikidata: a free collaborative knowledgebase. CACM (2014)
48. Wang, S., et al.: R 3: Reinforced ranker-reader for open-domain question answering. In: AAAI (2018)
49. Weikum, G., Dong, X.L., Razniewski, S., Suchanek, F., et al.: Machine knowledge: Creation and curation of comprehensive knowledge bases. Found, Trends Databases (2021)
50. Xin, R.S., Crankshaw, D., Dave, A., Gonzalez, J.E., Franklin, M.J., Stoica, I.: GraphX: Unifying data-parallel and graph-parallel analytics. CoRR (2014)
51. Yao, X., Van Durme, B.: Information extraction over structured data: Question answering with freebase. In: ACL (2014)
52. Yasunaga, M., Ren, H., Bosselut, A., Liang, P., Leskovec, J.: Qa-gnn: reasoning with language models and knowledge graphs for question answering. arXiv preprint arXiv:2104.06378 (2021)
53. Yu, D., et al.: Kg-fid: infusing knowledge graph in fusion-in-decoder for open-domain question answering. arXiv preprint arXiv:2110.04330 (2021)
54. Zaharia, M., Chowdhury, M., Franklin, M.J., Shenker, S., Stoica, I.: Spark: cluster computing with working sets. In: HotCloud (2010)
55. Zaharia, M., et al.: Apache Spark: a unified engine for big data processing. CACM (2016)
56. Zhang, L., et al.: A survey on complex factual question answering. AI Open (2023)
57. Zhu, S., Cheng, X., Su, S.: Knowledge-based question answering by tree-to-sequence learning. Neurocomputing (2020)

STLGCN: Spatial-Temporal Graph Convolutional Network for Long Term Traffic Forecasting

Xuewen Chen, Peng Peng, and Haina Tang[✉]

School of Artificial Intelligence, University of Chinese Academy of Sciences,
No. 19A, Yuquan Road, Beijing, China
{chenxuewen20,pengpeng21}@mails.ucas.ac.cn, hntang@ucas.ac.cn

Abstract. As an essential part of intelligent transportation, accurate traffic forecasting helps city managers make better arrangements and allows users to make reasonable travel plans. Current mainstream traffic forecasting models are developed based on spatial-temporal graph convolutional neural networks, in which appropriate graph structures must be generated in advance. However, most existing graph generation approaches learn graph structures based on local neighborhood relationships of urban nodes, which cannot capture complex dependencies over long spatial ranges. To solve the above problems, we propose Spatial-Temporal Graph Convolutional Neural Network (STLGCN) for long-term traffic forecasting, in which a novel graph generation method is developed by measuring multi-scale correlations among vertices. Meanwhile, a new graph convolution method is proposed for extracting valuable features and filtering out the irrelevant ones, which significantly optimizes the process of spatial information aggregation. Extensive experimental results on two real public traffic datasets, METR-LA and PEMS-BAY, demonstrate the superior performance of our algorithm.

Keywords: traffic forecasting · spatial-temporal graph neural network · long-term forecasting · graph generation

1 Introduction

Intelligent Transportation System (i.e., ITS) effectively applies computer technology and artificial intelligence in transportation and service control, strengthening the connection among vehicles, roads, and users, thus forming a safe, efficient, and accurate comprehensive transportation system. As a critical task in intelligent transportation, traffic prediction significantly impacts traffic management, vehicle allocation, travel time prediction, and other downstream tasks and has become an important research direction in ITS.

The existing traffic forecasting methods can be divided into three categories: statistical methods, traditional machine learning methods, and deep learning

© ICST Institute for Computer Sciences, Social Informatics and Telecommunications Engineering 2024
Published by Springer Nature Switzerland AG 2024. All Rights Reserved
Z. Tan et al. (Eds.): BDTA 2023, LNICST 555, pp. 49–61, 2024.
https://doi.org/10.1007/978-3-031-52265-9_4

methods. Statistical methods predict future traffic conditions through historical averages or probability modeling. The former corresponds to the historical
average model, which assumes that traffic at the exact location has similar daily
patterns; Therefore, the historical average can be used as the prediction result.
The latter's representative is the Auto-Regressive Integrated Moving Average
model (ARIMA) [1,2], which uses ARIMA to model the time series of traffic
volume. However, unexpected situations such as traffic congestion and accidents
often occur in the transportation system. In this case, statistical methods may
be unable to make accurate predictions.

Machine learning-based methods, which generally rely on support vector
machines (SVM) [3] and hidden Markov models for modeling, can better handle unexpected conditions than statistical methods. However, the performance
of machine learning-based methods is heavily determined by the effectiveness
of feature extraction. Thus, with the popularization of the Global Positioning
System (GPS) and the development of traffic sensors, traffic data has accumu-
lated rapidly. These methods are no longer suitable for processing increasingly
expanding datasets. In this case, deep learning has gradually gained attention
and become the mainstream research direction.

Deep learning methods mainly use Convolutional Neural Networks (CNN)
[4,5] or Graph Convolutional Networks (GCN) [6–8] to extract spatial features
of nodes and use Recurrent Neural Networks (RNN) [10], CNN, and Attention mechanisms to extract temporal features of nodes. Compared to CNN-
based models that only apply to grid format data, Graph Convolutional Networks (GCNs) can extract spatial features from data with non-Euclidean structures. However, its effectiveness highly depends on the quality of the graph and
requires prior knowledge of physical topology or traffic networks. In addition,
graph structures generated by adjacent relationships typically reflect local correlations between nodes, which is insufficient to capture complex dependency
over a long spatial range. In practice, the state of a node may be affected by
other non-adjacent nodes. For example, an accident vehicle may cause congestion
in the entire transportation network. Therefore, the global correlation between
non-adjacent nodes is crucial for long-term prediction, which has been largely
ignored in previous models.

To solve the above issues, we propose a new spatio-temporal Graph Neural Network (STLGCN) for long-term traffic prediction. Different from existing
methods that require the pre-generation of graph structures, our model adaptively generates multi-scale feature maps by calculating node correlations based
on time information. To improve the effectiveness of graph generation, we have
designed a self-generated position encoding method. In addition, we propose a
new graph convolution method to optimize the use of traffic information. Our
contributions are summarized as follows:

- An adaptive graph generation method is proposed for learning a multi-scale
  feature graph based on temporal information. This method uses self-generated
  position encoding to improve the effectiveness of the generated graph.

- A novel graph convolution method is proposed to optimize the utilization of related traffic information. This method can better extract valuable features and filter out irrelevant features.
- Extensive experiments conducted on real-world datasets prove that our proposed method achieves higher precision than other baseline methods.

2   Related Work

This section briefly introduces methods used in graph convolution, graph generation, and traffic forecasting.

2.1   Graph Convolution

Graph convolution is a commonly used technology in applications, including natural language processing and social network analysis. It is specifically designed to aggregate information from neighboring nodes through a convolution kernel for processing graph structured data. Based on the way of processing the adjacency matrix, there are two main graph convolution methods: spectral-based and spatial-based [9].

The spectral-based method originates from graph spectral theory. This method defines the graph Fourier transform based on the concept of the graph Laplacian and then establishes the graph filter following the traditional signal processing method. For example, Bruna et al. [8] first defined spectral-based graph convolution based on graph theory. However, this method involves the eigendecomposition of the Laplacian matrix and multiple matrix multiplications. Thus its computational cost is enormous. At the same time, the quantity of learnable parameters defined by its convolutional kernel is equivalent to the number of graph nodes, which might lead to high computational complexity and make the method less effective. Therefore, until the proposal of ChebNet [9], graph convolution had not received attention and development. ChebNet uses Chebyshev polynomials to parameterize convolutional kernels, which significantly reduces time and spatial complexity and gives the characteristics of Spatial Localization.

Similar to traditional CNN convolution on images, spatial-based graph convolution is defined based on the spatial relationships of graph nodes. This method, whose essence is the transmission of node information along the graph edges, integrates the information of the central node and its neighboring nodes to update the feature representation of the central node. There are several main methods in this category. Micheli et al. [9] defined spatial convolution operations through message passing. Atwood et al. [12] proposed that graph convolution is a diffusion process of information between different nodes, and they defined a convolution on a graph based on diffusion theory. And, Velickovic et al. [6] introduced an attention mechanism that uses attention weights to aggregate information about neighboring nodes.

2.2   Graph Generation

Graph generation methods can be divided into two categories [18]. The first generates an adjacency matrix based on the spatial features, while the second is based on the temporal features. In general, most methods are based on the former method regarding the spatial distance or the status of road connections as spatial features. Such spatial graphs generated in this way can effectively capture local correlation in transportation networks. However, it often performs poorly in capturing the global correlation, which is even more crucial for long-term prediction.

There are three main methods for generating graph structures based on temporal features: 1. Metric Learning [22], 2. Probabilistic Modeling [19], and 3. Directly Optimizing [20].

Among them, metric learning aims to learn a metric function that calculates the correlation between nodes. Common methods for metric learning include kernel-based methods and attention-based methods. The former method commonly uses Gaussian or polynomial kernel functions and neural networks. However, attention-based methods use attention mechanisms to calculate correlations, which are more dynamic than metric-based methods.

Probabilistic modeling aims to learn the probability distribution of edges. This method assumes that graphs can be generated by sampling edges, whose probabilities can be modeled by learnable parameters. Probabilistic modeling is often combined with the Bayesian theorem to filter out irrelevant edges.

Direct optimization methods are based on the prior knowledge of the graph and handle the adjacency matrix directly. This method assumes that similar nodes are connected and generates the graph based on this assumption. Direct optimization methods are often combined with GCN for graph generation and use regularization for optimization.

2.3   Traffic Forecasting

Traffic prediction problems aim to predict future traffic status given historical traffic information. The information here is usually provided by sensor networks on the road, and the states between sensor nodes are generally strongly correlated in time and space. Thus, how to capture the implicit spatial and temporal dependencies in data is a critical issue in this field.

In recent years, deep learning-based methods have become the focus of this field. In the early stages, CNN-based methods typically converted urban traffic data into grid format to meet the requirements of image convolution. For example, Guo [21] designed a 3D CNN for capturing spatial-temporal correlations. Yu [15] combined CNN with LSTM for traffic forecasting. Although these methods have achieved improvements over traditional machine learning methods, the transformation process results in the loss of topological information about roads.

Considering the importance of spatio-temporal dependence in traffic prediction problems, spatio-temporal graph convolution is a more suitable choice for processing traffic data. These methods use GCN to capture spatial correlations between nodes and use CNN, RNN, or Attention Mechanisms to capture temporal correlations, effectively utilizing the topological information of the road. One representative is the DCRNN model proposed by Li [14], which embeds graph convolution in GRU to solve the task of spatio-temporal prediction. And Yu et al. obtained spatio-temporal correlation by stacking spatio-temporal modules constructed by TCN [10] and GCN. In addition, there are methods to directly use graph convolution to get spatio-temporal correlation by generating a spatio-temporal graph [16].

3   Methods

In this section, after introducing some basic concepts, we provide a detailed introduction to the proposed model's network framework, focusing on the graph generator and spatio-temporal blocks.

3.1   Preliminary

One of the most important goals of traffic forecasting is to predict the future traffic condition given historical features. These traffic features (e.g., velocity, flow, volume) can basically reflect the real-time traffic conditions of road segments in a city.

In this article, we denote the sensor networks as a weighted undirected graph $G = (V, E, W)$, where V is the set of sensor nodes with a number of elements $|V| = N$, while W is the weights of Nodes, and E denotes the set of edges. Based on the above assumptions, the traffic features observed at time t can be denoted by $X_t^p = (x_{i,t}), i = 1, \ldots, N$, where i represents the i-th node. The primary purpose of traffic forecasting is to learn a function $f(\cdot)$ which establishes a mapping from T historical signals to T' future signals, i.e.:

$$f : x_{future} = f(x_{historical}), \tag{1}$$

where:

$$x_{future} = [x_{t+1}, ..., x_{t+T'}] \in R^{T' \times N \times d},$$

$$x_{historical} = [x_{t-T+1}, \ldots, x_t] \in R^{T \times N \times d},$$

and d is the dimension of the feature.

3.2   Framework

The proposed Spatial-Temporal graph convolutional network framework is shown in Fig. 1, which consists of a Graph Generating block, a Spatial-Temporal block, and a Prediction block.

Among them, the graph generation block generates multi-scale graphs by redefining the neighbors of each node and generating a multi-order neighborhood graph. Additionally, self-generated position encoding is used in the process

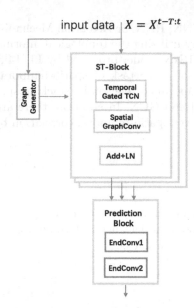

input data $X = X^{t-T:t}$

Fig. 1. Framework of STLGCN, consisting of Graph Generator block, Spatial-Temporal blocks and Prediction block.

of graph generating. In the Spatial-Temporal blocks, dilated causal convolutions are utilized to extract the temporal correlation. And a novel graph convolution method is used to capture the spatial dependency of graphs generated in the Graph Generator block. And in the prediction block, two temporal convolutions are used for prediction. The graph-generating module and spatio-temporal module will be introduced in detail in the following text.

3.3 Graph Generation Block

Figure 2 shows the framework of the graphic generation block. The definition of multi-level neighbors, self-generated position encoding methods, and graph generating methods involved in this module will be introduced in this section.

Definition of Multi-order Neighbors. For each pair of nodes $v, u \in V$ in a given graph $G = (E, V)$, if there is a path:

$$p_{v,u}^{(S)} = (e_{v,s_1}, e_{s_1,s_2}, \ldots, e_{s_{k-2},s_{k-1}}, e_{s_{k-1},u}), \tag{2}$$

such that connects v, u, then v, u are called multi-order neighbors on graph G; where $S = \{s_1, ..., s_{k-1}\}$ represents intermediate nodes that the path $p_{v,u}^{(S)}$ passes through, and $e_{i,j} \in E, \{i,j\} \subset \{v, u, s_1, ..., s_{k-1}\}$. In addition, the length of the shortest path:

$$k = \min_S |p_{v,u}^{(S)}|, \tag{3}$$

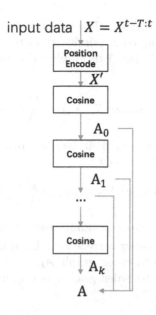

Fig. 2. Graph Generator Block.

connecting v and u on graph G is called the order of the neighbor v, u; Meanwhile, v, u are called k-hops neighbor to each other.

Self-generated Position Encoding. The success of the Transformer can be attributed, in part, to its ingenious design of position encoding, which enables the model to distinguish different nodes and obtain unique relationships between them. Inspired by this, we propose a self-generated position encoding method, which can simultaneously determine the temporal and spatial patterns of the data and enables the encoding process to be learnable. By applying this method in the graph representation, the model proposed in this article can more effectively capture the temporal and spatial correlations between nodes.

Specifically, let $X_i^{(T)} \in R^{d \times T}$ be the feature of node i at time slot T, where d denotes the dimension of node features. To capture time patterns, a convolutional layer with a kernel size of 1×1 is used for temporal encoding. In terms of spatial encoding, a learnable parameter P is used to distinguish the differences between nodes, which will be adaptively optimized during the training process. Overall, The entire process can be represented as:

$$X' = Conv(X) + P, \tag{4}$$

where $Conv(\cdot)$ represents convolutional layer, and P represents learnable position encoding.

Graph Generation Algorithm. The graph-generation algorithm adopts a metric learning method, using cosine similarity as the kernel function. The original adjacency matrix cap A. sub 1 of graph script cap G is calculated first in graph generating.

$$A_{i,j}^{(1)} = cosine(X_i, X_j) = \frac{(X_i \cdot X_j)}{\|X_i\|\|X_j\|}, \tag{5}$$

Then, for each pair of nodes v, u, their k-order correlation is generated by all $(k-1)$-order correlations of v, u, i.e.:

$$A^{(k)}(v, u) = A_{i,j}^{(k)} = cosine(A_{i,:}^{(k-1)}, A_{j,:}^{(k-1)}), \tag{6}$$

where $A_{i,:}^{(k-1)}$ represents the corresponding rows of the i-th nodes v in matrix $A^{(k)}$, that is, all its $(k-1)$-order correlations. By iteratively solving the above recursive equation, any multi-order graph $A_k, k = 1, 2, ...$ can be obtained. Finally, the final set of multi-order graphs is obtained by combining all the generated adjacency matrix, i.e.:

$$A = [A^{(1)}, ..., A^{(k)}], \tag{7}$$

3.4   Spatial-Temporal Blocks

This block sequentially uses dilated convolution and a new graph convolution method to capture temporal and spatial correlations. The framework of the convolution module proposed in this article for capturing spatial correlation is shown in Fig. 3.

Temporal Correlation Capturing. Compared to RNN, CNN-based methods have fewer parameters and are easier to optimize. Therefore, we utilize gated causal convolution with dilation to capture a temporal correlation. The dilated causal convolution increases the Receptive field by increasing expansion, which improves efficiency. In addition, by stacking dilated causal convolutional layers with different kernel sizes, various scale temporal correlations can be effectively captured. This process can be represented as:

$$x \star f(t) = \sum_{s=0}^{K-1} f(s)x(t - d \times s), \tag{8}$$

where d is the size of dilation. In addition, the gating mechanism is adopted to control the transmission of information. Specifically, assuming that the input is $X \in R^{N \times d \times S}$, this final output can be represented as:

$$h = \tau(\theta_1 \star X + b) \odot \sigma(\theta_2 \star X + c), \tag{9}$$

where $\tau(\cdot), \sigma(\cdot)$ represent $Tanh$ and $Sigmoid$ activation function.

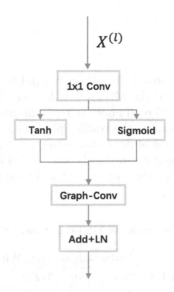

Fig. 3. Spatial-temporal Block.

Spatial Correlation Capturing. Global features, usually implicit, refer to the overall dependency information between nodes, which is crucial for revealing the global correlation between data. Existing GCN methods typically use a spatial graph to aggregate information, which may result in neglecting these global features. For example, when dealing with a fully connected graph, previous methods usually choose a threshold to filter out the irrelated neighbor information, such as the degree of relevance or the number of neighbors. However, if the threshold value is set inappropriately, the irrelated information may be included or the valuable information may be ignored while aggregating information from neighbors.

To solve this problem, we propose a novel graph convolution method. When sampling the neighborhoods of nodes, we assume that highly correlated nodes should exist in all graphs with different sampling rates, while unrelated nodes may only exist in those graphs with high sampling rates. Based on this assumption, we use different sampling rates on the sub-graphs generated by the graph generator module to filter out irrelevant influences and enhance the effect of highly correlated neighbors. In addition, the sampling strategy is the same in all sub-graphs. The sampling frequency is $a_1, a_2, ..., N$, where $a_1 < a_2 < ... < N$ and N is the total number of neighbors. We then use these sampled subgraphs to aggregate information from neighbors. As a result, STLGCN can aggregate more useful information from highly related neighbors and ignore the irrelated information more efficiently.

4 Experiments

4.1 Datasets

Experiments in this paper are conducted on two public transportation datasets: the PEMS-BAY dataset and the METR-LA dataset. The PEMS-BAY dataset records the speed data of 325 road nodes in the California highway network, and the METE-LA dataset contains the traffic speed data of 207 nodes on the Los Angeles expressway. In terms of data processing, the time window size adopted in this paper is 5 min. The data in the dataset is divided into a training set, a validation set, and a test at the ratio of 6:2:2. The specific data are shown in Table 1.

Table 1. The statics of METR-LA and PEMS-BAY

Data	Nodes	edges	Time Window
META-LA	207	1515	34272
PEMS-BAY	325	2369	52116

4.2 Baseline Algorithms

The dynamic spatial-temporal graph convolution is compared with the following models.

- T-GCN [15], which integrates GCN into GRU, is used for traffic forecasting.
- STGCN [13], which combines GCN with one-dimensional causal convolution and adopts a sandwich structure for spatial-temporal relationship acquisition.
- DCRNN [12], which uses diffusion graph convolution and integrates it with an RNN. It adopts an encoder-decoder structure for traffic forecasting.
- STSGCN [14], which generates the spatial-temporal adjacency matrix of nodes and obtains the spatial-temporal relationship through graph convolution.
- AGCRN [11], which proposes a learnable node encoding method.
- Graph WaveNet [2], which adopts improved diffusion graph convolution to obtain spatial relationships, uses dilated graph convolution to obtain temporal relationships, and extracts spatial-temporal relationships through iterative temporal relationship acquisition and spatial relationship acquisition.

4.3 Experiment Settings

All experiments are conducted on a hardware platform equipped with an Intel(R) Xeon(R) Gold 6138 CPU @ 2.00 GHz and an NVIDIA GeForce RTX 2080 Ti. The dilation sizes are defined as 1, 2, 1, 2, 1, 2, 1, 2. There are a total of four spatial-temporal convolution blocks and two diffusion steps. The graph generator block generates zero-order and first-order neighbors. The sampling frequency is set to 50 nodes, 100 nodes, and all nodes, respectively. The Dropout is set to 0.3, and the Adam optimizer is used. One hundred training rounds are conducted, and the decay index is 0.0001. Besides, the loss function is MAE. The evaluation indexes include MAE, RMSE, and MAPE, where MAE and RMSE reflect the fitting of the model to the extreme values, and MAPE reflects the average prediction of the model.

4.4   Experimental Results

Table 2. Performance of STLGCN and other baselines.

data	model	30 min			45 min			60 min		
		MAE	MAPE	RMSE	MAE	MAPR	RMSE	MAE	MAPE	RMSE
METR-LA	TGCN	5.67	14.09%	9.89	6.21	15.81%	10.81	6.68	17.37%	11.53
	STGCN	3.62	10.43%	7.27	4.05	12.04%	8.24	4.44	13.53%	9.00
	DCRNN	5.11	12.85%	9.89	5.92	15.01%	11.20	6.66	16.94%	12.22
	STSGCN	4.07	10.37%	9.64	4.68	12.15%	11.00	5.18	13.62%	12.07
	AGCRN	4.79	10.56%	12.08	5.58	11.92%	13.80	6.21	13.08%	14.96
	Graph WaveNet	3.16	8.55%	**6.31**	3.45	9.54%	7.03	3.67	10.28%	7.53
	STLGCN	**3.14**	**8.51%**	**6.31**	**3.40**	**9.41%**	**6.91**	**3.58**	**10.17%**	**7.30**
PEMS-BAY	TGCN	2.48	5.58%	4.53	2.77	6.33%	5.04	3.06	7.04%	5.50
	STGCN	1.94	4.41%	4.27	2.25	5.31%	5.02	2.50	6.06%	5.63
	DCRNN	1.80	4.07%	3.91	2.05	4.79%	4.52	2.24	5.31%	4.92
	STSGCN	1.89	4.28%	4.19	2.15	5.05%	4.85	2.36	5.60%	5.28
	AGCRN	1.74	4.01%	3.90	1.92	4.53%	4.37	2.07	4.93%	4.70
	Graph WaveNet	1.77	3.92%	3.72	1.97	4.50%	**4.20**	2.12	4.90%	4.78
	STLGCN	**1.68**	**3.77%**	**3.78**	**1.87**	**4.39%**	4.24	**2.02**	**4.84%**	**4.56**

This paper mainly compares the long-term forecasting ability of the models. To this end, the time window sizes of 30 min, 45 min, and 60 min are adopted in the selection of the forecast horizon. The experiments of all models are conducted in the same environment, and the training parameters of the models are kept consistent. The prediction results of the models are shown in Table 2. It can be seen that STLGCN shows the best result in all indexes. With the increase in the prediction time, the improvement of MAPE is more significant. On the METR- LA dataset, compared with the optimal model, the MAPE of STLGCN at 30 min, 45 min, and 60 min is improved by 0.04%, 0.13%, and 0.11%, respectively. On the PEMS-BAY dataset, compared with the optimal model, the MAPE of STL-GCN at 30 min, 45 min, and 60 min is improved by 0.08%, 0.06%, and 0.03%, respectively. In the baseline models, the performance of the models using the RNN is poor. For example, the three models (TGCN, DCRNN, and AGCRN) perform worse than the TCN-based model. Among the baseline models, the best-performing model is Graph WaveNet, and this is highly related to the diffusion graph convolution it used. STSGCN builds a spatial-temporal graph and exploits the spatial-temporal correlations more powerfully, so its performance is relatively better.

5 Conclusions

In this study, we propose a novel spatial-temporal graph convolutional network for long-term traffic forecasting (STLGCN). Our model adaptively generates a multi-order graph using a graph generator that incorporates self-generated position encoding to enhance the effectiveness of the generated graph. Additionally, we propose a graph convolution method to extract useful traffic information from the generated graph while filtering out irrelevant data, improving the model's ability to capture spatial-temporal correlations.

Acknowledgement. This work is supported by the National Natural Science Foundation of China (NSFC) (Grant No. 52071312), and the Open Program of Zhejiang Lab (Grant No. 2019KE0AB03).

References

1. Fattah, J., Ezzine, L., Aman, Z., Moussami, H., Lachhab, A.: Forecasting of demand using ARIMA model. Int. J. Eng. Bus. Manag. **10** (2018). https://doi.org/10.1177/1847979018808673
2. Xie, Y., Zhang, P., Chen, Y.: A fuzzy ARIMA correction model for transport volume forecast. Math. Problems Eng. **2021**, 6655102, 10 p. (2021). https://doi.org/10.1155/2021/6655102
3. Kim, K.: Financial time series forecasting using support vector machines. Neurocomputing **551**, 307–319 (2003). https://doi.org/10.1016/S0925-2312(03)00372-2
4. He, K., Zhang, X., Ren, S., Sun, J.: Deep residual learning for image recognition. In: IEEE Conference on Computer Vision and Pattern Recognition (CVPR), Las Vegas, NV, USA (2016). https://doi.org/10.1109/CVPR.2016.90
5. Szegedy, C., et al.: Going deeper with convolutions. In: IEEE Conference on Computer Vision and Pattern Recognition (CVPR), Boston, MA, USA, pp. 1–9 (2015). https://doi.org/10.1109/CVPR.2015.7298594
6. Veličković, P., Cucurull, G., Casanova, A., Romero, A., Liò, P., Bengio, Y.: Graph attention networks. In: International Conference on Learning Representations (2018). http://openreview.net/forum?id=rJXMpikCZ
7. Kipf, T.N., Welling, M.: Semi-supervised classification with graph convolutional networks. In: International Conference on Learning Representations (2016). http://openreview.net/forum?id=SJU4ayYgl
8. Bruna, J., Zaremba, W., Szlam, A., LeCun, Y.: Spectral networks and deep locally connected networks on graphs. In: 2nd International Conference on Learning Representations, ICLR, Banff, Canada (2014)
9. Michael, D., Xavier, B., Pierre, V.: Convolutional neural networks on graphs with fast localized spectral filtering. In: International Conference on Neural Information Processing Systems (NIPS), pp. 3844–3852 (2016)
10. Shi, X., Chen, Z., Wang, H., Yeung, D., Wong, W., Woo, W.: Convolutional LSTM network: a machine learning approach for precipitation nowcasting. In: International Conference on Neural Information Processing Systems (NIPS), 802–810 (2015)

11. Wu, Z., Pan, S., Long, G., Jiang, J., Zhang, C.: Graph WaveNet for deep spatial-temporal graph modeling. In: International Joint Conference on Artificial Intelligence, pp. 1907–1913 (2019). https://doi.org/10.5555/3367243.3367303

12. Atwood, J., Towsley, D.: Diffusion-convolutional neural networks. In: Neural Information Processing Systems, pp. 2001–2009, Barcelona, Spain (2016). https://doi.org/10.5555/3157096.3157320

13. Bai, L., Yao, L., Li, C., Wang, X., Wang, C.: Adaptive graph convolutional recurrent network for traffic forecasting. In: Neural Information Processing Systems (2020). https://doi.org/10.5555/3495724.3497218

14. Li, Y., Yu, R., Shahabi, C., Liu, Y.: Diffusion convolutional recurrent neural network: data-driven traffic forecasting. In: 6th International Conference on Learning Representations (ICLR) (2018). http://openreview.net/forum?id=SJiHXGWAZ

15. Yu, B., Yin, H., Zhu, Z.: Spatio-temporal graph convolutional networks: a deep learning framework for traffic forecasting. In: International Joint Conference on Artificial Intelligence (IJCAI) Stockholm, Sweden (2018). https://doi.org/10.5555/3304222.3304273

16. Song, C., Lin, Y., Guo, S., Wan, H.: Spatial-temporal synchronous graph convolutional networks: a new framework for spatial-temporal network data forecasting. In: Proceedings of the AAAI Conference on Artificial Intelligence **3401**, 914–921 (2022). https://doi.org/10.1609/aaai.v34i01.5438

17. Zhao, L., et al.: T-GCN: a temporal graph convolutional network for traffic prediction. IEEE Trans. Intell. Transport. Syst. **21**(9), 3848–3858 (2020). https://doi.org/10.1109/TITS.2019.2935152

18. Zhu, Y., et al.: A survey on graph structure learning: progress and opportunities. In: International Joint Conference on Artificial Intelligence (2021)

19. Franceschi, L., Niepert, M., Pontil, M., He, X.: Learning discrete structures for graph neural networks. In: International Conference on Machine Learning (ICML) pp. 1972–1978 (2019). https://proceedings.mlr.press/v97/franceschi19a.html

20. Gao, X., Hu, W., Guo, Z.: Exploring structure-adaptive graph learning for robust semi-supervised classification. In: 2020 IEEE International Conference on Multimedia and Expo (ICME), pp. 1–6, London, UK (2020). https://doi.org/10.1109/ICME46284.2020.9102726

21. Guo, S., Lin, Y., Li, S., Chen, Z., Wan, H.: Deep spatial-temporal 3D convolutional neural networks for traffic data forecasting. IEEE Trans. Intell. Transp. Syst. **2010**, 3913–3926 (2019). https://doi.org/10.1109/TITS.2019.2906365

22. Shao, Z., et al.: Decoupled dynamic spatial-temporal graph neural network for traffic forecasting. Proc. VLDB Endow. 2733–2746 (2022). https://doi.org/10.14778/3551793.3551827

23. Jiang, J., Han, C., Zhao, W., Wang, J.: PDFormer: propagation delay-aware dynamic long-range transformer for traffic flow prediction. In: AAAI (2023)

Image Forgery Detection Using Cryptography and Deep Learning

Ayodeji Oke and Kehinde O. Babaagba$^{(\boxtimes)}$ ⓘD

School of Computing, Engineering and the Built Environment, Edinburgh Napier
University, Edinburgh EH10 5DT, UK
40524773@live.napier.ac.uk, K.Babaagba@napier.ac.uk

Abstract. The advancement of technology has undoubtedly exposed
everyone to a remarkable array of visual imagery. Nowadays, digital technology is eating away the trust and historical confidence people have in
the integrity of imagery. Deep learning is often used for the detection of
forged digital images through the classification of images as original or
forged. Despite many advantages of deep learning algorithms to predict
fake images such as automatic feature engineering, parameter sharing
and dimensionality reduction, one of the drawbacks of deep learning
emanates from parsing bad examples to deep learning models. In this
work, cryptography was applied to improve the integrity of images used
for deep learning (Convolutional Neural Network - CNN) based prediction using SHA-256. Our results after a hashing algorithm was used at a
threshold of 0.0003 gives 73.20% image prediction accuracy. The use of
CNN algorithm on the hashing image dataset gives a prediction accuracy
of 72.70% at 0.09 s. Furthermore, the result of CNN on the raw image
dataset gives a prediction accuracy of 89.08% at 2 s. The result shows
that although a higher prediction accuracy is obtained when the CNN
algorithm is used on the raw image without hashing, the prediction using
the CNN algorithm with hashing is faster.

Keywords: Image Forgery Detection · Machine Learning · Deep
Learning · Cryptography · Hashing

1 Introduction

The availability of multiple tools for image editing, enhancement, correction,
alteration, and reconstruction continue to stimulate the perpetration of crimes.
The widespread distribution of forged faces and videos on the Internet has caused
several cultural, moral, and security problems, including fraud and fake news
[8]. Synthesising whole face, identity exchange, manipulation of attribute, and
expression, are various ways picture forgery is propagated by criminal elements
in the manipulation of faces of victims. Research on image forgery indicates that
these kinds of crimes are typically committed to spread false information, obtain
political power, and create unsavoury notoriety and benefits. It is critically necessary to either put an end to the spread of false information or find a remedy

Z. Tan et al. (Eds.): BDTA 2023, LNICST 555, pp. 62–78, 2024.
https://doi.org/10.1007/978-3-031-52265-9_5

for it [35]. This suggests that potential image forgery detection systems focus on establishing the consistency and authenticity of electronic images.

Over the years, several investigation outputs have emerged with a view to mitigating and restoring the integrity and trust of digital images. Two basic approaches being employed are blind or passive image forgery and non-blind or active image forgery detection [11]. The non-blind or active image forgery detection uses a watermark and digital signature to authenticate digital images [10]. This approach simply implies that a watermark has to be inserted at the point of storage. However, a digital camera will need to be specially equipped to make this approach a reality. A digital signature is an approach used to ensure the authenticity and integrity of information that possesses a key or signature [32]. Cryptography is a subset of digital signatures, and it is a communication technique for conveying information securely [22] through the use of a private key and hash extracted from typical digital signature.

In blind detection of image forgery, the authenticity of an image is verified and confirmed without requiring further action for the purpose of authenticity. Pixel-based techniques are one of the techniques in passive image forgery detection for deciphering manipulated images. It comprises parameters such as noise, blurring, color, and scaling from which tampered images can be distinguished from the original ones. In images, the color of an observed light, which is an interaction between the illumination and the reflection of the object surface, obeys certain structures that are consistent with the physical phenomenology of color [38]. When an image is manipulated, the consistency of the color pixels with color phenomenology is also manipulated.

In addition, deep learning is an integral part of machine learning [36] used for the detection of forged digital images [37] through the classification of images as original or forged. It commonly uses digital image splicing [23], which originated from a pixel-based technique, to develop a new classifier aimed at detecting inconsistencies stemming from image manipulations that affect the object's color appearance. Thus, this study focuses on the use of a subset of features in passive and active fake image detection. This research proposes an anomalous image detection system with the use of cryptography and deep learning techniques.

The research questions that this work will address are as follows:

- Can hashing algorithms be used in detecting image forgeries?
- When hashing is used in conjunction with deep learning does it outperform a model that does not use hashing?

We answer these two questions by carrying out experiments that first check the efficacy of an hashing algorithm in detecting image forgery. We then compare the performance of the CNN algorithm without hashing. Then, we test for performance improvement of the CNN algorithm using hashing.

The rest of the paper is structured as follows. Section 2 provides a review of related works. In Sect. 3, we describe the methodology of our research. Then we explain our experimental design in Sect. 4. We present and discuss our results in Sect. 5. Section 6 summarises and concludes the paper, it also provides direction for future research.

2   Related Work

Images are an essential part of the digital world and are vital for both storing and disseminating data. They can easily be edited using a variety of tools [24]. These tools were originally developed in order to enhance photographs. Some individuals, however, use the functionalities of these tools to distort photos and spread myths rather than improving the image [2]. This poses a serious risk because falsified photographs often result in severe and often irreparable harm [3]. Image splicing (copying a section of a donor image into a legacy image) and copy-move (creating forged image from only one image) are the two main types of image forgeries [3].

To combat the problem of picture distortion in many fields, digital image forgery detection has substantially expanded [27]. Techniques for image forgery detection are used for both copied and spliced pictures. In order to protect digital photographs, [20] presented a hybrid cryptographic and electronic technique for watermarking. While protecting the image content with cryptography, they employed the watermarking approach to authenticate the image. [19] worked on identifying JPG, PDF, PNG, and GIF file types for digital forensics and employed computational intelligence techniques to do so. They also used these algorithms to expose the right file type if the JPG, PDF, PNG, or GIF was changed. They assessed chrominance, brightness, and grayness and claimed that their method outperformed other cutting-edge forgery detection methods. [21] developed an innovative hybrid discrete cosine conversion and visual encryption technique for protecting digital photos. They condensed the image that was encrypted using the discrete cosine transform after encrypting the image's RGB channel as n shares. The method used was reversed to produce the plain image, but pixel values were lost.

Deep artificial neural networks are referred to as deep learning. Deep learning has become increasingly popular over the past few years, largely due to recent developments in machine learning and signal/information processing research as well as dramatically improved chip processing capabilities (e.g., GPU units), significantly lower hardware costs, and other factors. Autoencoder (AE) [29], Convolutional Neural Network (CNN) [15], Deep Belief Network (DBN) [12], Recurrent Neural Network (RNN) [34], and Direct Deep Reinforcement Learning [16] are examples of common deep learning approaches. Researchers can utilize a variety of deep learning frameworks to implement any deep learning technique.

The literature has suggested a number of strategies to combat picture forgery. In contrast to modern strategies based on deep learning such as CNN, which are detailed below, the majority of older techniques are based on specific artefacts left by image forgeries. Before discussing deep learning-based strategies, we first discuss different conventional methodologies. For instance [40] presented Error Level Analysis (ELA) that identify fake image. The ELA technique operates on JPEG images based on a grid, changing a portion of a grid to affect the entire grid square. However, ELA is limited in its capability to detect single pixel modifications or minor color adjustments [31]. [28] used the illumination of objects to determine whether an image is fake. Based on the difference in illumination direction between the authentic and fake portions of digital image, it attempts to identify forgery. Different conventional methods for detecting forged image have been compared in [9]. The contourlet transform is used in [17] to regain the edge pixels for detection of forgery. Though the contourlet transform is advantageous in multi-resolution, discrete domain implementation and multi-direction, redundancy reduction, the disadvantages are the shift variant, which leads to the pseudo-Gibbs phenomenon, poor frequency selectivity, and poor temporal stability [33].

In terms of deep learning models, [7] developed a technique for identifying fake images by using resampling characteristics and deep learning. A technique for detecting manipulated images by clustering the features of camera-based CNN was proposed by [6]. [24] invented Compression Artefact Tracing Network (CAT-Net) that simultaneously captures forensic features of artefact compression on the RGB and DCT domains. HR-Net is their principal network (high resolution). As sending DCT coefficients straight to a CNN would not effectively train it, they employed the method suggested in [42], which explains how the DCT coefficient can be used. In their Dual-Order Attentive Generative Adversarial Network (DOA-GAN), [18] suggested using a GAN with dual attention to locate copy-move forgeries in an image. The generator's first-order attention is made to gather copy-move location data, whilst the second-order attention for patch co-occurrence takes advantage of more discriminative characteristics. The co-occurrence and location-aware features are combined for the final localization branches and detection for the network by using the affinity matrix to retrieve both attention maps.

[5] describes the construction of a Dual-encoder U-Net using an unfixed encoder and a fixed encoder (D-Unet). The picture fingerprints that distinguish between authentic and altered regions are learned by the unfixed encoder on its own. The fixed encoder, on the other hand, provides direction information to aid network learning and detection. A deepfake detection technique was introduced by [25]. Only fixed-size images of the face may be produced using deepfake techniques, and these images have to be affinely twisted to match the facial layout of the source image. This warping creates various artefacts because of the different resolution between the surrounding environment and the warped face area. As a result, these artefacts can be used to recognize deepfake videos. Other authors such as [26,41] among others, have used deep learning for image forgery detection.

In summary, numerous strategies have been put forth by researchers to identify image forgeries. Traditional methods of detecting image forgeries focus on the various artefacts that can be found in forged images, such as variations in illumination, compression, contrast, sensor noise, and shadow. The use of CNN for a variety of computer vision tasks, such as picture object recognition, semantic segmentation, and image classification, has grown in popularity recently. CNN's accomplishments in computer vision is mostly due to two characteristics. Firstly, CNN makes use of the strong correlation between nearby pixels. CNN favours connections that are grouped locally over the connection on one-to-one bases between every pixel. Secondly, a convolution process using shared weights is used to create each output feature map. Additionally, CNN employs learned characteristics from training photos and can generalize itself to detect unseen forgery, in contrast to old techniques, which rely on manufactured features to detect specific fabrication.

CNN is a promising approach for identifying image forgeries because of these benefits. A CNN model can be trained to learn the numerous artefacts present in a fake picture. Additionally, using image artefacts with hashing has been shown to achieve integrity [13]. In order to learn the tampered image artefacts as a result of changes in original image features and ensure highly confidential images that are tamper-proof, we propose an authentication system for identifying anomalies in images using cryptography and deep learning techniques.

3 Methodology

The alteration of images using various technological approaches may have an impact on aspects of images that are challenging for humans to recognize. Using an image editor, an image effect, or any other tool to alter the imaging features can result in a bogus image. Our goal is to identify such tampered images by training a model on a dataset of real and tampered images. We employ CNN to boost prediction accuracy and efficiency and cryptography to preserve the integrity of the image.

3.1 Dataset Summary

The dataset employed in this research is the Casia dataset[1] comprising of 3416 images. The images are of the format BMP, JPG and TIF which comprises of 2391 real images and 1025 tampered images. Among the pictorial content of these images includes architectures, plants, articles, animals, textures, nature, indoor and scenes images. These images are of different sizes varying from 384×256 pixels to 800×600 pixels.

A deep learning model was developed using CNN to carry out learning and prediction firstly on the raw image dataset and on an image dataset that had undergone hashing. The image dataset after data cleaning consists of 3,247 images including real (2,376) and fake (871) images. In terms of the type of images in the dataset, a total of 2563 images were .JPG, 559 images were .TIF and there were 125 .BMP images. The details of the information regarding how image is distributed is presented in Table 1.

3.2 Image Processing

The process of color image segmentation and the identification of reference points are explained in this section. The procedures to achieve this are as follows:

---

[1] Casia Dataset - https://www.kaggle.com/datasets/sophatvathana/casia-dataset.

Table 1. Image Distribution after Data Cleaning

Format	Real Image	Fake Image	Total
.JPG	1989	574	2563
.TIF	333	226	559
.BMP	54	71	125
Total	2376	871	3247

Resize the RGB Image. In this phase, bi-cubic interpolation was used for the resizing of the input images to $M \times M$ matrix. The resizing of image lay credence to the fact that the input images have variety of sizes, and it is desirable that hashes of images must be of the same length. This infers that images with different sizes tend to have different length of hashes [1]. The resizing process therefore ensures that digital images that have different resolution can be identified with hashing. After the resizing of image, gaussian low-pass was then applied for the filtering of the image. The filtering process is with a view to reduce minor manipulation influence such as noise contamination which further enhance certain features in an image [39].

The source of an image contributes to the features of the image. Images derived from digital cameras or scanners have a metadata standard attaching to it which is knows as Exchangeable image file format (Exif). This Exif data consists of broad range of features such as camera settings which includes rotation, shutter speed, camera model, aperture, ISO speed information, metering mode, focal length and so on. It also includes image metrics such as color space, pixel dimensions, file size and resolution. Other features are copyright, date and time and location information. These features are mainly direct data that can be extracted from digital image. Furthermore, these digital images are stored in a computer in form of a matrix or an array of square pixels in which each element are arranged in rows and column, that is, in a 2-dimensional matrix. There is possibility of having smoother or pixelated (mosaic-like) images otherwise called image resolutions which determine the size of the square pixels. The information contained in the pixels are color and intensity. These pixels are represented as RGB in coloured images, that is, two dimensional arrays with three layers. These layers in the images depicts red, green, and blue channels together with their equivalent 8-bit digit for the intensity.

Feature Selection. In this phase, after the importing features of the digital image, the interested data from the image features were selected. The basic features selected from the image data includes image shape (width, height, and size), object type (image array) and image dimension which is basically the number of array dimensions of the image which is usually three for coloured images (RGB channels). All the information in the selected features are necessary for the image pre-processing to ensure the main objective of the study is achieved.

RGB Color Pixel Normalization. In this phase, the numeric values in the columns of the dataset were normalized to reduce data redundancy and improve the performance of the result expected to be derived from our implementation. The purpose of the normalization is to change the dataset value into common scale without distorting differences in the ranges of values or losing information [4]. Therefore, the pixel values which range from 0 to 255 are divided by 255 to convert it to range 0 to 1 which gives numbers with small values and makes computation faster and easier. The typical objective of normalizing image is to change the range of intensity values in the pixel. This converts the range of value in the pixel of the input image into a normal scale. Hence, this work performs normalization on the input image to scale down the pixel value without distorting or losing information in the input image. Let R, G, and B be the red, green, and blue component of a pixel, the ranges of R, G, and B are then converted from $[0, 255]$ to $[0, 1]$.

Computation of Mean from RGB Color Space. In each component, every representation of RGB were divided into non-overlapping block of dimension $b \times b$. For instance, if N is the block number and Bi is the ith block ($i = 1, 2, ..., N$). Thus, the mean m was calculated to represent the block.

$$m = 1/b^2 \sum_{j=1}^{b^2} B_i(j) \tag{1}$$

The $B_i(j)$ represents the value of the jth element of the ith block. The statistical selection above is based on the consideration that the mean and variance can indicate the average energy and the fluctuation of the block. The formulas in equation (1) were applied to each channel of RGB color, and thus the color feature vector v_i of the ith block was obtained.

$$v_i = [m_R, m_G, m_B]^T \tag{2}$$

where m_R is the mean of the R channel of RGB, m_G is the mean of the G channel, and m_B is the mean of the B channel. By ordering these vectors v_i, matrix V was obtained from the feature.

$$V = [v_1, v_2, v_3, ..., v_N] \tag{3}$$

During this process, instances of images that were not in image format and possess three-dimensional space were removed. The total number of images at the end of the phase was 3247, with real images comprising of 2376 while tampered images were 871.

3.3 Hash Generation

The RGB colour channel was parsed to the SHA-256 hash function to generate the hash value for each image in the dataset. SHA-256 is a 256-bit encryption hash function that may also be represented as a 64-digit number system in base 16 [30]. Firstly, 512 bits are added to the entry message Q to pad it. In order to generate a length that is multiples of 512 bits, a bit "1" and a variable number of zero bits are appended to a 64-bit binary denoting the length of Q. The length of the actual message is stored as a 64-bit value in the final 64 bits of the padded message. The padded message is broken up into 512-bit blocks $B^{(0)}$, $B^{(1)}$, $B^{(2)}$, ..., $B^{(N-1)}$ and each block of data $B^{(i)}$ is sequentially processed by the main function over the course of 64 loops. The final hash HN is computed and supplied after the last block of data $B^{(N-1)}$ is computed, and a hashing H_i having partial 256-bit is obtained when a whole execution of the present $B^{(i)}$ is completed [14].

Hash Similarity. To measure the similarity between hashes of the original and the attacked images, the d norm is computed. Let h_1 and h_2 be two image hashes. Thus, the d norm is defined as:

$$d = \sqrt{\sum_{i=1}^{N} |h_1(i) - h_2(i)|^2} \tag{4}$$

Here $h_1(i)$ and $h_2(i)$ are the ith element of h_1 and h_2. The more similar the input images of the hashes, the smaller the d value. If d is smaller than a pre-defined threshold T, the original and the fake images are classified as a pair of images that are visually identical. Otherwise, they are different.

Evaluation of the Hashing. The hashing was evaluated to determine its ability to differentiate between real images and anomalous images. The following are the evaluation terms used for the experimentation: Total images (T_{IMG}) - the total number of tested images, True positive (T_p) - properly labeled real images, True negative (T_N) - properly labeled manipulated image, False negative (F_N) - incorrectly labeled manipulated images, the manipulated images that have been proven to be real images, False positive (F_P) - incorrectly labeled real images, the real image that have been proven to be fake images. Thus, the accuracy ($\frac{T_p+T_N}{T_{IMG}} \times 100$), recall ($\frac{T_p}{T_p+F_N}$), and precision ($\frac{T_p}{T_p+F_P}$) are calculated to evaluate the comparative performance of hashing at different threshold levels to set the benchmark for the hash function. Table 2 represents the result of the evaluation of the hashing algorithm for accuracy, recall, and precision.

Table 2. Hashing Evaluation

Threshold	T_p	F_N	F_p	T_N	Recall (%)	Precision (%)	Accuracy (%)
0.0001	2376	870	0	0	73.20	1.0	73.20
0.0002	2375	870	1	0	73.19	99.96	73.17
0.0003	2375	869	1	1	73.21	99.96	73.20

4 Experimental Design

The experimental procedure taken to carry out the model formulation and prediction is explained in this section.

4.1 Deep Learning Experiment

After the dataset preparation as explained in Sect. 3, in order to predict a tampered image, CNN was used to train the dataset of real and tampered images. The process followed to achieve this is described in the following sections.

Pre-processing. Since the real and tampered images were of varying sizes, the first step in data pre-processing was to resize them. This strikes a balance between offering sufficient resolution for real and manipulated image detection by the machine learning algorithm and for efficient training. To meet ImageNet[2] requirements, all images were normalized. For the purpose of standardizing the experiments, the same image size used in the experiment with hashing is deployed in the experiment without hashing. Hence, the image size used in our work is 150 by 150 pixels, and those images are converted to RGB color space. For the experiment that uses the hashing dataset, the derived hash value from the image dataset from Sect. 3 was deployed. The length of the hash value was established, and this information was used to modify the input tensor's shape. This entails altering CNN's Keras input layer using the Input() function.

Splitting of Dataset. The training, validation, and testing sets were created from the data by splitting the dataset. The validation set is used to modify the hyperparameters, the testing set is used to assess how well the trained model performed, and the training set is used to train the network. The ratio of training to testing dataset used was 80:20.

Data Augmentation. If more data are generated, the model will often be more robust and minimize overfitting. A huge dataset is necessary for the algorithm used for deep learning to function effectively. Data augmentation was used on the training image dataset to increase the model's performance. Deep learning systems typically include a library of tools for enhancing the data. Rescale, horizontal flip, and vertical flip was used to create fresh training sets. The image is rotated right or left on a plane within 1° and 360° to perform rotation augmentations. The rotating degree parameter has a significant impact on the reliability of rotation augmentations. Images can be transformed to capture extra information about things of interest by shifting and flipping them.

---

[2] ImageNet - https://www.image-net.org/.

CNN Architecture. The CNN architecture was defined for the training image dataset for the purpose of classification. We built a model with six convolutional layers, followed by a fully connected hidden layer. In order to output a probability for each class, the output layer utilizes SoftMax activation. The Adam optimization algorithm and a rate of learning were employed to optimize the network. During the training process, the model iterates across batches of the dataset for training, for each batch size. Gradients are then calculated for each batch, and the weighting of the network is automatically updated. Typically, training is continued until the algorithm converges. A checkpoint was employed to save the model with the highest level of validation accuracy. This is helpful because, after a given number of epochs, the network can begin to overfit. The Keras library's callback functionality was used to enable this functionality. A sequence of functions known as a callback is used at specific points in the training process, such as the conclusion of an epoch. Model check-pointing and learning rate scheduling are both built-in features of Keras.

For the experiment with the hashing dataset, to create a CNN architecture that can take a training image dataset with hash codes as an input for classification, CNN's input shape was defined to match the shape of the hash codes the hashing function produces. As a result, the input layer was shaped in a way that matches the length of the hash codes. The CNN's convolutional layers were made to work with hash codes. This was accomplished by modifying the convolutional operation's stride, number of filters, and filter size to take the lower input size into account. In general, the CNN's architecture was selected to capture the pertinent characteristics of the hashed data. The size of the pooling windows was carefully chosen to prevent losing too much information from the hashed data because the pooling layers of the CNN can be used to down sample the feature maps produced by the convolutional layers. The CNN's output layer was created to deliver the results required for the task at hand. For instance, as the assignment involved classifying images, it was desirable to set the output layer to be a Sigmoid layer with as many nodes as there were classes in the dataset.

The model was created with four convolutional layers, followed by a fully connected hidden layer. The SHA-256 hash codes, which have a length of 64, were defined to have a shape that matches the input shape of the CNN. This indicates that the input layer's shape should be (64, 1). The CNN's convolutional layers were made to work with SHA-256 hash codes. One strategy is to employ a 1D convolutional layer with a modest kernel size, like 3 or 5 since the input contains binary data. A limited number of filters, such as 16 or 32, may be present in this layer. To decrease the spatial dimensions of the feature maps while retaining the most crucial features, we employed a max pooling layer with a pool size of 2. The CNN's output layer was created to deliver the results required for the task at hand. The output layer was made up of a single node with a sigmoid activation function as our objective was binary classification. As explained earlier, a checkpoint was used to preserve the model with the best validation accuracy.

Training and Validating the Models. Using backpropagation and the Adam optimizer, the dataset was trained using the defined CNN architecture. The training of model involves setting the model parameters, such as the learning rate and the number of iterations, and then using an optimization algorithm, such as Adam, to adjust the parameters and minimize the error between the predicted and actual values. In the same vein, model validation was carried out after the model had been trained to evaluate its performance on the validation data. This involved measuring metrics such as accuracy, precision, recall, and F1 score. The model was trained and retrained with different parameters to optimize the model's performance on the validation data until the model's performance was satisfactory.

5 Results and Discussion

This section focuses on presenting the results obtained from the implementation and comparing them in a progressive manner as per the research methodology.

5.1 Deep Learning Without Hashing

The model was trained and verified until the highest possible training and validation accuracy was achieved. The network's learning curve throughout training and validation is depicted in Fig. 1(a). In the training and validation phases, accuracy both increased, reaching 97.68% training accuracy and 98.62% validation accuracy, as can be observed. Also, the training and validation losses were 0.0548 and 0.0404, respectively. Figure 1(b) represents the network's loss curve during training and validation, while Fig. 1(c) represents the network's F1 curve during training and validation. The result shows that both validation loss and training loss decreased with an increasing number of iterations, which demonstrated the model's effectiveness.

Evaluation of the Model. For the testing of the model, the testing dataset comprising the same image features used in the training phase but different from the images that were used in original dataset for training, are used to test the model. By loading the test images dataset and identifying the classes utilizing the model, the models were tested. Through the use of the predict_classes() function, it was possible to determine whether an image was real or artificially altered based on whether it represented 1 or 0. The model shows the prediction accuracy, precision, recall, F-score, and loss to be 89.08%, 0.88.89%, 89.07%, 88.94%, and 34.7%, respectively.

Figure 2 represents the result of the confusion matrix. From the confusion matrix we can gain better understanding of the classifiers. It can be seen from Fig. 2 that the classifier classifies 133 (76%) of the real instances correctly and 42 (24%) of the real instances incorrectly. However for the tampered instances, it classifies 446 (94%) of those instances correctly and 29 (6%) incorrectly.

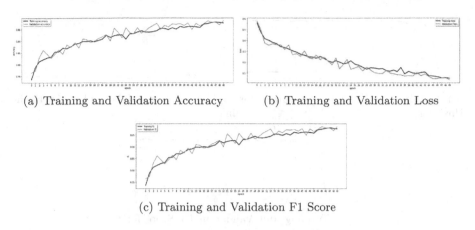

(a) Training and Validation Accuracy   (b) Training and Validation Loss

(c) Training and Validation F1 Score

Fig. 1. Training and Validation Performance

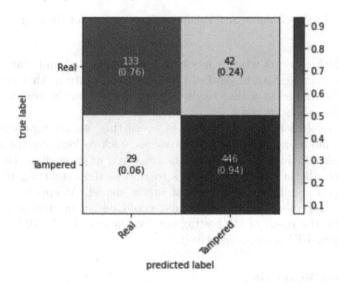

Fig. 2. Performance Evaluation of Image Prediction

5.2 Deep Learning with Cryptography

To obtain the desired accuracy during training and validation, the model was trained and tested. Figures 3(a), 3(b) and 3(c) represent the network's learning curve, loss curve and F1 curve for the hash image dataset respectively.

It can be seen that pattern of line on validation training, loss and F1 for the CNN learning model shows a straight-line pattern. A straight line for the validation loss or accuracy indicates that the model is not improving its performance on the validation set even though the training loss is still decreasing. This can mean that the model has already learned everything it can from the training data and is overfitting, but it also means that it is unable to generalize to new

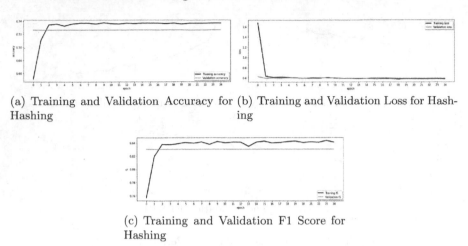

(a) Training and Validation Accuracy for (b) Training and Validation Loss for Hash-
Hashing   ing

(c) Training and Validation F1 Score for
Hashing

Fig. 3. Training and Validation Performance for Hashing

data. Overfitting occurs when a model is too complicated and starts to fit the
noise in the training data instead of the underlying patterns that generalize to
new data. The model may thus begin to perform well on the training data but
poorly on the validation data.

To find a solution to the problem of overfitting, an attempt was made to
simplify the model using different approaches, such as lowering the number of
layers or nodes, including regularization strategies, or expanding the validation
set. However, all the possible attempts to resolve the overfitting problem did
not result in a significant improvement in the model. At epoch 20, the highest training and validation accuracy that could be achieved were 73.69% and
72.66%, while the result of the testing and evaluation were 72.70% and 83.90%
for accuracy and F1 score, respectively.

5.3   Results Evaluation

Going by the result of the hashing evaluation, which showed 73.20% accuracy,
99.96% precision, and 73.21% recall at 0.0003 threshold, which is surprisingly
within the same range as the result of the deep learning algorithm, indicates that
a more robust hashing algorithm that ensures high euclidean distance is required
to achieve high prediction performance. This implies that to use cryptography to
improve the integrity of image prediction in deep learning, more effort is needed
at the hashing phase to ensure the accuracy of prediction.

In the overall assessment of our result, the hashing algorithm at the threshold
0.0003 gives 73.20% image prediction accuracy. The use of the CNN algorithm
on the hashing image dataset of 3247 at epoch 20 gives a prediction accuracy of
72.70% at 0.09 s. In the same vein, the result of CNN on the raw image dataset
at epoch 50 gives a prediction accuracy of 89.08% at 2 s. The result shows the
high capacity of deep learning prediction accuracy on the raw image without

hashing. However, the prediction on hashing image dataset is faster on CNN, though with less accuracy.

6   Conclusion

The advancement in technological and image generation techniques have provided the possibility to create fake images. Many approaches have been developed to predict fake images using different approaches such as through the use of cryptography and deep learning algorithms. Despite many advantages in deep learning algorithms to predict fake images such as automatic feature engineering, parameter sharing and dimensionality reduction, one of the deep learning drawbacks emanates from parsing of bad examples to deep learning models.

This work investigated applying cryptography - hashing to an image based on the RGB channel and how this could be used to improve the integrity of the image prediction as fake or real by deep learning. The hashing was performed on the RGB channel of the image dataset of both real and manipulated images using SHA-256 hash function and the euclidean distance was used to differentiate between the real and manipulated images. The lower the hash value the higher the possibility of the image to be classified as fake while the higher the hash value the higher the possibility of the image to real. Based on this, a threshold was set to determine the accuracy of the hashing to predict fake image. The generated hash value of the image dataset was parsed to a deep learning model - CNN algorithm for image prediction. The raw image dataset without hashing was also parsed into CNN algorithm for prediction for the purpose of comparison.

The result of our experimental analysis shows the viability of hashing to improve the integrity of images that a deep learning model will predict provided a robust hashing algorithm with a very high accuracy is used. This will go a long way in reducing the adversarial attack on CNN through the feeding of bad examples into deep learning networks and make prediction at lesser time. Hence, using cryptography on an image before deep learning can guarantee the integrity of the image being predicted, which can be done at a lesser time. However, the cryptography algorithm to be applied must be robust enough to give high euclidean distance between real and manipulated images to guarantee high accuracy.

For future work, it is desirable to investigate more hashing algorithms and their prediction accuracy on deep learning models with a view to establish which hashing algorithm has better performance for the purpose of integrity of image prediction. Furthermore, more data-sets could also be used to test the efficacy of the developed model.

References

1. Ali, N.H.M., Mahdi, M.E.: Detecting similarity in color images based on perceptual image hash algorithm. IOP Conf. Ser.: Mater. Sci. Eng. **737**(1), 012244 (2020). https://doi.org/10.1088/1757-899X/737/1/012244

2. Ali, S.S., Baghel, V.S., Ganapathi, I.I., Prakash, S.: Robust biometric authentication system with a secure user template. Image Vis. Comput. **104**, 104004 (2020). https://doi.org/10.1016/j.imavis.2020.104004

3. Ali, S.S., Ganapathi, I.I., Vu, N.S., Ali, S.D., Saxena, N., Werghi, N.: Image forgery detection using deep learning by recompressing images. Electronics **11**(3) (2022). https://doi.org/10.3390/electronics11030403

4. Azure: Algorithm & component referencefor azure machine learning designer. Python SDK Azure-Ai-Ml V2 (2023)

5. Bi, X., et al.: D-Unet: a dual-encoder u-net for image splicing forgery detection and localization. CoRR abs/2012.01821 (2020). https://doi.org/10.48550/arXiv.2012.01821

6. Bondi, L., Lameri, S., Güera, D., Bestagini, P., Delp, E.J., Tubaro, S.: Tampering detection and localization through clustering of camera-based CNN features. In: 2017 IEEE Conference on Computer Vision and Pattern Recognition Workshops (CVPRW), pp. 1855–1864 (2017). https://doi.org/10.1109/CVPRW.2017.232

7. Bunk, J., et al.: Detection and localization of image forgeries using resampling features and deep learning. In: 2017 IEEE Conference on Computer Vision and Pattern Recognition Workshops (CVPRW), pp. 1881–1889. IEEE Computer Society, Los Alamitos, CA, USA (2017). https://doi.org/10.1109/CVPRW.2017.235

8. Chaitra, B., Reddy, P.B.: A study on digital image forgery techniques and its detection. In: 2019 International Conference on Contemporary Computing and Informatics (IC3I), pp. 127–130 (2019). https://doi.org/10.1109/IC3I46837.2019.9055573

9. Christlein, V., Riess, C., Jordan, J., Riess, C., Angelopoulou, E.: An evaluation of popular copy-move forgery detection approaches. IEEE Trans. Inf. Forensics Secur. **7**(6), 1841–1854 (2012). https://doi.org/10.1109/TIFS.2012.2218597

10. Devi Mahalakshmi, S., Vijayalakshmi, K., Priyadharsini, S.: Digital image forgery detection and estimation by exploring basic image manipulations. Digit. Investig. **8**(3), 215–225 (2012). https://doi.org/10.1016/j.diin.2011.06.004

11. Easow, S., Manikandan, D.L.C.: A study on image forgery detection techniques. Int. J. Comput. (IJC) **33**(1), 84–81 (2019). https://ijcjournal.org/index.php/InternationalJournalOfComputer/article/view/1411

12. Feng, W., Wu, S., Li, X., Kunkle, K.: A deep belief network based machine learning system for risky host detection. CoRR abs/1801.00025 (2018). https://doi.org/10.48550/arXiv.1801.00025

13. Gadamsetty, S., Ch, R., Ch, A., Iwendi, C., Gadekallu, T.R.: Hash-based deep learning approach for remote sensing satellite imagery detection. Water **14**(5) (2022). https://doi.org/10.3390/w14050707

14. García, R., Algredo-Badillo, I., Morales-Sandoval, M., Feregrino-Uribe, C., Cumplido, R.: A compact FPGA-based processor for the secure hash algorithm SHA-256. Comput. Electr. Eng. **40**(1), 194–202 (2014). https://doi.org/10.1016/j.compeleceng.2013.11.014, 40th-year commemorative issue

15. Ghosh, A., Sufian, A., Sultana, F., Chakrabarti, A., De, D.: Fundamental concepts of convolutional neural network. In: Balas, V.E., Kumar, R., Srivastava, R. (eds.) Recent Trends and Advances in Artificial Intelligence and Internet of Things. ISRL, vol. 172, pp. 519–567. Springer, Cham (2020). https://doi.org/10.1007/978-3-030-32644-9_36

16. Guan, Y., Li, S.E., Duan, J., Li, J., Ren, Y., Sun, Q., Cheng, B.: Direct and indirect reinforcement learning. Int. J. Intell. Syst. **36**(8), 4439–4467 (2021). https://doi.org/10.1002/int.22466

17. Habibi, M., Hassanpour, H.: Splicing image forgery detection and localization based on color edge inconsistency using statistical dispersion measures. Int. J. Eng. **34**(2), 443–451 (2021). https://doi.org/10.5829/IJE.2021.34.02B.16

18. Islam, A., Long, C., Basharat, A., Hoogs, A.: DOA-GAN: dual-order attentive generative adversarial network for image copy-move forgery detection and localization. In: 2020 IEEE/CVF Conference on Computer Vision and Pattern Recognition (CVPR), pp. 4675–4684 (2020). https://doi.org/10.1109/CVPR42600.2020.00473

19. Karampidis, K., Papadourakis, G.: File type identification for digital forensics. In: Krogstie, J., Mouratidis, H., Su, J. (eds.) CAiSE 2016. LNBIP, vol. 249, pp. 266–274. Springer, Cham (2016). https://doi.org/10.1007/978-3-319-39564-7_25

20. Kester, Q.A., Nana, L., Pascu, A.C., Gire, S., Eghan, J.M., Quaynor, N.N.: A hybrid image cryptographic and spatial digital watermarking encryption technique for security and authentication of digital images. In: 2015 17th UKSim-AMSS International Conference on Modelling and Simulation (UKSim), pp. 322–326 (2015). https://doi.org/10.1109/UKSim.2015.85

21. Kester, Q.A., Nana, L., Pascu, A.C., Gire, S., Eghan, J.M., Quaynor, N.N.: A novel hybrid discrete cosine transformation and visual cryptographic technique for securing digital images. In: 2015 17th UKSim-AMSS International Conference on Modelling and Simulation (UKSim), pp. 327–332 (2015). https://doi.org/10.1109/UKSim.2015.101

22. Kumar, M., Soni, A., Shekhawat, A.R.S., Rawat, A.: Enhanced digital image and text data security using hybrid model of LSB steganography and AES cryptography technique. In: 2022 Second International Conference on Artificial Intelligence and Smart Energy (ICAIS), pp. 1453–1457 (2022). https://doi.org/10.1109/ICAIS53314.2022.9742942

23. Kuznetsov, A.: Digital image forgery detection using deep learning approach. J. Phys.: Conf. Ser. **1368**(3), 032028 (2019). https://doi.org/10.1088/1742-6596/1368/3/032028

24. Kwon, M.J., Yu, I.J., Nam, S.H., Lee, H.K.: CAT-Net: compression artifact tracing network for detection and localization of image splicing. In: 2021 IEEE Winter Conference on Applications of Computer Vision (WACV), pp. 375–384 (2021). https://doi.org/10.1109/WACV48630.2021.00042

25. Li, Y., Lyu, S.: Exposing deepfake videos by detecting face warping artifacts. CoRR abs/1811.00656 (2018). https://doi.org/10.48550/arXiv.1811.00656

26. Liu, X., Liu, Y., Chen, J., Liu, X.: PSCC-Net: progressive spatio-channel correlation network for image manipulation detection and localization. IEEE Trans. Cir. and Sys. for Video Technol. **32**(11), 7505–7517 (2022). https://doi.org/10.1109/TCSVT.2022.3189545

27. Mahdian, B., Saic, S.: Blind methods for detecting image fakery. In: 2008 42nd Annual IEEE International Carnahan Conference on Security Technology, pp. 280–286 (2008). https://doi.org/10.1109/CCST.2008.4751315

28. Matern, F., Riess, C., Stamminger, M.: Gradient-based illumination description for image forgery detection. IEEE Trans. Inf. Forensics Secur. **15**, 1303–1317 (2020). https://doi.org/10.1109/TIFS.2019.2935913

29. Michelucci, U.: An introduction to autoencoders. CoRR abs/2201.03898 (2022). https://doi.org/10.48550/arXiv.2201.03898

30. Okeyinka, A., Alao, O., Gbadamosi, B., Ogundokun, R., Oluwaseun, R.: Application of SHA-256 in formulation of digital signatures of RSA and Elgamal cryptosystems, pp. 61–66 (2018). https://api.semanticscholar.org/CorpusID:195800765

31. Pierluigi, P.: Photo Forensics: detect photoshop manipulation with error level analysis (2023). https://resources.infosecinstitute.com/topic/error-level-analysis-detect-image-manipulation/

32. Raja, A.: Active and passive detection of image forgery: A review analysis. IJERT-Proc **9**(5), 418–424 (2021). https://www.ijert.org/research/active-and-passive-detection-of-image-forgery-a-review-analysis

33. Ravi, J., Durga, M.G.S., Kartheek, Y.D.R.C., Begum, M.S., Raju, T., Raju, T.V.S.: Image fusion using non subsampled contourlet transform in medical field. Int. J. Eng. Adv. Technol. (IJEAT) **9**(3), 3829–3832 (2020). https://doi.org/10.35940/ijeat.C6268.029320

34. Salehinejad, H., Baarbe, J., Sankar, S., Barfett, J., Colak, E., Valaee, S.: Recent advances in recurrent neural networks. CoRR abs/1801.01078 (2018). https://doi.org/10.48550/arXiv.1801.01078

35. Sharma, P., Kumar, M., Sharma, H.: Comprehensive analyses of image forgery detection methods from traditional to deep learning approaches: an evaluation. Multimedia Tools Appl. **82**(12), 18117–18150 (2023). https://doi.org/10.1007/s11042-022-13808-w

36. Shinde, P.P., Shah, S.: A review of machine learning and deep learning applications. In: 2018 Fourth International Conference on Computing Communication Control and Automation (ICCUBEA), pp. 1–6 (2018). https://doi.org/10.1109/ICCUBEA.2018.8697857

37. Singh, A., Singh, J.: Image forgery detection using deep neural network. In: 2021 8th International Conference on Signal Processing and Integrated Networks (SPIN), pp. 504–509 (2021). https://doi.org/10.1109/SPIN52536.2021.9565953

38. Stanton, J., Hirakawa, K., McCloskey, S.: Detecting image forgery based on color phenomenology. In: Proceedings of the IEEE/CVF Conference on Computer Vision and Pattern Recognition (CVPR) Workshops (2019). https://etd.ohiolink.edu/apexprod/rws_etd/send_file/send?accession=dayton15574119887572&disposition=inline

39. Tang, Z., Li, X., Zhang, X., Zhang, S., Dai, Y.: Image hashing with color vector angle. Neurocomputing **308**, 147–158 (2018). https://doi.org/10.1016/j.neucom.2018.04.057

40. Verdoliva, L.: Media forensics and deepfakes: an overview. IEEE J. Selected Top. Signal Process. **14**(5), 910–932 (2020). https://doi.org/10.1109/JSTSP.2020.3002101

41. Wu, Y., AbdAlmageed, W., Natarajan, P.: ManTra-Net: manipulation tracing network for detection and localization of image forgeries with anomalous features. In: 2019 IEEE/CVF Conference on Computer Vision and Pattern Recognition (CVPR), pp. 9535–9544 (2019). https://doi.org/10.1109/CVPR.2019.00977

42. Yousfi, Y., Fridrich, J.: An intriguing struggle of CNNs in JPEG steganalysis and the OneHot solution. IEEE Signal Process. Lett. **27**, 830–834 (2020). https://doi.org/10.1109/LSP.2020.2993959

Revocable Attribute-Based Encryption Scheme with Cryptographic Reverse Firewalls

Yang Zhao[1,2], Xing-Yu Ke[1,2], Yu-Wei Pang[1,2], Hu Xiong[1,2], Guo-Bin Zhu[1,2], and Kuo-Hui Yeh[3(✉)]

[1] School of Information and Software Engineering, University of Electronic Science and Technology of China, Chengdu 610054, China
[2] Network and Data Security Key Laboratory of Sichuan Province, University of Electronic Science and Technology of China, Chengdu 610054, China
[3] Department of Information Management, National Dong Hwa University, Hualien, Taiwan
khyeh@gms.ndhu.edu.tw

Abstract. With the prevalence of information sharing, preserving the confidentiality of sensitive data has become paramount. Attribute-based encryption (ABE) has become a viable option to tackle this problem. Using a set of attributes, data owners can encrypt data with ABE, and data is only accessible by users with the required attributes and authorization. However, there are various limitations associated with the traditional CP-ABE scheme, such as embedding user-sensitive information in the access structures without any hidden operations, an inability to effectively address the issue of user attribute changes, and vulnerability to internal attacks from cryptography devices. To address these limitations, researchers have proposed various enhanced ABE schemes. Mironov presented a concept of cryptographic reverse firewall (CRF) in Eurocrypt 2015, which could resist certain compromised machines from leaking secret information. The CRF has been deployed in many cryptographic systems, but its application in the ABE field has been relatively limited. This paper presents a novel attribute-based encryption scheme which incorporates attribute revocation, hidden policy components, and CRF mechanism to prevent attackers from internal attacks on cryptography devices. This scheme is applicable in various applications, such as cloud computing, where secure data sharing is required.

Keywords: Attribute-based Encryption · Attributes revocation · Partial Hidden policy · Cryptographic Reverse Firewalls · Data sharing

1 Introduction

While traditional encryption methods suffer from three major drawbacks: (1) To ensure secure encryption, resource providers need the user's genuine public key certificate before proceeding with encryption. (2) messages must be encrypted

Z. Tan et al. (Eds.): BDTA 2023, LNICST 555, pp. 79–94, 2024.
https://doi.org/10.1007/978-3-031-52265-9_6

individually using the public key of each user, resulting in high processing over-heads and bandwidth consumption issues; and (3) broadcast encryption technology, while partially solving the efficiency problem [5], requires resource providers to obtain the user list before encryption, creating two secondary problems: distributed applications cannot obtain the size of the receiving group at once, and listing user identities may compromise user privacy.

Shamir and Boneh et al. [4,19] introduced identity-based encryption (IBE) mechanisms to address the issue that resource providers are required to acquire a user's public key certificate, while Sahai and Waters presented attribute-based encryption (ABE) mechanisms built upon IBE technology to solve issues of high processing overhead and bandwidth consumption [18]. ABE mechanisms have four key features that make them promising for fine-grained access control [9, 22], targeted broadcasting [9], group key management [7,8], privacy protection [22,23], and other fields. These features include the ability for resource providers to encrypt messages based on attributes, without paying attention to group size or identity, ensuring only group members with required attributes can decrypt messages, preventing collusion attacks by users, and supporting flexible access control policies based on attribute conjunctions, disjunctions, negations, and threshold operations.

In 2013, Edward Snowden released a large number of documents to the media revealing various surveillance programs of the US government. These programs allowed the government to monitor user privacy on a large scale by obtaining data from super-large internet companies such as Microsoft and Google. Additionally, the NSA installed backdoor programs in widely used public encryption standards and intercepted hardware sent to users to tamper with programs for monitoring purposes [10]. Bellare et al. [2] presented an algorithm replacement attack. Mironov and Stephons-Davidowitz [15] introduced the CRFs in 2015 that intercepts and modifies both inbound and outbound messages to enhance security protection. However, few papers have proposed a cryptographic reverse firewall suitable for ABE, and its addition may increase time overhead and require further study on algorithm efficiency.

1.1 Related Work

ABE [18] is an encryption scheme that allows access control based on user attributes rather than their identity. ABE is commonly categorized into key-policy ABE [9] and ciphertext-policy ABE [3]. KP-ABE embeds access policy into secret key, and attributes set into ciphertext. On the contrary, CP-ABE embeds attribute set into the key, while access policy into ciphertext. In order to successfully decrypt and access a secret message, their attribute set must satisfy the access policy requirements.

Within context of attribute-based encryption (ABE), user attributes may change frequently, leading to the revocation of certain attributes. Two types of revocation can be implemented: user revocation and attribute revocation. Revoking user entails invalidating all attributes that have been assigned to a particular user. The term attribute revocation, on the other hand, refers to the situation where a user's access rights are restricted because a particular attribute has been revoked. To achieve attribute revocation, Pirretti et al. [17] presented a method in 2010 that utilizes a timed update key mechanism. Subsequently, Wang et al. [20] introduced group key forms and binary trees to implement attribute revocation in their respective schemes in 2018. Notably, none of these schemes support decryption testing. Zhang [25] presented a different method that reduces the reliance on bilinear pairing. However, this scheme lacks support for attribute revocation. In 2021, a scheme was proposed by Zeng et al. [24] that can handle large attribute domains, but lacks support for attribute revocation.

Chen et al. [6] put forward cryptographic reverse firewall (CRF) and suggested a smooth projective hash function (SPHF) as a technique for building CRFs. However, their CRF construction is not applicable to attribute-based encryption due to its complexity. To address this limitation, Yuyang Zhou [26] presented a CRFs method for certificateless public key encryption, while Mengdi Ouyang [16] presented a non-monotonic access structure-based scheme with CRFs for identity-based signature. In addition, BO HONG et al. [11] presented a Multi-Authority KP-ABE scheme with Cryptographic Reverse Firewalls, and Hui Ma [14] designed a CRFs scheme based on online/offline CP-ABE. Although various attempts have been made, a CRF scheme appropriate for CP-ABE that includes attribute revocation and partial policy hiding has yet to be proposed. Xiong et al. [21]introduced a secure efficient revocable PRS (R-PRS) scheme

Therefore, there is still a need to develop a CRFs scheme that can address the challenges associated with CP-ABE, such as attribute revocation and policy partial hiding. This will be an great improvement for CP-ABE and enhancing the security of attribute-based encryption schemes.

1.2   Our Contribution

To overcome these challenges, this paper presents a novel ABE scheme with reverse firewall, called RH-CPABE-CRF. Our proposed scheme provides a robust security framework for data sharing in dynamic environments by supporting attribute revocation and hidden policy delegation. The cryptography reverse firewall ensures that our scheme can support protection from malicious attacks from within the device.

Resist Internal Attacks. We extended the CRFs insecure for the base scheme which are used to recalculate important parameters to against the leakage of inner attack and also keep functionality.

Partial Policy Hiding: We have implemented partial policy hiding in our scheme by only hiding attribute values, while keeping attribute names visible. This ensures efficient implementation while maintaining a level of security.

Attribute Revocation: Our scheme supports attribute-level revocation for users. The CA creates a group key for each user attribute, which are organized in a binary tree structure. This enables efficient storage and retrieval of user attributes, while also allowing for easy revocation of specific attributes as needed.

Large Attribute Universe: Our scheme has public parameters of constant size, ensuring that its performance remains efficient and scalable even with an increasing number of user attributes.

2 Preliminary

2.1 Bilinear Groups

Assume $\mathbb{G}$ and $\mathbb{G}_T$ denotes two cyclic groups of prime order p. Bilinear pairing e between these groups is rigorously defined when certain conditions are met:

1. Bilinearity: $\forall g_1, g_2 \in \mathbb{G}$, $\forall m, n \in \mathbb{Z}_p^*$, such that $e\left(g_1^m, g_2^n\right) = e(g_1, g_2)^{mn}$.
2. Non-degeneracy: e is non-degenerate meaning that $P \in \mathbb{G}$ and $e(P, P) \neq 1$.
3. Computability: $\forall g_1, g_2 \in \mathbb{G}$, $e(g_1, g_2)$ must be efficiently computable.

2.2 Access Structures

The collection of participants $T = \{P_1, \cdots, P_n\}$ is defined in our scheme. Access structure is then defined as $B \subseteq 2^T$ of non-empty subsets of T with monotonicity, meaning that if $E \in B$ and $E \subseteq R$, then $R \in B$. This access structure is used to determine which participants have access to encrypted data.

2.3 Linear Secret Sharing Schemes

Definition 1. *Linear Secret Sharing Scheme (LSSS): To qualify as a LSSS over the field $\mathbb{Z}_p$, certain requirements must be met:*

1. *Each participant is assigned a vector over $\mathbb{Z}_p$ for their share.*
2. *Let M be a $d \times n$ matrix that serves as the shared generating matrix. For each $i \in 2, \ldots, d$, let $\rho(i)$ denote the party labeling row i. Each column vector $v = (s, r_2, \ldots, r_n)$, where s is the secret to be shared and r_2 to r_n are randomly selected variables in $\mathbb{Z}_p$, produces a vector M_v of d shares of the secret $s.s$*

In [1], the authors proved that a LSSS satisfying definition 1 has the linear reconstruction property. Specifically, given an access structure $\mathbb{A}$ corresponding to an LSSS scheme, and an authorized set $S \in \mathbb{A}$, one can find constants $\omega_i \in \mathbb{Z}_p, i \in I$ in polynomial time, where $I = i : \rho(i) \in S$, such that λ_i is a valid share and $\sum_{i \in I} \omega_i \lambda_i = s$. This means that the authorized parties are able to rebuild s using their shares, while unauthorized parties cannot.

3 System Model

Our proposed Revocable CP-ABE Scheme with CRFs (RH-CPABE-CRF) consists of six entities (Fig. 1):

Central Authority (CA): The Central Authority creates and manages the global public parameters used in the cryptographic system, as well as generating secret keys and sent to users.

Cloud Service Provider (CSP): CSP stores and manages access to data and also provides assistance with the re-encryption or updating of ciphertext when attribute revocation occurs.

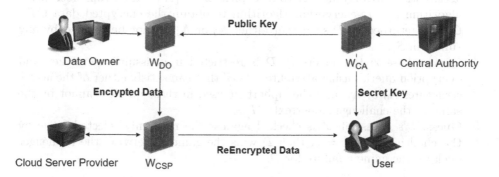

Fig. 1. System Model

Data Owner (DO): DO selects access policy for attributes and performs encryption accordingly, without relying on the CSP for access control. User decryption privileges based on attributes are used for access control within the cryptography.

User: Users are assigned with attributes. Decryption is only allowed when attributes meet access policy, and this can be done using their corresponding secret keys.

Firewall of CA (W_{CA}): W_{CA} intercepts the public parameters published by the CA, modifies a portion of them, and then republishes them. When a user obtains their secret key, W_{CA} also scrambles the user's secret key.

Firewall of CSP (W_{CSP}): W_{CSP} intercepts the encrypted message sent by the DO, performs pre-re-encryption processing, and then forwards it to the CSP for re-encryption. Once the CSP completes re-encryption, W_{CSP} performs post-re-encryption processing on the message before forwarding it to the user.

Firewall of DO (W_{DO}): After the DO encrypts the message, W_{DO} re-randomizes the encrypted message before sending it to the CSP.

3.1 Security Model

Our security model involves a challenger $\mathcal{C}$ and an adversary $\mathcal{D}$.

1. **SetUp:** Upon execution of SetUp, the party $\mathcal{C}$ obtains public parameters PK and master key MSK. PK are disclosed to $\mathcal{D}$.
2. **Query phase 1:** $\mathcal{D}$ can issue two kind of queries.
   (a) Secret keys query: $\mathcal{C}$ generates the secret key $sk_{id,\mathcal{S}}$ using the KeyGen algorithm with the given id and attribute set $\mathcal{S}$ provided by $\mathcal{D}$, and then sends $sk_{id,\mathcal{S}}$ back to $\mathcal{D}$ in response to a secret key query.
   (b) Decryption query: $\mathcal{C}$ can run the KeyGen and Decrypt algorithms on the ciphertext provided by $\mathcal{D}$ to obtain the corresponding plaintext M, which it then sends to $\mathcal{D}$ as a response.
3. **Challenge:** $\mathcal{D}$ sends two messages S_0 and S_1 of same length, along with two access structures $\mathbb{A}_0$ and $\mathbb{A}_1$ to $\mathcal{C}$. $\mathcal{C}$ picks $\omega \xleftarrow{R} \{0,1\}$, then runs encryption algorithm and re-encryption algorithm to obtain the encrypted data CT'_ω. CT'_ω is returned to $\mathcal{D}$ such that either $\mathbb{A}_0$ or $\mathbb{A}_1$ cannot be fulfilled by any subset in $\mathcal{S}$).
4. **Query phase 2:** the adversary $\mathcal{D}$ is restricted from issuing secret key and decryption queries using attribute sets $\mathcal{S}'$ that can satisfy either of the access structures $\mathbb{A}_0$ or $\mathbb{A}_1$, and the ciphertext used in these queries cannot be the same as the challenge ciphertext CT'_ω.
5. **Guess:** $\mathcal{D}$'s guess bit ω' is checked against the randomly selected bit ω by the challenger. If $\omega' = \omega$, then $\mathcal{D}$ wins the game, otherwise, the challenger declares the game a failure for $\mathcal{D}$.

If $\mathcal{D}$ can correctly guess the value of ω with a significant advantage, then the security of this scheme is compromised (Fig. 2).

4   Our Construction

- **Setup:** It produced bilinear pairing $(\mathbb{G}, \mathbb{G}_T, e)$ over a composite order $N = p_1 p_2 p_3 p_4$, given security parameter λ as input. It initializes the attribute universe $\mathcal{U}$ as $\mathbb{Z}_N$, then it selects random values $\beta, b \xleftarrow{R} \mathbb{Z}_N$, $g \xleftarrow{R} \mathbb{G}p_1$, $p \xleftarrow{R} \mathbb{G}p_3$, and $q, r \xleftarrow{R} \mathbb{G}p_4$. Lastly, it returns public parameters $PK = (N, \mathbb{G}, \mathbb{G}_T, e, g, g^b, e(g,g)^\beta, p, q, r)$ and master key $MSK = \beta$.
- **KeyGen:** TA selects random values $k \xleftarrow{R} \mathbb{Z}_N$ and $d, \eta, \mu_i \xleftarrow{R} \mathbb{G}p_2$, where $\forall i \in \mathcal{I}_\mathcal{S}$. It takes PK, MSK, id, and $\mathcal{S}$ as input to return the private key

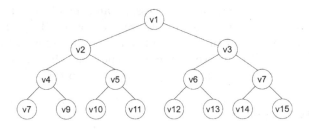

Fig. 2. $Tree_x$ for attribute x

$sk_{id,\mathcal{S}} = \left(\mathcal{S}, K, K'', \{K_i\}_{i\in\mathcal{I}_S}\right)$, in which $K = g^k d$, $K'' = g^\beta g^{bk}\eta$, and $K_i = (g^{s_i})^k \mu_i$, $\forall i \in \mathcal{I}_S$, and $\mathcal{I}_S$ is attribute name index.

- **AttrGroupKeyGen**: $AttrGroupKeyGen(x) \rightarrow (KEK_{TREE_x}, AGK)$: It takes an attribute x as input and generates the necessary keys for the attribute user group AG_x. TA creates a binary state tree $TREE_x$ [13] to represent the attribute and maintains the group AG_x which includes all users possessing the attribute. Every node v_j in the tree corresponds to a random key $KEK_j \in \mathbb{Z}_p$, and the leaf nodes corresponds to the elements of AG_x. For a user u in the group, $PATH_u$ represents the path from leaf node assigned to u to root node, and u stores $PATH_u$ as its path keys. The CA also generates a unique attribute group key $AGK_x \in \mathbb{Z}_p$, which is shared with CSP after encrypting it using KEK as a symmetric key.

- **Encryption**: It inputs message M, public key PK, access policy $\mathbb{A}$ which corresponds to the LSSS (with dimensions $\ell \times n$), a vector $\mathcal{T}$ representing attribute values, and a mapping ρ from $\{1, 2, \ldots, \ell\}$ to the attribute name universe. It then picks random vectors v and v' in attribute name space, along with $2(\ell+1)$ random subgroup elements r_1, r_2, $r_{1,x}$, and $r_{2,x}$, where $x \in \{1, 2, \ldots, \ell\}$. Lastly, a message $R \in \mathbb{G}_T$ is randomly selected to compute the ciphertext CT:

$$CT = \left((\mathbb{A}, \rho), \hat{W}, W_1, W_2, \hat{W}_1, \hat{W}_2, \{W_{1,x}, W_{2,x}\}_{x\in[\ell]}\right) \tag{1}$$

where we have $\hat{W} = p^{H(M)}q^{H(R)}$ ($'H'$ is a hash function), $W_1 = M \cdot e(g,g)^{\beta \cdot s}$, $\hat{W}_1 = g^s r_1$, $W_{1,x} = g^{bA_x \cdot v}g^{-s \cdot t_{\rho(x)}}r_{1,x}$, $W_2 = R \cdot e(g,g)^{\beta \cdot s'}$, $\hat{W}_2 = g^{s'} r_2$, $W_{2,x} = g^{bA_x \cdot v'}g^{-s' \cdot t_{\rho(x)}} \cdot r_{2,x}$, then sends to CSP.

- **ReEncryption**: $ReEncrypt(CT, \{AGK_i\}_{i\in\mathcal{I}_S}) \rightarrow CT'$: CSP obtains the CT from data owner generated by $Encryption$, and $\{AGK_i\}_{i\in\mathcal{I}_S}$ from CA generated by $KeyGeneration$. This algorithm applies re-encryption on CT using $AGK_{\rho(i)}$ corresponding to each attribute $\rho(i)$ in $\mathbb{A}$ and obtains CT'.

$$CT' = \left((\mathbb{A}, \rho), \hat{W}, W_1, \hat{W}_1, W_2, \hat{W}_2, \{W'_{1,x}, W'_{2,x}\}_{x\in[\ell]}\right) \tag{2}$$

where $W'_{1,x} = W_{1,x}^{AGK_{\rho(x)}}$, $W'_{2,x} = W_{2,x}^{AGK_{\rho(x)}}$.

- **Decryption**: $Decryption(CT', \mathcal{S}, PK, \{AGK_i\}_{i\in\mathcal{I}_S}, sk_{id,\mathcal{S}}) \rightarrow (m/\perp)$: For attribute $\rho(x)$ in S, the user recovers $AGK_{\rho(x)}$ using the specific path keys $\{KEK_i\}_{i\in\mathcal{I}_S}$, and then calculates $K^* = (K)^{1/AGK_{\rho(x)}}$. Finally it computes:

$$W_2 \cdot \frac{\prod_{x\in\mathcal{X}}\left(e\left(W'_{2,x},K^*\right)\cdot e\left(\hat{W}_2,K_{\rho(x)}\right)\right)^{w_x}}{\hat{e}\left(\hat{W}_2,K''\right)}$$

$$= W_2 \cdot \frac{\prod_{x\in\mathcal{X}}\left(e\left(W_{2,x},K\right)\cdot e\left(\hat{W}_2,K_{\rho(x)}\right)\right)^{w_x}}{\hat{e}\left(\hat{W}_2,K''\right)} \tag{3}$$

$$= R\cdot e(g,g)^{\beta\cdot s'}\cdot \frac{\prod_{x\in\mathcal{X}}\left(e(g,g)^{bA_x v'k}\right)^{w_x}}{\hat{e}\left(g^{s'},g^\beta\cdot g^{bk}\right)}$$

$$= R\cdot e(g,g)^{\beta\cdot s'}\cdot \frac{e(g,g)^{\sum_{x\in\mathcal{X}}(A_x\omega_x v')bk}}{\hat{e}\left(g^{s'},g^\beta\cdot g^{bk}\right)}$$

$$= R$$

$$W_1 \cdot \frac{\prod_{x\in\mathcal{X}}\left(e\left(W'_{1,x},K^*\right)\cdot e\left(\hat{W}_1,K_{\rho(x)}\right)\right)^{w_x}}{\hat{e}\left(\hat{W}_1,K''\right)}$$

$$= W_1 \cdot \frac{\prod_{x\in\mathcal{X}}\left(e\left(W_{1,x},K\right)\cdot e\left(\hat{W}_1,K_{\rho(x)}\right)\right)^{w_x}}{\hat{e}\left(\hat{W}_1,K''\right)} \tag{4}$$

$$= M\cdot e(g,g)^{\beta\cdot s}\cdot \frac{\prod_{x\in\mathcal{X}}\left(e(g,g)^{bA_x vk}\right)^{w_x}}{\hat{e}\left(g^s,g^\beta\cdot g^{bk}\right)}$$

$$= M\cdot e(g,g)^{\beta\cdot s}\cdot \frac{e(g,g)^{\sum_{x\in\mathcal{X}}(A_x\omega_x v)bk}}{\hat{e}\left(g^s,g^\beta\cdot g^{bk}\right)}$$

$$= M$$

It returns M if $\hat{W}=p^{H(M)}q^{H(R)}$.

- **Revocation**: CA update the membership of AG_u and select a new attribute group key $AGK'_u \in \mathbb{Z}_p$ for the affected attribute. Then, CA computes a new minimum cover set G_u, which consists of descendant nodes covering unrevoked users. To update the keys for attribute u, the CA encrypts AGK'_u using KEK_v for the affected attribute and sends to the unaffected users. Attribute-level revocation can be achieved using the following two algorithms. $KeyReGen\left(\mathcal{S},sk_{id,\mathcal{S}},u,AGK'_u\right)\to sk'_{id,\mathcal{S}}$: If u is the attribute be revoked, $\rho(j')=u$. Unaffected users obtain AGK'_u from $\{AGK'_u\}_{KEK_{G_u}}$ by using KEK, where $KEK\in(KEK_{G_u}\cap PATH_{gid})$. It updates $sk'_{id,\mathcal{S}}=(\mathcal{S},K,K'',\{K^*_j\}_{j\in\mathcal{I}_\mathcal{S}})$, where

$$\forall j\in[l]\backslash\{j'\}:K^*_j=\left((g^{s_i})^k\mu_i\right)^{\frac{1}{AGK_{\rho(j)}}},j=j':K^*_j=\left((g^{s_j})^k\mu_j\right)^{\frac{1}{AGK'_u}} \tag{5}$$

$CTReGen(CT', u, AGK'_u) \rightarrow CT^*$: It randomly picks vectors $v'' = (s'', v''_2, \ldots, v''_n)^T$, $v''' = (s''', v'''_2, \ldots, v'''_n)^T$. Updates CT^*:

$$CT^* = \left((A,\rho), \hat{W}, W''_1, \hat{W}''_1, W''_2, \hat{W}''_2, \{W''_{1,x}, W''_{2,x}\}_{x \in [\ell]}\right) \qquad (6)$$

where $W''_1 = M \cdot \hat{e}(g,g)^{\beta \cdot s''}, \hat{W}''_1 = g^{s''} r_1, W''_{1,x} = \left(g^{bA_x \cdot v''} g^{-t_{\rho(x)}s''} r_{1,x}\right)^{AGK_{\rho(x)}}, W''_2 = R \cdot \hat{e}(g,g)^{\beta \cdot s'''}, \hat{W}''_2 = g^{s'''} r_2, W''_{2,x} = \left(g^{bA_x \cdot \hat{v}} g^{-t_{\rho(x)}s'''} r_{2,x}\right)^{AGK_{\rho(x)}}$.

5   Our Construction with CRFs

To enhance the confidentiality and integrity of TA, CSP, and DA, we introduce a revocable CP-ABE scheme with CRFs that builds upon the basic revocable CP-ABE. Three reverse firewalls are introduced: W_{TA}, W_{CSP} and W_{DO}. These firewalls are used to rerandomize PK, MK, $sk_{id,S}$, CT and CT'.

- *Setup*: TA runs setup algorithm to generate $PK = (N, \mathbb{G}, \mathbb{G}_T, e, g, g^b, e(g,g)^\beta, p, q, r)$ sent to other entities and master key $MSK = \beta$ kept secret.
- W_{TA}.*Setup*: W_{TA} receives PK and MSK, then randomly choose z_1, z_2, β' from $\mathbb{Z}_N$, let $\tilde{p} = p^{z_1}, \tilde{q} = q^{z_2}$, get updated

$$\tilde{PK} = \left(N, \mathbb{G}, \mathbb{G}_T, e, g, g^b, e(g,g)^{\beta'}, \tilde{p}, \tilde{q}, r\right) \qquad (7)$$

and $\tilde{MSK} = \beta'$.
- Key Generation: TA takes $\tilde{PK}, \tilde{MSK}$, user identity id and S as input to run $KeyGen$ to obtain $sk_{id,S}$ and sends to user. CA takes attribute set $\{x\}$ as input to run $AttrGroupKeyGen(x)$.
- W_{TA}.*KenGen*: W_{TA} receives $sk_{id,S}$ from TA, W_{TA} randomly chooses m, n from $\mathbb{Z}_N$, let $\tilde{K} = g^m K, \tilde{K}_i = g^n (g^{s_i})^k \mu_i, i \in \mathcal{I}_S, \tilde{K}'' = g^{m+n} K'', \tilde{sk}_{id,S} = \left(S, \tilde{K}, \tilde{K}'', \{\tilde{K}_i\}_{i \in \mathcal{I}_S}\right)$ and sends to user.
- Encryption: Data owner takes message M, public key PK, access policy $\mathbb{A}$ as input to generate $CT = \left((\mathbb{A}, \rho), \hat{W}, W_1, W_2, \hat{W}_1, \hat{W}_2, \{W_{1,x}, W_{2,x}\}_{x \in [\ell]}\right)$, then sends to CSP.
- W_{DO}.*Encrypt*: W_{DO} receives CT, then randomly choose $\{h_{1,x}, h_{2,x}\}_{x \in [\ell]}$ and h_1, h_2 from $\mathbb{Z}_p$, where we have $\sum_{x \in [\ell]} h_{1,x} = h_1, \sum_{x \in [\ell]} h_{2,x} = h_2$. then we compute $\tilde{W}_1 = g^{h_1} W_1, \tilde{W}_2 = g^{h_2} W_2, \tilde{\hat{W}}_1 = g^{h_1} \hat{W}_1, \tilde{\hat{W}}_2 = g^{h_2} \hat{W}_2, \tilde{W}_{1,x} = (g^b)^{h_{1,x}} \frac{W_{1,x}}{i}, \tilde{W}_{2,x} = (g^b)^{h_{2,x}} \frac{W_{2,x}}{i}$. get updated

$$\tilde{CT} = \left((\mathbb{A}, \rho), \hat{W}, \tilde{W}_1, \tilde{W}_2, \tilde{\hat{W}}_1, \tilde{\hat{W}}_2, \{\tilde{W}_{1,x}, \tilde{W}_{2,x}\}_{x \in [\ell]}\right) \qquad (8)$$

- $W_{CSP}.PreReEncrypt$: W_{CSP} obtains the $\{AGK_x\}_{x \in [\ell]}$ from CSP, then randomly picks $\{t_x\}_{x \in [\ell]} \in \mathbb{Z}_p$, get updated $\{A\tilde{G}K_x\}_{x \in [\ell]}$ where $A\tilde{G}K_x = t_x AGK_x$, and save t_x.
- ReEncryption: CSP takes $\tilde{C}T$ generated by $Encryption$, and $\{AGK_i\}_{i \in \mathcal{I}_s}$ generated by $KeyGeneration$ as input to run $ReEncrypt$ and obtains CT'.

$$\text{CT}' = \left((\mathbb{A}, \rho), \hat{W}, W_1, \hat{W}_1, W_2, \hat{W}_2, \{W'_{1,x}, W'_{2,x}\}_{x \in [\ell]} \right) \qquad (9)$$

where $W'_{1,x} = (W_{1,x})^{A\tilde{G}K_{\rho(x)}}, W'_{2,x} = (W_{2,x})^{A\tilde{G}K_{\rho(x)}}$.
- $W_{CSP}.AfterReEncrypt$: W_{CSP} obtains the CT' from CSP, then use the stored $\{t_x\}_{x \in [\ell]} \in \mathbb{Z}_p$ to compute

$$\tilde{\text{CT}}' = \left((A, \rho), \hat{W}, W_1, \hat{W}_1, W_2, \hat{W}_2, \{\tilde{W}'_{1,x}, \tilde{W}'_{2,x}\}_{x \in [\ell]} \right) \qquad (10)$$

where $\tilde{W}'_{1,x} = W'_{1,x}{}^{\frac{1}{t_x}}, \tilde{W}'_{2,x} = W'_{2,x}{}^{\frac{1}{t_x}}$.
- Decryption: Data user takes $\tilde{P}K$, $\tilde{C}T'$, and $sk_{\widetilde{id},S}$ as input to run $Decryption$ to get R and M, if $\hat{W} = p^{H(M)}q^{H(R)}$, it returns M.
- Revocation: It does the same as algorithms $Revocation$ in basic revocable CP-ABE.

6   Secure Analysis

6.1   Proof of RH-CPABE

Theorem 1. Suppose there exists the attacker $\mathcal{A}$ can break our method with non-negligible advantage e, then we can create an attacker $\mathcal{B}$ to break method [24].

Proof. We define attacker $\mathcal{A}$, challenger $\mathcal{B}$ of our scheme, also an attacker of scheme [24], $\mathcal{C}$ as an challenger of scheme [24].

1. Setup, $\mathcal{A}$ sends a access control policy to $\mathcal{B}$. Then $\mathcal{B}$ get $\text{PK}_c = \left(N = p_1 p_2 p_3 p_4, \mathbb{G}, \mathbb{G}_T, e, g, g^b, e(g,g)^\beta \right)$ from $\mathcal{C}$ in scheme [24]. $\mathcal{B}$ selects p from G_{p_3} and q, r from G_{p_4}, it returns the public parameters $\text{PK} = \left(N, \mathbb{G}, \mathbb{G}_T, e, g, g^b, e(g,g)^\beta, p, q, r \right)$ to the adversary $\mathcal{A}$ and key master key $MSK = \beta$ secret.
2. Query phase 1: $\mathcal{A}$ send some queries.
   (a) Secret keys query: $\mathcal{A}$ sends attributes sets S to $\mathcal{B}$ and $\mathcal{B}$ delivery it to $\mathcal{C}$, $\mathcal{C}$ launch key generation algorithm in [24] to produce $sk_{id,S}$ and returns to $\mathcal{B}$, $\mathcal{B}$ then sends it to $\mathcal{A}$.
   (b) Decryption query: With ciphertext CT as input, $\mathcal{B}$ runs $Decrypt$ to get message M, it then sends M to $\mathcal{A}$.

3. Challenge: $\mathcal{A}$ sends two messages M_0, M_1 and two access structure $\mathbb{A}_i$: $(A, \rho, \mathcal{T}_i)\,(i = 0, 1)$ to $\mathcal{B}$ and delivery to $\mathcal{C}$. $\mathcal{C}$ picks bit $\omega \xleftarrow{R} \{0, 1\}$, launch Encrypt $(PK, M_\omega, \mathbb{A}_\omega)$ and ReEncrypt (CT_ω, AGK) and give ciphertext CT'_ω back to $\mathcal{B}$. $\mathcal{B}$ sends to $\mathcal{A}$ where $\mathbb{A}_0$ or $\mathbb{A}_1$ cannot be satisfied by any set sub $(sub \subseteq \mathcal{S})$.
4. Query phase 2: $\mathcal{A}$ repeats Query phase 1, with restrictions that attribute set $\mathcal{S}'$ cannot satisfy $\mathbb{A}_0$ or $\mathbb{A}_1$ and $CT = CT'$.
5. Guess: $\mathcal{A}$ guesses bit $\omega' \in \{0, 1\}$. If $\omega' = \omega$, $\mathcal{A}$ wins the game.

Our scheme achieves selective security since it shares the same properties and security advantage as the method presented in [24].

6.2 Proof of RH-CPABE-CRF

For some damage caused by central authority, data owner, Cloud Server Provider, we utilize tampering algorithms $Setup^*$, $KeyGeneration^*$, $DataEncryption^*$, $DataReEncryption^*$ to verify selective CPA-secure through the indistinguishability of Rh-CPABE-CRF security game and Rh-CPABE scheme security game. In addition, the weak security resistance and weak resistance leakage of the reverse firewall can also be proved in this part:

Game 0: Its aligns with the security game in 3.1.

Game 1: Aligns with Game 0, but with the generation of PK and MSK occurs exclusively within the basic construction, as opposed to involving $Setup^*$ and $W_{TA}.Setup$.

Game 2: Aligns with Game 1, but with the difference that in the $KeyGeneration$ phase, the generation of SK is carried out solely by the $KeyGeneration$ process in the basic construction, rather than involving $KeyGeneration^*$ and $W_{TA}.KeyGen$.

Game 3. Aligns with Game 2, but with CT generated by the basic construction's $DataEncryption$, not $DataEncryption^*$ and $W_{DO}.Encrypt$.

Game 4. Aligns with Game 3, but with CT' are generated by $DataReEncryption$ in the basic construction, not $W_{CSP}.PreReEncrypt$ and $W_{CSP}.AfterReEncrypt$.

We prove indistinguishability between Game 0 and Game 1, Game 1 and Game 2, Game 2 and Game 3, and Game 3 and Game 4. After using the reverse firewall $W_{TA}.Setup^*$ on any tampered algorithm, the public parameters PK remain uniformly random, preserving the original algorithm's behavior and ensuring security.

Game 0 and Game 1 are indistinguishable. Game 1 and Game 2 are indistinguishable because user secret key also have key malleability. For the pair Game 2 and Game 3, for any tampered algorithm $Dataencryption^*$, after the post-processing of $W_{DO}.Encrypt$. The updated ciphertext CT are uniformly regenerated, which is smae as encryption algorithm in the basic construction. And also, after pre-processing by $W_{CSP}.PreReEncrypt$ and $W_{CSP}.AfterReEncrypt$. Game 3 and Game 4 are indistinguishable since the updated ciphertext CT' are uniformly reproduced. Thus, we can deduce that Game 0 and Game 4 are indistinguishable. As the basic construction ensures selective CPA-security, the proposed Rh-CPABE-CRF scheme also achieves selective CPA-security.

The selective CPA security implies that the reverse firewalls maintain weakly preserved security. Additionally, the indistinguishability between Game 0 and Game 4 demonstrates their effectiveness in weakly resisting exfiltration attempts. This completes the proof of the proposed scheme's security.

7 Performance

In Table 1, the primary procedures of our scheme are juxtaposed with those of other methods for comparison. Our scheme proposes an encryption-based access control scheme that addresses the critical issue of data sharing and protection. In comparison with [11, 12, 14], our scheme exhibits several notable advantages. Firstly, it supports reverse firewall, which provides more reliable protection against internal attack. Secondly, it supports attribute revocation, enabling attributes to be revoked when they are no longer needed, ensuring data controllability and security. Thirdly, it supports partial policy hiding, which enables data owners to protect data privacy and confidentiality by hiding part of the access policy. Fourthly, it supports large universe attributes, which enables a wider range of attributes to be used, thereby increasing system flexibility and scalability. Finally, our scheme uses a secret sharing scheme based on LSSS for access control, which is more efficient and flexible compared to the Tree structure used in [11].

In contrast, [11, 14] only support reverse firewall with no support for attribute revocation, partial policy hiding, or large universe attributes. Similarly, paper [12] does not support reverse firewall or attribute revocation, but it does support attribute hiding and uses LSSS for access control. Thus, the proposed access control scheme in this paper offers superior support and security compared to the three comparison papers, making it a significant contribution to the field of data sharing and protection.

Regarding time efficiency, Table 2 indicates that our scheme outperforms other solutions at encryption and decryption. Specifically, in terms of key generation, our scheme ranks in the middle. Regarding CRFs' performances, our scheme demonstrates superior efficiency compared to all the solutions listed in Table 2. In the $W_{TA}Setup$ setup, three schemes from Table 2 remain unchanged with an increase in the number of attributes, whereas our scheme outperforms others during the $W_{TA}KeyGen$ and $W_{DO}Enc$ procedures.

We evaluated the efficiency of our proposed schema using the JPBC library and conducted experiments on Windows 10 operating system with an i7-11700 2.50GHz CPU. The performance of our scheme is shown in Fig. 3, while Figs. 3(a), 3(b), and 3(c) display the performance of KeyGen, Encryption and Decryption. Additionally, Figs. 3(d), 3(e), 3(f), and 3(g) demonstrate time cost of CRFs. The experimental outcomes consistently corroborate the efficiency comparison table, as depicted in Table 2.

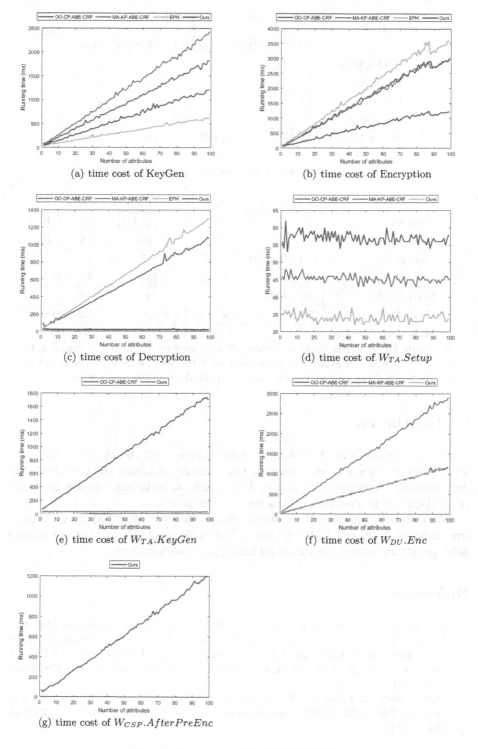

(a) time cost of KeyGen

(b) time cost of Encryption

(c) time cost of Decryption

(d) time cost of $W_{TA}.Setup$

(e) time cost of $W_{TA}.KeyGen$

(f) time cost of $W_{DU}.Enc$

(g) time cost of $W_{CSP}.AfterPreEnc$

Fig. 3. Time cost of Rh-CPABE-CRF

Table 1. Function comparison

	OOCAC [14]	AKAC [11]	EPH [12]	Ours
With CRFs	✓	✓	×	✓
Revocable	×	×	×	✓
Policy hiding	×	×	✓	✓
Large Universe	×	×	×	✓
Access structure	LSSS	LSSS	Tree	LSSS

Table 2. Efficiency comparison

	OOCAC [14]	AKAC [11]	EPH [12]	Ours
$KeyGen$	$(3l+4)E$	$(4l+2)E+P$	$(l+4)E$	$(2l+3)E$
$Encryption$	$(5l+2)E$	$(5l+2)E$	$(6l+4)E$	$(2l+6)E$
$Decryption$	$E+(3l+1)P$	$E+P$	$lE+2lP$	E
$W_{TA}.Setup$	$7E+P$	$5E+P$	×	$3E+P$
$W_{TA}.KeyGen$	$(3k+5)E$	×	×	$3E$
$W_{DO}.Enc$	$2lE$	$(5l+2)E+P$	×	$(2l+2)E$
$W_{CSP}.AfterReEnc$	×	×	×	$2lE$

E stands for modular exponentiation. P represents a bilinear pairing. l indicates the number of attributes associated with the user. k denotes the count of attributes in the access structure that fulfill the decryption requirement.

8   Conclusion

This paper proposes an ABE scheme with revocable attributes and hidden policy, enhanced with a reverse firewall. Our scheme addresses the confidentiality and integrity challenges of existing ABE schemes, including efficient attribute revocation and protection of the access control policy.

We evaluated the properties of our scheme and demonstrated its advantages over existing ABE with CRFs schemes. The experiments shows that our scheme achieves strong security while maintaining good performance.

References

1. Beimel, A., et al.: Secure schemes for secret sharing and key distribution (1996)
2. Bellare, M., Paterson, K.G., Rogaway, P.: Security of symmetric encryption against mass surveillance. In: Garay, J.A., Gennaro, R. (eds.) CRYPTO 2014. LNCS, vol. 8616, pp. 1–19. Springer, Heidelberg (2014). https://doi.org/10.1007/978-3-662-44371-2_1
3. Bethencourt, J., Sahai, A., Waters, B.: Ciphertext-policy attribute-based encryption. In: 2007 IEEE Symposium on Security and Privacy (SP 2007), pp. 321–334. IEEE (2007)

4. Boneh, D., Franklin, M.: Identity-based encryption from the Weil pairing. In: Kilian, J. (ed.) CRYPTO 2001. LNCS, vol. 2139, pp. 213–229. Springer, Heidelberg (2001). https://doi.org/10.1007/3-540-44647-8_13

5. Boneh, D., Gentry, C., Waters, B.: Collusion resistant broadcast encryption with short ciphertexts and private keys. In: Shoup, V. (ed.) CRYPTO 2005. LNCS, vol. 3621, pp. 258–275. Springer, Heidelberg (2005). https://doi.org/10.1007/11535218_16

6. Chen, R., Mu, Y., Yang, G., Susilo, W., Guo, F., Zhang, M.: Cryptographic reverse firewall via malleable smooth projective hash functions. In: Cheon, J.H., Takagi, T. (eds.) ASIACRYPT 2016. LNCS, vol. 10031, pp. 844–876. Springer, Heidelberg (2016). https://doi.org/10.1007/978-3-662-53887-6_31

7. Cheung, L., Cooley, J.A., Khazan, R., Newport, C.: Collusion-resistant group key management using attribute-based encryption. Cryptology ePrint Archive (2007)

8. Cheung, L., Newport, C.: Provably secure ciphertext policy ABE. In: Proceedings of the 14th ACM Conference on Computer and Communications Security, pp. 456–465 (2007)

9. Goyal, V., Pandey, O., Sahai, A., Waters, B.: Attribute-based encryption for fine-grained access control of encrypted data. In: Proceedings of the 13th ACM Conference on Computer and Communications Security, pp. 89–98 (2006)

10. Green, M., Hohenberger, S., Waters, B.: Outsourcing the decryption of {ABE} ciphertexts. In: 20th USENIX Security Symposium (USENIX Security 11) (2011)

11. Hong, B., Chen, J., Zhang, K., Qian, F.H.: Multi-authority non-monotonic KP-ABE with cryptographic reverse firewall. IEEE Access **7**, 159002–159012 (2019)

12. Lai, J., Deng, R.H., Li, Y.: Expressive CP-ABE with partially hidden access structures. In: ACM Asia Conference on Computer and Communications Security (2012)

13. Liu, Z., Jiang, Z.L., Wang, X., Yiu, S.M.: Practical attribute-based encryption: outsourcing decryption, attribute revocation and policy updating. J. Netw. Comput. Appl. **108**, 112–123 (2018)

14. Ma, H., Zhang, R., Yang, G., Song, Z., Sun, S., Xiao, Y.: Concessive online/offline attribute based encryption with cryptographic reverse firewalls—secure and efficient fine-grained access control on corrupted machines. In: Lopez, J., Zhou, J., Soriano, M. (eds.) ESORICS 2018. LNCS, vol. 11099, pp. 507–526. Springer, Cham (2018). https://doi.org/10.1007/978-3-319-98989-1_25

15. Mironov, I., Stephens-Davidowitz, N.: Cryptographic reverse firewalls. In: Oswald, E., Fischlin, M. (eds.) EUROCRYPT 2015. LNCS, vol. 9057, pp. 657–686. Springer, Heidelberg (2015). https://doi.org/10.1007/978-3-662-46803-6_22

16. Ouyang, M., Wang, Z., Li, F.: Digital signature with cryptographic reverse firewalls. J. Syst. Architect. **116**, 102029 (2021)

17. Pirretti, M., Traynor, P., McDaniel, P., Waters, B.: Secure attribute-based systems. In: Proceedings of the 13th ACM Conference on Computer and Communications Security, pp. 99–112 (2006)

18. Sahai, A., Waters, B.: Fuzzy identity-based encryption. In: Cramer, R. (ed.) EUROCRYPT 2005. LNCS, vol. 3494, pp. 457–473. Springer, Heidelberg (2005). https://doi.org/10.1007/11426639_27

19. Shamir, A.: Identity-based cryptosystems and signature schemes. In: Blakley, G.R., Chaum, D. (eds.) CRYPTO 1984. LNCS, vol. 196, pp. 47–53. Springer, Heidelberg (1985). https://doi.org/10.1007/3-540-39568-7_5

20. Wang, W., Zhang, G., Shen, Y.: A CP-ABE scheme supporting attribute revocation and policy hiding in outsourced environment. In: 2018 IEEE 9th International Conference on Software Engineering and Service Science (ICSESS), pp. 96–99. IEEE (2018)

21. Xiong, H., Zhou, Z., Wang, L., Zhao, Z., Huang, X., Zhang, H.: An anonymous authentication protocol with delegation and revocation for content delivery networks. IEEE Syst. J. **16**(3), 4118–4129 (2021)
22. Yu, S., Ren, K., Lou, W.: Attribute-based content distribution with hidden policy. In: 2008 4th Workshop on Secure Network Protocols, pp. 39–44. IEEE (2008)
23. Yu, S., Ren, K., Lou, W.: Attribute-based on-demand multicast group setup with membership anonymity. In: Proceedings of the 4th International Conference on Security and Privacy in Communication Networks, pp. 1–6 (2008)
24. Zeng, P., Zhang, Z., Lu, R., Choo, K.K.R.: Efficient policy-hiding and large universe attribute-based encryption with public traceability for internet of medical things. IEEE Internet Things J. **8**(13), 10963–10972 (2021)
25. Zhang, Y., Zheng, D., Deng, R.H.: Security and privacy in smart health: efficient policy-hiding attribute-based access control. IEEE Internet Things J. **5**(3), 2130–2145 (2018)
26. Zhou, Y., Guo, J., Li, F.: Certificateless public key encryption with cryptographic reverse firewalls. J. Syst. Architect. **109**, 101754 (2020)

IoT Attacks Countermeasures: Systematic Review and Future Research Direction

Joshua Teddy Ibibo$^{(\boxtimes)}$ [ID]

School of Computing, Edinburgh Napier University, Edinburgh, UK
joshua.ibibo@napier.ac.uk

Abstract. In order to connect heterogeneous nodes, objects, and smart devices of a network, such as e-transportation, e-health, e-education, e-home, and e-grip, the Internet of Things (IoT) has emerged as an efficient technology. This technology makes things easier, safer, and more productive for us all. These nodes are often resource-constrained because of their involvement in a huge network of heterogeneous devices, making them the weakest link in the chain for a cyber attacker because they generate enormous amounts of data despite a number of limitations, including memory, power, and low processor of the device. So these limitations make IoT devices vulnerable to a variety of security attacks. In this paper, we presented a survey on attacks IoT countermeasures, systematic reviews, and analyses of various IoT attacks that are occurring, classified them, discussed their defences, and identified the most significant IoT attacks countermeasures. A state-of-the-art analysis of the different attacks, including their effectiveness and degree of damage in IoT devices, has been given and contrasted. We identify the advantages and disadvantages of IoT Attack Countermeasures and proposed a Novel IoT Attack Countermeasures. Finally, we identify the open-research issue in the domain and provide directions for future research.

Keywords: IoT · Attacks · Countermeasures · privacy · security · IoT application

1 Introduction

The Internet of Things (IoT) was first used some 23 years ago by Kelvin Ashton while working on his newly developed sensor project in a presentation for Procter & Gamble in the context of RFID supply chains in 1999 [1] and David L. Brock [2] in 2001. However, Since 1832, there has been a theory of connected devices. It was possible to directly communicate between two devices by sending electrical signals when the first electromagnetic transmission was created. But the creation of the Internet in the late 1960s marked the beginning of the real Internet of Things. According to B. Ghaleb, IoT is defined as follows. "IoT is a network of connected smart objects that may exchange data over a wired network without the need for human-to-human (H2H) or human-to-computer (H2C) interaction [3]." There have been different applications that using the IoT technology have risen across all spheres of life attributed to its effectiveness and autonomy. Such applications include e-homes [4], e-offices [5], e-cities [6], e-education

Z. Tan et al. (Eds.): BDTA 2023, LNICST 555, pp. 95–111, 2024.
https://doi.org/10.1007/978-3-031-52265-9_7

[7], e-transportation systems [8], e-banking [9], and e-healthcare [10]. The implementation of this applications will be hampered by the lack of confidentiality, integrity, and data security. Majorities of the IoT attacks in the domain have received comments and discussions from [11–14]. IoT Attacks have been cited as an emerging concern to smart gadgets in a number of earlier papers [21–28]. These publications do not, however offer a taxonomy nor an analysis of the vulnerabilities and attacks implications. We provide a thorough analysis of the threats and exploits that are now being made against IoT devices in comparison to earlier works, and we offer a systematic analysis of threats to help people understand the attack methods and their effects on IoT devices. We looked at scientific publications on security, threats, and defenses in well-known databases like Google Scholar, Elsevier, the Edinburgh Napier University Library Search, the IEEE Xplore digital library, Rearchgate, and Science Direct. Out of the 500 journal and conference papers that were initially reported over the past ten years, 289 were picked for full-text examination after duplicate entries were removed and the abstract was examined. Only 85 articles were ultimately chosen for the study after 200 publications were excluded after reviewing the entire report. Below are six key contributions made by this work:

1. The research limits, unresolved issues, and potential paths for further research are mentioned.
2. The study offers knowledge about IoT architectures and infrastructure networks.
3. IoT security goals and problems are systematically clarified in the study.
4. We proposes a four-tier architecture for the Internet of Things
5. In order to secure IoT networks, it offers comprehensive and cutting-edge security novel IoT attack countermeasures.
6. Finally, it discusses the applicability of current defenses for various security attacks and offers possibilities for further research.

The rest of the paper is divided into the following sections. We look at the introduction of the domain, background and computing surveys. In Sect. 2, we go over IoT countermeasures overview, advantages and disadvantages of IoT attack countermeasures of each approach. We focus on the comparative systematic analysis of the Study in Sect. 3 and describe their overall IoT Attacks architecture and Its security challenges in Sect. 4. In Sect. 5, we provide a brief overview of the threats models on application domain and possible attacks within IoT. While in Sect. 6, we provide the countermeasures and threat models for security attacks in IoT.

1.1 Background and Statistics

Since the first theory of interconnected devices over the network was discovered in the 1980s, the concept of smart objects has been circulating. In the 1960s, the first attempts at automating smart objects that we use every day were made. Many industries tried to transfer tiny amounts of data in the 1990s transfer of packets between nodes [15]. The IoT goal has advanced significantly since then from a hypothetical idea to a top priority for many enterprises. Organizations over the world are searching for innovative methods to use and manage the data they acquire as they integrate IoT devices into their network infrastructures. Devices with IoT functionality can connect to a larger network and perform a wide range of functions. Securing all that data, though, presents a completely new difficulty. If an IoT connection is not properly secured, it could lead to major occurrences. Most recently in the year 2022, there are statistics of industry IoT as fellow;

1. There are currently over seven (7) billion active IoT devices. However, the number of IoT devices is anticipated to more than triple by 2030 to reach 25.44 billion around the globe [17]. In 2030, there will likely be more than triple the figure 25.4 billion active Internet of Things (IoT) devices in the world
2. There will be 152,200 IoT devices connecting to the internet every minute by the year 2025 [17].
3. In the six years between 2019 and 2025, it is predicted that global IoT spending could approach 15 Dollars trillion [17].
4. By 2025, it is anticipated that IoT devices would produce 73.1 ZB (zettabytes) of data [16].
5. In the healthcare industry, where there will be a significant increase in the number of IoT-connected devices in 2020, COVID-19 stimulates further investment in the technology. As anticipated by statistics and IoT projections from years ago, the FreeStyle Libre smart CGM communicates diabetic patients' data to an app on iPhone, Android, and Apple Watch devices, and remote monitoring by caregivers [16].

However, according to IoT statistics, the CAGR decreased to 8.2% in 2020, which is a nearly twice as low increase as the predicted 14.9% at the end of 2019. With a CAGR of 11.3% from 2020 to 2024, things are anticipated to get back to normal in 2023 [18].

1.2 Computing Survey

There are many computing review survey papers on IoT attacks countermeasures, which Table 1 has summarized them.

The survey by Lin, Jie, et al. [12] improves user-friendly environments and network nodes in the event of failures, fog/edge computing has been proposed to be connected with the Internet of Things (IoT) to enable computing services devices installed at the network edge. Fog/edge computing can offer a better quality of service and quicker reaction times for IoT applications. Another author [7] purpose of this study is to describe the most recent advancements in utilizing IoT applications in education and to present opportunities and challenges for subsequent experiments. As stated researchers have neglected to offer a comprehensive review study on IoT in education, which is a component of the domain. This review study provides an overview of the potential for incorporating wearable technologies, green IoT, medical education and training, vocational education and training, and IoT in education. Since IoT adoption and applications are still in their infancy in underdeveloped countries, further research is definitely encouraged. The author [13] divided the survey into four sections, focusing on the most recent network node constraints, IoT network procedures and designs for device authentication, and an analysis of security vulnerabilities at various layers. The IoT is introduced in this paper [19] together with its well-known system design, enabling technologies, security problems, and objectives. The analysis of security flaws and the provision of modern security methods are additional features of the study [20]. A proactive network technology [21] solution dubbed "PROSE," designed by the author of this paper, is used. It focuses on building reliable IoTs by proactively identifying critical nodes in the network so that they may be protected by deploying backups. We assume the worst-case scenario, where the attacker is able to capture/disable a section of the nodes, has comprehensive knowledge of the network architecture and traffic patterns, and is attempting to lower the maximum network throughput.

In [21], the researcher talks about several IoT attacks that are occurring, categorizes them, examines their defenses, and identifies the most notable IoT attacks in the network nodes. A cutting-edge analysis of the many attacks in the IoT has been given and compared, including their effectiveness and the degree of harm caused by the attacker. In this paper, [22], the author address the potential security threat and risks to industries using IoT devices, as well as the numerous attacks that could be made against the layered IIoT architecture's component parts and some safeguards. Finally, they proposed modern taxonomy to help reduce the risks of flaws in the IoT environment. This article [23] provided a thorough layer-by-layer analysis of IoT security vulnerabilities and the AI-based security models to mitigate such attacks within the domain. The protection of the IoT network is a big threat and future research goals are then discussed. In [24] Review the IoT's processes, goals, platforms, and methods. In order to classify IoT, we first introduce a brand-new classification system that ranks its approaches according to the relevant categories. To categorize the IoT literature, we second develop a classification strategy. In our third section, we look at the most significant IoT security breaches and the suggested defenses. Finally, we outline the unsolved problems in IoT security and privacy research and offer suggestions for future paths. However, [25] conducted a survey on IoT security in this report and examined the most pressing recent issues and Multi-layer attacks that are related to it. This study examines the IoT's security objectives and offers a taxonomy of attacks along with their remediation based on layer theory. The primary goal is to determine how, when, and why an IoT was penetrated or engaged in an attack. This [26] reviews the current defences against isolated side-channel attacks (SCA) before delving into unified defenses that help IoT devices overcome their power and footprint limitations. We also suggested using 3D integration as an IoT platform to protect the IoT system from advanced SCA. The ideal option for IoT systems is 3D integration because of its numerous benefits, including heterogeneous integration, split manufacturing, support for different IoT technologies like MEMS sensors, etc. the study [27, 28] examined machine- and deep learning-based security mechanisms for IoT and noted the drawbacks of each approach.

2   IoT Attack Countermeasures Background

The IoT uses diverse communication protocols for networks and objects, enabling M2M, T2T, H2T, and H2H interactions [29, 30]. Intelligent objects gather and transmit global data. Actuators enhance data processes and computer connections. Given IoT's scale, security is crucial, demanding attention from both business and academic experts [31].

Table 1. A Summary of Related Survey Papers

Reference	Input of Author	Attacks	Multi-layer Attacks	Threats	Privacy	Counter Measures	Threat Model
Lin, Ji et al. [12]	To research IoT centered on fog/edge technologies	1	0	2	1	0	0
Al-Emran et al. [7]	Highlight the most current developments in using IoT applications in education	0	0	0	2	0	0
Jie et al. [13]	examines how cyber-physical systems and IoT are related	1	0	2	1	0	0
Khanam et al. [19]	The author evaluates security flaws and provides modern security taxonomy	1	0	1	1	1	0
Ashraf [20]	This paper proposes PROSE-a proactive network fortifying solution in IoT	1	0	2	2	2	0
Deogirikar et al. [21]	The research analyzes several IoT threats, classifies them, and their defenses	1	0	1	0	2	0
Panchal et al. [22]	An IIoT attack taxonomy that we suggest	1	0	1	2	1	0
Zaman et al. [23]	This report provided a thorough layer-by-layer analysis of IoT security concerns	1	0	1	1	1	1

(continued)

Table 1. (*continued*)

Reference	Input of Author	Attacks	Multi-layer Attacks	Threats	Privacy	Counter Measures	Threat Model
Algarni [24]	Reviewing the SHS's approaches, goals, platforms, and methods	1	0	2	1	1	0
Gautam et al. [25]	We discussed a survey on IoT security and conducted an analysis	1	0	2	2	2	0
Dofe et al. [26]	We suggested using 3D integration as an IoT platform	1	0	1	0	1	0
Al-Garadi et al. [27]	examine ML/DL techniques for Internet networks	1	0	1	1	0	0
Hussain et al. [28]	Author discuss the existing ML and DL solutions for IoT network	1	0	1	1	2	1
Our	we presented a survey on attacks IoT countermeasures, systematic reviews, and analyses of various IoT network	1	1	1	1	1	1

Note: 1 = Fully Implemented, 2 = Partially Implemented, 0 = Not Implemented

2.1 Advantages of IoT Attack Countermeasures

1. Enhanced Security: The primary advantage of IoT attack countermeasures is the improved security they provide. By implementing security protocols and measures, the likelihood of successful attacks on IoT devices and systems decreases significantly.
2. Preventing Unauthorized Access: Countermeasures help prevent unauthorized access to IoT devices and networks, reducing the risk of data breaches and unauthorized control of connected devices.

3. Monitoring and Detection: Countermeasures include monitoring and detection systems that can identify potential threats and suspicious activities in real-time. Early detection allows for a quicker response and minimizes the impact of attacks.
4. Privacy Protection: IoT attack countermeasures help protect the privacy of users and organizations by ensuring that data is collected, stored, and processed in compliance with relevant regulations and policies.

2.2 Disadvantages of IoT Attack Countermeasures

1. Resource Constraints: Many IoT devices have limited processing power, memory, and battery life. Implementing strong security measures can consume additional resources, impacting the device's performance and battery life. Balancing security with resource constraints is a delicate challenge.
2. Potential Backdoors: While countermeasures are designed to improve security, if not implemented correctly, they may unintentionally create new vulnerabilities or backdoors that attackers could exploit.
3. Dependency on Third-Party Providers: Many IoT solutions rely on third-party services and cloud providers for security measures. Depending heavily on external entities raises concerns about data privacy, reliability, and vendor trustworthiness.
4. Legal and Ethical Concerns: Some IoT attack countermeasures may raise privacy and ethical concerns. For instance, data collection and monitoring practices may be viewed as invasive, leading to potential legal or public relations issues.

3 Comparative Systematic Analysis of the Study

This study examines articles on the IoT device security, privacy, and cyber-attacks. Key objectives, application domains, approaches, methodologies, and limitations in the field are all identified through the comparative systematic analysis. Many authors of original research literature were taken into consideration for the collection of the pertinent data, including Scopus, IEEE, Google Scholar, Elsevier, Springer, and ACM. The selection of papers was done using the next methodology: (1) Search each electronic database, (2) Find papers about IoT attacks countermeasures using specific keywords, (3) Compile the journal articles from steps 1 and 2, (4) Remove sources that are not from reputable peer-reviewed journals or conferences, (5) Are not pertinent to IoT attacks countermeasures, security, and privacy and (7) Classify the papers with the help of an expert panel. However, in our research with Scopus citation database more than 1,996 pieces of literature were found using databases in the English language and the starting search term "smart healthcare system security," without quotation marks. Only peer-reviewed publications released in or after 2015 were kept in this initial dataset. The dataset was reduced to about 708 results after the second pruning. ("IoT") OR ("Countermeasures") OR ("Attacks") OR ("Security") OR ("Privacy") and other IoT-related subject phrases were removed from the dataset a third time. As a consequence, a dataset with 146 items was trimmed. Reviews were disregarded because this study is primarily focused on primary sources. A final pruning process eliminated any articles that did not specifically address IoT attacks, security, and privacy along with the years of publication which is from 2016–2022, as well as any that did not provide sufficient information on these subjects. The final dataset had 85 articles in it.

3.1 Classified by Publication Type

According to the distribution performance space, the articles chosen for review are categorised in this section. Figure 1 shows how the papers are distributed according to their broad type: 51.1% come from conferences, while 48.9% come from primary research published in reputable publications.

3.2 Classified by Publication Year

Figure 1 show how regularly articles are published in a certain field. Prior to 2015, there was little interest in the domain, and just 2% of the reviewed publications are published papers from that period. However, the number of publications that are declared in Figure 1 each year has increased significantly since 2015. In fact, 12% of the evaluated articles in 2017, the most recent complete year for which data were available, dealt with security and privacy in IoT attack defences. Given the availability of new wearable technologies and 5G networks, it is fair to anticipate that the quantity of articles discussing IoT attack defences will increase.

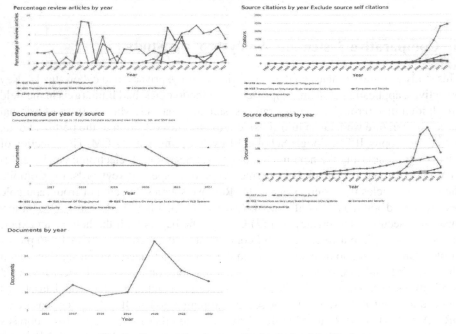

Fig. 1. Comparative Systematic Analysis of the Study

4 IoT Architecture and Its Security Challenges

Although there isn't a single accepted architecture for the IoT, there are a few unproven models with three, four, or five layers [?]. However, we will propose an acceptable model of the architecture of IoT together with their security operations as shown in Fig. 2 shows four basic layers such are, perception layer (PL), Middleware Layer (ML), Application Layer (AL), and Network Layer (NL).

4.1 Perception Layer (PL)

In IoT architecture, the PL also referred to Sensor Layer (SL), SL is a pivotal component in IoT architecture, facilitating device coordination, function control, data management, and user services [34, 35]. It employs protocols like Wireless Sensor Networks, RFID, and IDE. However, SL confronts significant security issues: weak device security, data tampering, encryption gaps, privacy risks, communication disruptions, and unauthorized access. Device impersonation and software vulnerabilities further threaten IoT [36]. Overcoming these challenges is vital for ensuring IoT ecosystem safety.

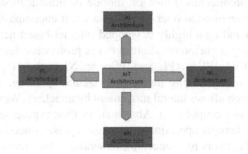

Fig. 2. An overview of IoT Architecture Within Network

4.2 Middle-Ware Layer (ML)

The ML is a subset of the IoT network architecture, related to the PL and TL [32]. The PL collects processed information from the TL, offers services using protocols, and passes data upwards. The TL handles network technologies like Wifi and Bluetooth. The ML focuses on network infrastructure, utilizing IPv6 for IoT device IP addresses. Security challenges confront the ML, which acts as a link between IoT devices and apps, attracting attackers [33]. Vulnerable middleware can lead to leaks and unauthorized access. Protocol vulnerabilities enable attacks like man-in-the-middle. Weak authentication and authorization risk data integrity. Middleware can suffer from buffer overflows and injection vulnerabilities. Securing configurations, strong encryption, and regular audits are vital for ML, ensuring overall IoT ecosystem security.

4.3 Application Layer (AL)

The AL in IoT architecture, also known as the Business Layer (BL), is the top-most layer that addresses user needs and technical standards across platforms. AL's functionality relies on key network protocols like HTTP, CoAP, and AMQP [38]. However, the AL encounters significant security challenges. Weaknesses in IoT applications can result in data breaches and unauthorized access. Insecure data handling risks sensitive information compromise. Flawed access controls may permit unauthorized manipulation of devices or data. Insufficient validation and input filtering can lead to code injection. Inadequate secure coding practices expose apps to exploitation. API vulnerabilities enable unauthorized access. Poor authentication jeopardizes identity protection. Robust security measures, secure coding, and regular assessments are vital for AL defense against threats. AL is user-oriented, managing tasks for end-users like controlling and monitoring. IoT applications span smart cars, health, home, office, banking, electricity, and environment, enhancing user experiences [37].

4.4 Network Layer (NL)

The NL within IoT architecture relies on mobile communication tools and internet technology for data transmission over long distances. It encompasses various communication networks, including a highly developed internet-based network. NL transfers data to users, processing it via intermediate network protocols originating from the Processing Layer (PL). IPV4, IPV6, RPL, and IPSec are NL tools [44]. Security challenges exist due to its critical role, facing threats like DDoS, spoofing, and traffic analysis. Inadequate segmentation allows lateral movement by attackers. Weak routing protocols risk data interception or manipulation. Absent encryption exposes data, while unauthorized network access disrupts operations. To address these concerns and ensure secure data transmission and network resilience, implementing robust access controls, intrusion detection systems, and secure routing protocols is crucial.

4.5 Security Challenges and Threat Model

For IoT applications to be safe and secure, there are certain security challenges, and threat models at each level of the IoT architecture must be addressed before the design and implementation of such layers [39]. Based on the architecture that is shown, we evaluate and analyse the current security threats that exist in the IoT architecture in Table 2 critically analysis different attacks in the architecture.

The studies carried out in [50, 53] indicate the security challenges, Multi-layer attacks, and ruthless cyber-threats enterprises have encountered recently. They detailed the security lapses and attacks that major and small firms in the UK have experienced from 2017–2022. According to statistics, there are 424 charities and 1,243 UK enterprises. 185 charities and 658 UK companies. Nearly four out of ten (42%) charities enable online donations, and just over four out of ten (44%) provide online service access for their beneficiaries [52].

5 Countermeasures and Threat Models for Security Attacks in IoT

Countermeasures and threat models play a vital role in securing the IoT ecosystem against security attacks. We propose four countermeasures and their corresponding threat models for security attacks in IoT:

1. Threat Model: Unauthorized Access Countermeasure: Implement strong authentication mechanisms, such as two-factor authentication or certificate-based authentication, to prevent unauthorized access to IoT devices and networks.
2. Threat Model: Denial-of-Service (DoS) Attacks Countermeasure: Implement traffic filtering, rate limiting, and anomaly detection to mitigate the impact of DoS attacks on IoT devices and networks.
3. Threat Model: Insecure APIs and Interfaces Countermeasure: Secure APIs and interfaces through proper authentication, access controls, and input validation to prevent API-based attacks.
4. Threat Model: Insider Threats Countermeasure: Implement role-based access controls, monitor user activities, and enforce the principle of least privilege to mitigate insider threats.

Table 2. Analytical comparisons of different attacks in IoT Network architecture

IoT Architecture					
S/N	Reference	Attack	Type	Action	Effect
1	[32–34]	Reply Attack	PL	Send signal to the network again and again	Availability of Data
2	[35, 36]	Port Scanning	ML	Obstruct the delivery and receipt of valid packages	Availability
3	[37, 38]	Poisoning Attack	AL	Maliciously injected code into network	Integrity
4	[39]	DoS	NL	Prevent legitimate to access the network	Availability

5.1 Novel IoT Attack Countermeasures

As technology advances and new IoT attack vectors are discovered, emerging IoT attack countermeasures are continuously being developed to address these evolving threats as shown in Table 3 [41–53]. We have proposed here are some of the emerging IoT attack countermeasures:

1. Hardware Security Modules (HSM) Countermeasure: Hardware Security Modules provide secure cryptographic processing and key management for IoT devices. HSMs

are tamper-resistant and protect sensitive cryptographic operations, ensuring the confidentiality and integrity of data.

2. Blockchain Technology Countermeasure: Blockchain technology is being explored to enhance IoT security by providing decentralized and tamper-resistant data storage and authentication mechanisms. It can help prevent unauthorized access and data manipulation in IoT networks.
3. Zero-Trust Architecture Countermeasure: Zero-trust architecture assumes that every device and user is untrusted until proven otherwise. This approach enforces strict access controls, continuously verifying the legitimacy of devices and users before granting access to resources.
4. Authentication and Authorization Countermeasure: Implement strong authentication mechanisms (e.g., two-factor authentication, certificate-based authentication) to ensure only authorized users and devices can access IoT systems and data.

Strengths of IoT Attack Countermeasures:

1. Diverse Defense Techniques: IoT attack countermeasures encompass a wide range of techniques, from encryption and authentication to intrusion detection systems and network segmentation. This diversity allows for a multi-layered defense approach that can effectively address various attack vectors.
2. Integration of AI and Machine Learning: AI-driven techniques, such as anomaly detection and behavior profiling, have the potential to identify new and previously unknown attack patterns. These technologies can adapt to changing attack methodologies, making them more robust against evolving threats.
3. Collaborative Solutions: Many IoT countermeasures encourage collaboration among devices and networks. Devices can share threat intelligence and collectively respond to attacks, thereby enhancing the overall security posture of the IoT ecosystem.

Weaknesses of IoT Attack Countermeasures:

1. Resource Constraints: Many IoT devices have limited computational power, memory, and energy resources. Implementing resource-intensive security mechanisms can lead to performance degradation and may not be feasible for all devices.
2. Regulatory and Compliance Challenges: Different regions and industries have varying regulations and compliance requirements for IoT security. This lack of standardization can complicate the implementation of consistent counter-measures.
3. Complexity and Usability: Some IoT security solutions can be complex to implement and manage. Complexity can lead to misconfigurations or neglect, reducing the effectiveness of countermeasures. Additionally, poor user interfaces can hinder proper configuration.

6   Future Direction, Summary and Conclusion

According to several surveys of literature studied above, the increased importance of IoT may grow over time. There are significant methods for protecting mobile mission-critical operations. A number of these could make the threat mitigation procedure more challenging and necessitate complete automation when it comes to individually or collectively safeguard the network. The following points provide a brief overview of our finding, recommendations and future direction.

Table 3. Comparative analysis of different countermeasures

Ref	Technology	Aim	Narration	Positive	Negative
[41]	Ultra-Low Power Public Key Cryptography	Reduced protocol overhead due PKC	PKC is beneficial to security services	Increased network/data security	It is a slow process
[42]	ICMetric Based Framework	Securing the IoT	Safeguard against threats	Preventing device unauthorized access	Potential for Direct Compromise
[43]	ICmetrics based security	Ensuring network integrity	Improving the security of IoT	Preventing device from cloning	Unauthenticated public keys
[44]	Anomaly-based intrusion detection systems	Proposed deep learning-based IDSs	IDSs with ML	Effective processing models	It is extremely expensive
[45]	Quality-Aware Streaming	D2D systems implementation	DASH technology	Solid network	IP spoofing
[46]	Intrusion Detection Technology in ML	Propose ML method for intrusion detection technology	Solve the safety risks of the system	Improve the detection accuracy	it is prone to DoS
[47]	Anomaly detection in IoT	Performances of ML models	IoT attack and anomaly detection	System accuracy	Incorrect Data Capture Difficulties
[48]	Symmetric and Asymmetric Key Cryptography	Proposed algorithms	Highly efficient in their respective domains	Effective network methods	High computational cost
[49]	IP-Base wireless sensor network	Propose SAKES	securing the IoT authentication model	Great inputs with security violations	May not be compactable with other IoT domain

1. More focus should be given to how to create a lightweight, reliable trust management system for both ultra-low power and powerful devices; further research must be done.
2. The security mechanisms should be updated to suit the system requirements and user needs better.
3. Resilience and Recovery Strategies: Developing strategies for IoT systems to quickly recover from attacks and restore normal operations is vital. This might involve redundancy, failover mechanisms, and rapid incident response plans.

4. Regulation and Standards: Collaborations between industry, researchers, and policy-makers are essential to establish security regulations and standards for IoT devices. Research could focus on defining best practices and guidelines for IoT manufacturers to ensure security by design.
5. Human-Centric Security: Considering the human factor in IoT security is often over-looked. Future research could investigate ways to design user interfaces that help users understand and manage the security settings of their IoT devices more effectively.
6. Device Authentication and Identity Management: Enhancing authentication methods for IoT devices and establishing robust identity management mechanisms are criti-cal. Future research could focus on developing lightweight yet secure authentication protocols and exploring the integration of blockchain technology for ensuring device identities and secure communication.

6.1 Conclusion

This article provides a thorough analysis of the Internet of Things, including its archi-tectures, supporting technologies, and privacy and security challenges. There have been discussions about various IoT architectures, including our proposed model of the archi-tecture of IoT along with their security operations. Figure 3 illustrates these operations with four fundamental layers: PL, ML, AL, and NL, in which our work analyzed the security issues and solutions. When employed in actual implementations, a number of applications, including the smart home, smart grid, smart health, smart transportation, and smart cities, are also vulnerable to dangers in the IoT application field. The main objectives of this study are to provide a clear, thorough, review, analysis, and deep understanding of IoT, explain the range of challenges it involves, and highlight areas that still need to be handled in order to promote the evolution of IoT. Furthermore, we have shown that little research is done in this area. We discussed security tactics while outlining unresolved issues and areas for further research.

References

1. Sundmaeker, H., Guillemin, P., Friess, P., Woelfflé, S.: Vision and challenges for realising the Internet of Things. Cluster of European research projects on the internet of things, European Commision, 3(3), pp. 34–36 (2010)
2. Brock, D.L.: The Electronic Product Code (EPC) - A naming scheme for physical objects. White paper (2001)
3. Ghaleb, B.: Lecture notes in Introduction to Internet of Things (IoT). School of Computing, Edinburgh Napier University (2022). Accessed November 2022
4. Santoso, F.K. Vun, N.C.: Securing IoT for smart home system. In: 2015 International Symposium on Consumer Electronics (ISCE), pp. 1–2. IEEE, June 2015
5. Rafsanjani, H.N., Ghahramani, A.: Towards utilizing internet of things (IoT) devices for understanding individual occupants' energy usage of personal and shared appliances in office buildings. J. Build. Eng. **27**, 100948 (2020)
6. Basford, P.J., Bulot, F.M., Apetroaie-Cristea, M., Cox, S.J., Ossont, S.J.: LoRaWAN for smart city IoT deployments: a long term evaluation. Sensors **20**(3), 648 (2020)

7. Al-Emran, M., Malik, S.I., Al-Kabi, M.N.: A survey of Internet of Things (IoT) in education: opportunities and challenges. In: Hassanien, A.E., Bhatnagar, R., Khalifa, N.E.M., Taha, M.H.N. (eds.) Toward social internet of things (SIoT): Enabling technologies, architectures and applications. SCI, vol. 846, pp. 197–209. Springer, Cham (2020). https://doi.org/10.1007/978-3-030-24513-9_12

8. Kaiser, M.S., et al.: Advances in crowd analysis for urban applications through urban event detection. IEEE Trans. Intell. Transp. Syst.Intell. Transp. Syst. **19**(10), 3092–3112 (2017)

9. Ebrahimi, P., Moghaddam, D.K., Mehrabani, Y.S.S.: Challenges and Opportunities of Big data and IoT in the Electronic Banking Industry: A Systematic Literature Review (2022)

10. Selvaraj, S., Sundaravaradhan, S.: Challenges and opportunities in IoT healthcare systems: a systematic review. SN Appl. Sci. **2**(1), 139 (2020)

11. Burhanuddin, M.A., Mohammed, A.A.J., Ismail, R., Hameed, M.E., Kareem, A.N., Basiron, H.: A review on security challenges and features in wireless sensor networks: IoT perspective. J. Telecommun. Electron. Comput. Eng. (JTEC) **10**(1–7), 17–21 (2018)

12. Lin, J., Yu, W., Zhang, N., Yang, X., Zhang, H., Zhao, W.: A survey on internet of things: architecture, enabling technologies, security and privacy, and applications. IEEE IoT J. **4**(5), 1125–1142 (2017)

13. Yang, Y., Wu, L., Yin, G., Li, L., Zhao, H.: A survey on security and privacy issues in Internet-of-Things. IEEE IoT J. **4**(5), 1250–1258 (2017)

14. Tewari, A., Gupta, B.B.: Security, privacy and trust of different layers in Internet-of-Things (IoTs) framework. Futur. Gener. Comput. Syst.. Gener. Comput. Syst. **108**, 909–920 (2020)

15. Martin, J.: Osborne, Postscapes, History of Internet of Things. http://postscapes.com/internet-of-things-history. Accessed 10 Nov 2022

16. Howarth, J.: DataProt, 80+ Amazing IoT Statistics 2022–2030, 20 July 2022. https://explodingtopics.com/blog/iot-stats. Accessed 10 Nov 2022

17. Jovanovic, B.: Internet of Things statistics for 2022 - Taking Things Apart. DataProt, 13 May 2022. https://dataprot.net/statistics/iot-statistics/. Accessed 10 Nov 2022

18. Viala, S.: Reva Solution, Internet Of Things: New Challenges And Practices For Information Governance, 8 April 2015. http://www.revasolutions.com/internet-of-things-new-challenges-and-practices-for-information-governance/. Accessed 10 Nov 2022

19. Khanam, S., Ahmedy, I.B., Idris, M.Y.I., Jaward, M.H., Sabri, A.Q.B.M.: A survey of security challenges, attacks taxonomy and advanced countermeasures in the Internet of Things. IEEE Access **8**, 219709–219743 (2020)

20. Ashraf, U.: PROSE–proactive resilience in Internet of Things: targeted attacks and countermeasures. IEEE Sens. J. **18**(24), 10049–10057 (2018)

21. Deogirikar, J., Vidhate, A.: Security attacks in IoT: a survey. In: 2017 International Conference on I-SMAC (IoT in Social, Mobile, Analytics and Cloud) (I-SMAC), pp. 32–37. IEEE, February 2017

22. Panchal, A.C., Khadse, V.M., Mahalle, P.N.: Security issues in IIoT: a comprehensive survey of attacks on IIoT and its countermeasures. In: 2018 IEEE Global Conference on Wireless Computing and Networking (GCWCN). pp. 124–130. IEEE, November 2018

23. Zaman, S., et al.: Security threats and artificial intelligence based counter-measures for internet of things networks: a comprehensive survey. IEEE Access **9**, 94668–94690 (2021)

24. Algarni, A.: A survey and classification of security and privacy research in smart healthcare systems. IEEE Access **7**, 101879–101894 (2019)

25. Gautam, S., Malik, A., Singh, N., Kumar, S.: Recent advances and countermeasures against various attacks in IoT environment. In: 2019 2nd International Conference on Signal Processing and Communication (ICSPC), pp. 315–319. IEEE, March 2019

26. Dofe, J., Nguyen, A., Nguyen, A.: Unified countermeasures against physical attacks in Internet of Things - a survey. In: 2021 IEEE International Symposium on Smart Electronic Systems (iSES) (Formerly iNiS), pp. 194–199. IEEE, December 2021

27. Al-Garadi, M.A., Mohamed, A., Al-Ali, A.K., Du, X., Ali, I., Guizani, M.: A survey of machine and deep learning methods for internet of things (IoT) security. IEEE Commun. Surv. Tut. **22**(3), 1646–1685 (2020)
28. Hussain, F., Hussain, R., Hassan, S.A., Hossain, E.: Machine learning in IoT security: current solutions and future challenges. IEEE Commun. Surv. Tut. **22**(3), 1686–1721 (2020)
29. Horrow, S., Sardana, A.: Identity management framework for cloud based internet of things. In: Proceedings of the First International Conference on Security of Internet of Things, pp. 200–203, August 2012
30. Al-Fuqaha, A., Guizani, M., Mohammadi, M., Aledhari, M., Ayyash, M.: Internet of things: a survey on enabling technologies, protocols, and applications. IEEE Commun. Surv. Tut. **17**(4), 2347–2376 (2015)
31. Wallgren, L., Raza, S., Voigt, T.: Routing attacks and countermeasures in the RPL-based internet of things. Int. J. Distrib. Sens. Netw.Distrib. Sens. Netw. **9**(8), 794326 (2013)
32. Wu, M., Lu, T.-J., Ling, F.-Y., Sun, J., Du, H.-Y.: Research on the architecture of internet of things. In: 2010 3rd International Conference on Advanced Computer Theory and Engineering (ICACTE), vol. 5, pp. V5-484–V5-487. IEEE (2010)
33. Yaqoob, I., Hashem, I.A.T., Mehmood, Y., Gani, A., Mokhtar, S., Guizani, S.: Enabling communication technologies for smart cities. IEEE Commun. Mag.Commun. Mag. **55**(1), 112–120 (2017)
34. Negash, B., Rahmani, A.-M., Westerlund, T., Liljeberg, P., Tenhunen, H.: LISA: lightweight internet of things service bus architecture. Procedia Comput. Sci. **52**, 436–443 (2015)
35. Chaqfeh, M.A., Mohamed, N.: Challenges in middleware solutions for the Internet of Things. In: 2012 International Conference on Collaboration Technologies and Systems (CTS), pp. 21–26. IEEE (2012)
36. Datta, S.K., Bonnet, C., Nikaein, N.: An IoT gateway centric architecture to provide novel M2M services. In: 2014 IEEE World Forum on Internet of Things (WF-IoT), pp. 514–519. IEEE (2014)
37. Seleznev, S., Yakovlev, V.: Industrial application architecture IoT and protocols AMQP, MQTT, JMS, REST, CoAP, XMPP, DDS. Int. J. Open Inf. Technol. **7**(5), 17–28 (2019)
38. Atzori, L., Iera, A., Morabito, G.: The Internet of Things: a survey. Comput. Netw. **54**(15), 2787–2805 (2010)
39. Kharrufa, H., Al-Kashoash, H.A., Kemp, A.H.: RPL-based routing protocols in IoT applications: a review. IEEE Sens. J. **19**(15), 5952–5967 (2019)
40. Yang, Z., Yue, Y., Yang, Y., Peng, Y., Wang, X., Liu, W.: Study and application on the architecture and key technologies for IoT. In: 2011 International Conference on Multimedia Technology, pp. 747–751. IEEE (2011)
41. Gaubatz, G., Kaps, J.-P., Ozturk, E., Sunar, B.: State of the art in ultra-low power public key cryptography for wireless sensor networks. In: Third IEEE International Conference on Pervasive Computing and Communications Workshops, pp. 146–150. IEEE (2005)
42. Tahir, R., Tahir, H., McDonald-Maier, K., Fernando, A.: A novel icmetric based framework for securing the Internet of Things. In: 2016 IEEE International Conference on Consumer Electronics (ICCE), pp. 469–470. IEEE (2016)
43. Hopkins, A.B., McDonald-Maier, K.D., Papoutsis, E., Howells, W.G.J.: Ensuring data integrity via ICmetrics based security infrastructure. In: Second NASA/ESA Conference on Adaptive Hardware and Systems, AHS 2007, pp. 75–81. IEEE (2007)
44. Aldweesh, A., Derhab, A., Emam, A.Z.: Deep learning approaches for anomaly-based intrusion detection systems: a survey, taxonomy, and open issues. Knowl. Based Syst. **189**, 105124 (2020)
45. Kim, J., Caire, G., Molisch, A.F.: Quality-aware streaming and scheduling for device-to-device video delivery. IEEE/ACM Trans. Netw. **24**(4), 2319–2331 (2015)

46. Fang, W., Tan, X., Wilbur, D.: Application of intrusion detection technology in network safety based on machine learning. Saf. Sci. **124**, 104604 (2020)
47. Hasan, M.M., Islam, M.M., Zarif, I.I., Hashem, M.M.A.: Attack and anomaly detection in IoT sensors in IoT sites using machine learning approaches. Internet Things **7**, 100059 (2019)
48. Shone, N., Ngoc, T.N., Phai, V.D., Shi, Q.: A deep learning approach to network intrusion detection. IEEE Trans. Emerg. Top. Comput. Intell. **2**(1), 41–50 (2018)
49. Chandra, S., Paira, S., Alam, S.S., Sanyal, G.: A comparative survey of symmetric and asymmetric key cryptography. In: 2014 International Conference on Electronics, Communication and Computational Engineering (ICECCE), pp. 83–93. IEEE (2014)
50. Hussen, H.R., Tizazu, G.A., Ting, M., Lee, T., Choi, Y., Kim, K.-H.: SAKES: secure authentication and key establishment scheme for M2M communication in the IP-based wireless sensor network (6L0WPAN). In: 2013 Fifth International Conference on Ubiquitous and Future Networks (ICUFN), pp. 246–251. IEEE (2013)
51. Jeba, A., Paramasivan, B., Usha, D.: Security threats and its countermeasures in wireless sensor networks: an overview. Int. J. Comput. Appl. **29**(6), 15–22 (2011)
52. Eisenbarth, T., Kumar, S., Paar, C., Poschmann, A., Uhsadel, L.: A survey of lightweight-cryptography implementations. IEEE Des. Test Comput. **24**(6), 522–533 (2007)
53. Baskar, C., Balasubramaniyan, C., Manivannan, D.: Establishment of light weight cryptography for resource constraint environment using FPGA. Procedia Comput. Sci. **78**, 165–171 (2016)

A Bibliometric Analysis and Systematic Review of a Blockchain-Based Chain of Custody for Digital Evidence

Belinda I. Onyeashie(✉), Petra Leimich, Sean McKeown, and Gordon Russell

Edinburgh Napier University, Edinburgh, Scotland
belinda.onyeashie@napier.ac.uk

Abstract. The effective management of digital evidence is critical to modern forensic investigations. However, traditional evidence management approaches are often prone to security and integrity issues. In recent years, the use of blockchain technology has emerged as a promising solution to enhance the security, transparency, and integrity of digital evidence. This systematic review critically evaluates the current state of research on blockchain-based chain of custody for digital evidence and its potential to transform the digital forensic community. By analysing papers from major databases, this study provides a bibliometric analysis of the research trends and opportunities for blockchain-based evidence management since 2015. The review highlights the benefits of blockchain technology in providing an immutable and decentralised structure for documenting and auditing evidence trails. Additionally, this research identifies the challenges and limitations of implementing a blockchain-based chain of custody and presents practical and scalable solutions for overcoming these challenges at Big Data scale.

Keywords: Bibliometric Analysis · Big Data · Chain of Custody · Digital Evidence · Digital Forensic

1 Introduction

There are challenges associated with the storage and sharing of digital evidence during an investigation. These challenges may include concerns about authenticity, integrity, privacy, and security, as well as difficulties with storing and sharing evidence. There have been significant delays for investigations involving digital evidence. Some cases may take up to six years to coordinate the handling and processing, and law enforcement personnel may be required to travel up to 4,500 times every week to physically obtain digital evidence [1]. Another significant challenge the police force is facing is how to securely store and share digital evidence during an investigation [2]. The volume of data generated and stored electronically is expanding at an exponential rate [3]; therefore, a secure and efficient method for storing and sharing evidence is required. However, the current procedures for storing and sharing digital evidence are inadequate and prone to errors [2] and threats, such as concerns about insider threats. This may compromise the integrity of the evidence and delay the investigation process.

Z. Tan et al. (Eds.): BDTA 2023, LNICST 555, pp. 112–131, 2024.
https://doi.org/10.1007/978-3-031-52265-9_8

Additionally, digital evidence monitoring, and documentation are still done manually, on paper, which is error-prone and time consuming [4]. Chain of custody is often a problem when dealing with digital evidence. The chain of custody plays a crucial role in digital forensic investigations by keeping track of every detail of digital evidence as it passes through different organisational levels [5]. Metadata on the method, time, place, and people who handled the data during its acquisition, processing, storage, and eventual use in investigations are all recorded by chain of custody. However, chain of custody is vulnerable to compromise if data is not retained and maintained during the life cycle of digitally recorded evidence, making it difficult to prove any situation relating to cybercrime in a court of law [6].

Digital evidence integrity relies on maintaining a verifiable chain of custody throughout an investigation. Furthermore, a chain of custody is incomplete if the evidence storage is inconsistent and unaccounted for [7]. Current systems inadequately track evidence trail and handling in a tamper-proof manner. Centralised evidence storage also poses risks of security breaches and system failures. This review examines the use of blockchain technology to strengthen the evidence chain of custody and interoperate with decentralised storage.

Research has demonstrated that blockchain can offer chain of custody immutability, and auditability [8–12]. A blockchain is a distributed database that creates a digital ledger (record) of timestamped transactions that is visible to everyone on a network [13]. Data on a blockchain are saved on a block and each block on a blockchain are linked to the previous block by the hash value. As a result of the unique feature of blockchain, application and research on blockchain is growing at an exponential rate.

Bibliometric analysis is a statistical method used to track research trends and measure academic output [14]. It was introduced by Garfield in 2007 and is used to assess the impact of research in various fields [15–17]. However, it has not yet been applied to blockchain for digital evidence chain of custody.

This paper provides a bibliometric analysis and literature review of blockchain's use in managing digital evidence chain of custody. It examines how blockchain technology can strengthen the evidential chain of custody and interoperate with actual evidence storage. The goal is to survey implementations that use blockchain to provide tamper-proof custody records and enable decentralised, verified evidence storage. The review also assesses current research, identifies gaps in knowledge, and provides direction for future research.

A literature search was conducted using Scopus, Google Scholar, and Web of Science, followed by a bibliometric analysis to investigate the relationship between article weight, content, co-occurrence, and search terms in the relevant publications. Subsequently, 58 most relevant articles were included in the systematic literature review. The study is structured into four main sections: Section 2 presents the Literature Search and Bibliometric Analysis, Sect. 3 provides a Systematic Review of the selected studies on blockchain-based chain of custody for digital evidence management, and Sect. 4 concludes the paper by summarising key findings and proposing future research directions.

2 Literature Search and Bibliometric Network

This section will introduce the literature search and bibliometric network related to the blockchain-based chain of custody. It aims to outline the research methodology and provide an overview of the interconnections and patterns within the existing body of literature in this field.

2.1 Literature Search

A review of the literature on blockchain-based chain of custody for digital evidence was conducted to answer the following research question: What is the current research on blockchain-based chain of custody for digital evidence? To find an answer, the scientific databases and search engines Scopus, Web of Science, and Google Scholar were used below. All three databases were subject to a time constraint from 2015 to the present. It was our goal to utilise both title, abstract, and keyword search queries in all three databases; however, this wasn't always feasible. It was not possible to do an abstract search on Google Scholar. Similarly, exporting search results from Google Scholar will require saving each search string individually before exporting. Also, the research results from google scholar overlapped search results already exported from Scopus and Web of Science. Therefore, we used Scopus and Web of Science to export the entire search string. Both databases required an exact-spelling search to avoid returning too many irrelevant papers. The search query returned a total of 104,324 articles from the three databases and search engines (below). The records from Scopus and Web of Science were imported into Mendeley.

Duplicates were excluded, leaving 10,134 articles to evaluate for title-based relevance. Following this preliminary screening, the remaining 2,440 articles were extracted and exported to VOSviewer for bibliometric analysis with author, title, abstract, source title, year, and volume.

2.2 Bibliometric Analysis

The bibliometric method was utilised in this study because it can objectively map out how a field's canon of literature has developed over time [18]. According to Khanra, et al. [15] a bibliometric technique is a multidisciplinary strategy for accurately charting the paths taken and areas researched as a field of study evolved. VOSviewer, an opensource tool to visualise bibliometric networks, was used to build and visualise co-occurrence networks of extracted terms from the literature. Research has shown that network visualisation is an efficient tool for analysing diverse bibliometric networks [19]; hence, it was utilised in this study.

There have been many innovative studies published because of the growing interest in blockchain technology. Numerous studies on blockchain have included a bibliometric examination of the data and trend. Zeng, et al. [20] conducted a bibliographic evaluation of blockchain-related studies between January 2011 and September 2017. Consequently, Dabbagh, et al. [21] used a bibliometric analysis to study the evolution of blockchain from 2013 to 2018. Numerous studies have also incorporated bibliometric analysis and a comprehensive literature assessment [17, 22, 23]. The bibliometric analysis in this study combines co-occurrence, and network analysis. We developed network visualisation to analyse the links between the search phrases' co-occurrence networks [19]. The overlay visualisation was also developed for the purpose of illustrating the frequency with which a particular keyword appears in the literature (Table 1).

Table 1. The number of articles based on search terms found in each database.

Keywords	Google Scholar	Scopus	Web of Science
Blockchain-based	30,700	8,865	11,528
Blockchain and Digital Forensic	7,740	205	132
Blockchain and Digital Evidence	28,200	344	337
Blockchain Chain of Custody	6,730	78	107
Blockchain Chain of Custody Evidence	4,780	34	29
Blockchain Chain of Custody Digital Evidence	4,448	31	24
Total Number of Articles	82,610	9,557	12,157

2.3 Blockchain and Digital Forensic Bibliometric Network

The total link strength represents the number of occurrences of a set of keywords in publications [24]. If two keywords are connected, it means they appear frequently together. The numerical value of each keyword indicates the relative importance of the link between two keywords. The relatedness of keywords is determined by how close they occur together. This network of associated keywords was constructed by calculating the frequency with which related publications contain the same keywords. As a result, the proximity of two terms indicates the degree to which they are related to one another. Clusters of highly related keywords are represented in the network by a variety of colours.

The visual representation of contents' co-occurrence networks is shown in Fig. 1. Each circle in the diagram signifies a different keyword. The greater the size of a circle, the greater the number of articles that include the matching term in their keywords. Words that appear together frequently are clustered in close proximity. The keywords were categorised, and the size of the group including the word "Blockchain" was exceptionally large. The red cluster encompasses blockchain, the light green cluster is comprised of digital forensics, chain of custody, cloud forensics, electronic crime countermeasures and investigative processes. The leaf-green cluster consists of big data, GDPR, privacy, and review, while the purple cluster contains several keywords related to digital storage, security, computer crime, and decentralisation.

The network contains 347 items and 8 clusters. The total link strength is 19591. Blockchain is the largest component in the network, with a total of 346 links, 4347 strong links, and 861 occurrences, indicating that it appeared at least once in every paper analysed, making it the keyword with the most occurrences in the network. Digital forensics consists of 204 links, 902 total link strengths, and 110 occurrences. Digital storage contained 118 links, 367 total strengths, and 47 occurrences, while chain of custody contained 94 links, 241 total link strengths, and 34 occurrences.

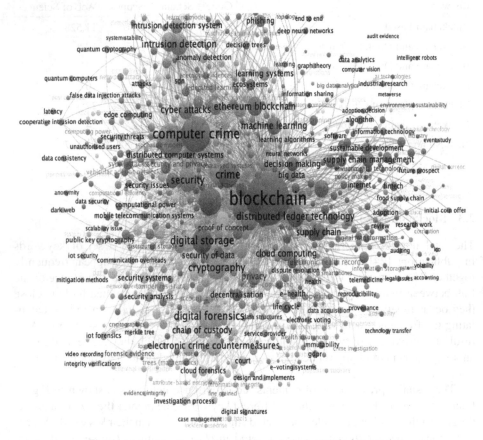

Fig. 1. Network visualisation of Blockchain for Digital Forensic.

Publication Year: The first article addressing the use of blockchain in digital evidence chain of custody was published in 2016, and the number of such publications has progressively increased since then, reaching a peak in 2021 with a total of thirty-four articles. The total number of articles published since 2016 is one hundred and three (Fig. 2).

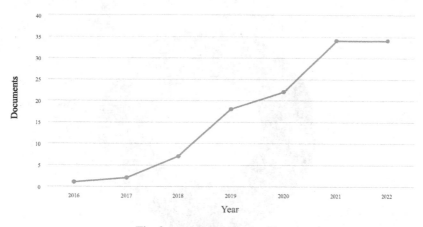

Fig. 2. Article Publication Year

Publication by Country: The paper counts from the Scopus dataset are displayed in Fig. 3, which ranks the top thirteen countries worldwide. The diversity of the countries represented on this graph demonstrates that blockchain-based chain of custody is an emerging, promising topic that is garnering interest from researchers all over the world.

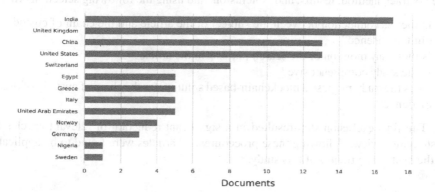

Fig. 3. Article Publication by Country

Document by Type: There have been 344 documents published for blockchain and digital evidence. 42.4% of the documents are articles. 41.5% are conference paper 4.2% are conference reviews and 8.5% are book chapters and 2.5% are review papers and one erratum paper (Fig. 4).

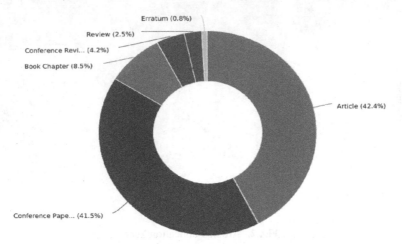

Erratum (0.8%)

Review (2.5%)

Conference Revi... (4.2%)

Book Chapter (8.5%)

Article (42.4%)

Conference Pape... (41.5%)

Fig. 4. Documents by source.

3 Systematic Review

Following the bibliometric analysis, the papers were reviewed in their entirety, including the abstract, method, results, and conclusion, and using the following selection criteria:

- Is there a connection between the subject of the article and the chain of custody for digital evidence?
- Is there any mention of the search phrases in the article?
- Is the study comprehensive?
- Does the study propose a blockchain-based solution for the chain of custody of digital evidence?

The final exclusion step resulted in a significant reduction of relevant articles for systematic review. Following these procedures, 58 articles were found to be applicable to the systematic review of this study.

3.1 Digital Evidence

Digital evidence encompasses any data in binary form that can serve as proof in an investigative or legal context [25, 26]. However, establishing the integrity and authenticity of digital evidence presents numerous challenges. Due to its latent and inherently volatile nature, digital evidence is susceptible to unintentional or deliberate alteration and degradation over time as technology evolves [26]. This poses threats to the reliability and admissibility of evidence.

To be admissible in court, digital evidence must be properly managed and preserved throughout its lifecycle, from initial acquisition to final disposal or destruction [27]. The digital evidence lifecycle contains various phases, including acquisition, analysis, and reporting [27, 28].

Maintaining a clear, comprehensive chain of custody is essential to verify the integrity of digital evidence as it moves between parties during an investigation [4]. Digital evidence is often handled by multiple departments and personnel, including first responders, forensic investigators, expert witnesses, law enforcement, and others [26]. The exchanges between these participants create vulnerabilities where the evidence could be unintentionally or deliberately compromised [29]. Meticulous documentation of custody transfers is therefore critical to ensure admissibility and reliability [29, 30].

Furthermore, the ephemeral properties of digital evidence raise concerns regarding integrity, authenticity, prevention of degradation, and assurance of chain of custody (Fig. 5).

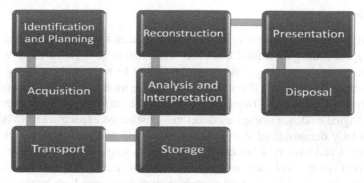

Fig. 5. Digital evidence processes [53]

3.2 Chain of Custody

Chain of custody sometimes referred to as (CoC) is a document that records sequential trail of evidence in each stage of an investigation evidence to establish provenance and authenticity [29]. For digital evidence, the chain of custody involves meticulously recording its complete lifecycle [4]. Comprehensive logs are necessary to ascertain integrity and enable admissibility. Unlike physical evidence, establishing chain of custody for inherently volatile digital artifacts presents unique challenges [30]. Phases must be comprehensively documented, incorporating, metadata and concerns about access control and security [7]. A break in the chain of custody or any questions about the authenticity or integrity of the evidence can weaken its value as evidence in a legal proceeding.

Cosic and Baca [31] proposed a digital evidence Management framework (DEMF) which aims to enhance the chain of custody of digital evidence throughout the entire process of a digital investigation. Their proposed framework made use of the SHA-2 hash function to create a digital fingerprint of the evidence, biometric traits to verify and identify the person who managed the scientific proof, a digital trusted timestamp to pinpoint the exact moment the evidence was found or was accessed, and global positioning system coordinates to pinpoint its location. Their framework comprises Five W's (and one H) in which five W represents What, Who, When, Where, Why and How.

To guarantee that digital evidence will be approved by the court, all these aspects must be used in the appropriate way to establish a safe and secure chain of custody.

The "where" of the five W's refers to the storage architecture involve in the investigation process. The storage system represents a crucial element in the effective management of digital evidence, particularly considering the voluminous nature of big data. Similar to the influence of the human factor, the storage architecture plays a crucial role in guaranteeing the security and accessibility of evidence as well as preserving the integrity of the chain of custody. As a result of this, it is imperative to improve storage systems as a preventative measure against potential threats that may inadvertently or deliberately impede the progress of an investigation.

3.3 Storage Architectures

Digital evidence storage architecture consists of technology, software, and methods for storing and managing digital evidence. The storage of digital evidence needs to be designed with the investigators' time and ability to work without being hindered by their location in mind [7]. The storage architecture for digital evidence encompasses the underlying technology, software, and protocols used to store and manage evidentiary data [32]. Digital evidence storage architectures exist across a spectrum from centralised servers to fully decentralised distributed networks. Centralised repositories simplify access control and oversight but concentrate risk in single points of failure [33, 34]. Decentralised systems enhance security through distribution but can impede holistic chain of custody views [35]. Hybrid models attempt to balance both approaches [34].

However, limitations remain with current standards alone for robust evidence custody. Centralised servers have inherent vulnerabilities while decentralised networks struggle to provide complete audit trails. This has driven interest in blockchain's tamper-proof ledgers for evidence custody management [33]. However, blockchain itself lacks native storage capacity for large evidence volumes.

An emerging solution proposes integrating decentralised storage backends with blockchain custody ledgers [35]. This allows distributing evidence across nodes for security while maintaining an immutable record of chain of custody events. This is important in evidence management, where the volume and range of digital evidence are rapidly growing, necessitating the use of flexible, scalable, and cost-effective storage systems. Decentralised storage and blockchain may fully address digital evidence security, integrity, resilience, and auditability challenges in a holistic architecture.

Subsequent sections present an overview on blockchain, blockchain's intersection with digital forensics, and a systematic review on blockchain in chain of custody for digital evidence. The literature review examines current research and open issues in unifying decentralised storage systems with blockchain for comprehensive digital evidence custody. A critical analysis of current research and implementations will reveal remaining gaps and opportunities to realise this promising convergence.

3.4 Blockchain Technology: Key Principles and Characteristics

Blockchain is a distributed ledger technology (DLT) that allows for synchronised sharing of data across multiple nodes [13]. This decentralised network reduces reliance on a single authoritative entity and increases data availability and resilience against single points of failure [36, 37].

One of the key features of blockchain is its ability to ensure data immutability. Once transactions are added to the chain through consensus, it becomes nearly impossible to alter their contents due to the cryptographic chaining of blocks [38]. This immutability provides a transparent and auditable transaction history.

Consensus algorithms, such as Proof-of-Work, Proof-of-Stake, etc., drive transaction validation and block creation within the blockchain [39]. These mechanisms ensure agreement among network nodes on the validity of transactions and prevent double-spending attacks. A network that is based on consensus ensures that every node has access to the same information. A consensus algorithm performs two functions: it ensures that the data on the ledger is the same for all the nodes in the network, which, in turn, prevents malevolent actors from manipulating the data; and it reaches a conclusion about what the data should be [13]. This precludes manipulation or unauthorised alteration of the blockchain, as any changes to the data would require consensus from the network. Guo, et al. [40] framework is grounded in post-Quantum theory, which protects the blockchain against outside attacks while also preserving its verifiability. The authors also used pre-image sampling process to produce secret keys that can be used to select a random value and sign the message. In addition, the consensus process can contribute to the blockchain's transparency and auditability by maintaining an immutable ledger of all transactions. This is particularly useful in the context of digital evidence chain of custody because it allows for straightforward tracking and tracing of the evidence's movement and management.

Consensus algorithm differs depending on the implementation of the blockchain being used [39] and the choice of consensus algorithm used will rely on the system's requirements, including security, efficiency, scalability, and cost. An analysis on consensus algorithms and their differences were highlighted in [39]. Proof of Work is the algorithm used in Bitcoin to achieve a consensus on the blockchain. However, other blockchain technologies use a wide variety of consensus algorithms [39], such as Proof of Stake, Proof of Burn, Practical Byzantine Fault Tolerance (PBFT), Proof of Elapsed Time, and a great number of others, depending on the specific requirements that they have.

Blockchain's versatility also includes the use of smart contracts, self-executing agreements with terms written directly into code. These digital protocols increase efficiency by automatically triggering actions when predefined conditions are met, eliminating the need for intermediaries [41]. Smart contracts operate on the simple rules "if, when, and then…" phrases that are encoded in the blockchain. Before smart contracts can be executed on the blockchain, they must be written with specific needs and specifications, including code, rules, objects, and data models [42]. A network of computers performs the actions at the time when pre-agreed conditions and rules have been verified and accomplished. These conditions and rules might comprise transfer of digital evidence to relevant participants, notification sending, and/or transfer of evidence ownership. Once a smart contract has been activated and carried out, the contract itself cannot be cancelled or erased from the blockchain once it has been recorded there [42]. Smart contracts will run, authenticate, and construct calls accordingly in the decentralised records without altering or amending the transactions itself. The blockchain is automatically updated whenever a transaction is successfully completed, and the participants will also be able to exchange, visualise data, information, and interact automatically without the need for an intermediary or time loss and the results of the implementation can be checked by authorised participant in the blockchain network (Table 2).

Table 2. Categories of Blockchain [36, 43]

Category	Definition
Public Blockchain	Anyone in the network can contribute and access information
Private Blockchain	Only one person or organisation has access to it
Consortium Blockchain	Only accessible to specified groups of people inside an organisation and, allows only authorised users to access the network and view data based on predefined permissions

Blockchain Frameworks, Features and Suitability for Chain of Custody: Public blockchains like Ethereum allow transparency and immutable custody records viewable by all participants [9]. Ethereum's native support for self-executing smart contracts enables reliable evidence handling rules and audit trails across open decentralised networks. However, public chains lack access controls and mechanisms to restrict sensitive forensic data, which could impede adoption.

Private blockchain architectures address these gaps through permissions and selective data sharing. Hyperledger Fabric utilises private channels, modular consensus, and membership services to conduct confidential custody transactions between authorised participants via chaincode contracts [37, 44]. Similarly, Corda propagates evidence exchange only between parties with a need to know [37].

Multichain facilitates interoperability between multiple private chains, allowing segmented custody trails across entities while preventing unauthorised access. These capabilities enhance privacy, throughput, and governance compared to fully public chains [45].

Hybrid approaches like Kadena bridge public verifiability and private data management [46]. The public chain provides transparent immutable records while its Kuro chain enables private smart contracts and restricted evidence access. Its partitioned architectures allow customisable security and performance based on use case needs [46].

In conclusion, the blockchain framework chosen for chain of custody should ensure privacy and non-repudiation while seamlessly interoperating with existing storage architectures that constitute the complete digital forensic processes for evidence management.

3.5 Blockchain's Intersection with Digital Forensics

This subsection highlights the potential synergistic alignment of blockchain technology with digital forensics, focusing on how blockchain's salient characteristics may engender a paradigm shift in current methodologies and offer cogent solutions to existing digital forensic challenges especially with digital evidence management.

Digital forensics involves identifying, extracting, and analysing digital evidence from electronic devices and systems for legal or investigative purposes [47]. It plays a critical role in law enforcement and cybersecurity, allowing organisations to identify and prosecute cybercriminals and protect against security threats [11]. The field has evolved rapidly with the widespread use of electronic devices [6, 48]. A key challenge is ensuring the integrity and authenticity of digital evidence, which can be volatile and easily altered [33, 49]. Stakeholders must follow established protocols to properly collect, preserve, and analyse evidence while being aware of legal and ethical considerations [7, 50]. In lieu of this, a system that guarantees accuracy, accessibility, privacy, and integrity of digital evidence is needed.

Blockchain's immutability generates a permanent record of digital evidence trails, ensuring authenticity from acquisition to its final disposition [33]. Integration of smart contracts can transform process automation, improving efficiency and reliability [51]. Blockchain's inherent transparency can bolster traceability of digital evidence, allowing authorised participants to audit interactions and validate evidence authenticity [38].

3.6 Blockchain in Chain of Custody for Digital Evidence

Blockchain is a focal solution where trust is lacking due to its transparency and traceability feature. Areas that have been researched includes Governance, finance sector, health, supply chains management, and digital forensics [52–54]. A blockchain-based evidence log keeps track of information such as the description of the evidence, its identification, the names of the creators, and the ownership history of the evidence [9]. The majority of previous research and studies on blockchain-based chain of custody propose a chain of custody system in which the evidence metadata is stored on the blockchain while the actual evidence is held on a different medium and is accessible to only permissioned participants [9, 33, 34, 55]. This is primarily because the evidence may be too large to be stored efficiently on a blockchain. The authors Bonomi, et al. [9] also explained that if the evidence is stored on a blockchain it will make it accessible to every node on the Blockchain. The sensitivity of chain of custody data restricts its disclosure to the public (unauthorised individuals), as doing so would compromise the confidentiality and privacy attributes that evidence data and trails should hold.

Research from Bonomi, et al. [9] and Lone and Mir [56] presented a chain of custody system based on a public Ethereum. In addition to the fact that creating a system on a public blockchain is costly, there is also the absence of privacy and confidentiality. Public blockchains are open and transparent, allowing anybody with an internet connection to access the blockchain's transactions. This may not be suitable for sensitive and confidential data, such as a digital evidence trail, as it may expose sensitive information to unauthorised individuals.

The authors [56] proposed another blockchain based chain of custody solution "Forensic-Chain" [33] based on permissioned Hyperledger Composer. In their system, system allows members' identities and roles to be known to other network members and is controlled by a consensus mechanism and a peer-to-peer network. The framework is made up of three components: a digital witness, a digital custodian, and a law enforcement organisation. A consensus mechanism is established to guard against system sabotage, and public-key cryptography is employed to uniquely identify all entities within the framework.

Ahmad, et al. [12] took the research a step further by proposing a prototype based on private Ethereum and introduced the concept of smart lock to link and secure access to the location of the physical evidence. Their framework uses predefined smart contracts to activate the smart locks in order to restrict and grant access to evidence. Tian, et al. [34] propose a blockchain-based digital evidence framework (Block-DEF) against file tampering. Their paper focuses on digital evidence security against file tampering that uses a multi-signature method that includes non-random and certificated key pairs for submitting and retrieving evidence. As opposed to the evidence framework proposed by Bonomi, et al. [9] the evidence in Block-DEF [34] must first be temporarily stored with its name and public key before establishing its validity.

Li, et al. [57] proposed LeChain, a system based on Ethereum blockchains and Proof of Authority as the consensus mechanism to record evidence trails and voting system to keep the jury anonymous. The system is intended to ensure the traceability of evidence while also protecting identities of witnesses and jurors. The authors employed Ciphertext Policy-Based Encryption (CP-ABE) to authenticate evidence access. CPABE is a form of encryption that enables users to selectively encrypt data depending on a set of predetermined policies [58]. These regulations specify who has access to encrypted data and under what circumstances. Furthermore, Lechain [57] used a short randomizable signature to authenticate the witness's identity. Additionally, their prototype aimed to address the issue of insider threats by invoking the access permissions of identified malicious participants.

Burri, et al. [59] study builds on their previous work [60] which used a trusted entity to improve e-Chain of Custody and public blockchain to safeguard specific blocks. They recommend that a private ledger be used to track chain of custody data, and the state of the private e-CoC ledger is frequently updated into a public blockchain. This according to the authors was to secure the trusted entity and ensure integrity of the data. Burri, et al. [59] framework for implementing a private blockchain hosted by a trusted institution is identical to the framework proposed by Ahmad, et al. [12] except that Ahmad, et al. [12] also propose installing smart locks to authenticate and authorise access for a requesting participant.

Khan, et al. [44] proposed the MF-Ledger, based on the Hyperledger Sawtooth framework, to form a private network for participants to communicate and decide on investigative activities before storing evidence metadata on a blockchain. The system incorporated smart contracts to authenticate access and focused on tracking and managing multimedia evidence. In a subsequent research [61], they designed a wireless

IoT-blockchain-enabled video surveillance chain of custody and evidence storage system, built on Hyperledger Sawtooth, that proposed storing actual evidence in IPFS, a decentralised storage system.

3.7 Existing Frameworks and Methodology

This subsection provides an overview of the blockchain frameworks, consensus mechanisms, and storage architectures employed in the existing literature on blockchain-based chain of custody. It aims to highlight the current methodologies and technologies used, thereby offering a comprehensive understanding of the prevailing trends and potential gaps in this research area.

Blockchain Frameworks Utilised: The surveyed literature employed a variety of blockchain frameworks, including permissioned, private, and consortium blockchains. Ethereum was used in 35% of the papers for experimental and analytical purposes. Despite the cost associated with using public Ethereum for experimentation, its ease of use justifies the expense. However, this necessitates a consideration of the trade-off between privacy and ease of use (Table 3).

Table 3. Blockchain frameworks

Framework	Reference	Year Framework was Introduced
DigiByte	[60]	2013
Ethereum (Private/Public)	[8, 9, 12, 56, 57, 62, 63]	2015
Hyperledger Composer	[33, 64]	2015 but declared end of life by August 2019
Hyperledger Sawtooth	[44, 61]	2015
Undisclosed Hyperledger Project	[65]	N/A
Unspecified	[10, 11, 30, 55, 59, 66, 67]	N/A

Consensus Mechanisms Utilised: The choice of consensus mechanism is largely contingent on the blockchain framework employed. Much of the current research on blockchain for digital evidence chain of custody is theoretical rather than experimental. As result, nearly half of the studies reviewed did not specify which consensus mechanisms they employed. Further practical testing is needed to evaluate different consensus algorithms within blockchain frameworks for digital evidence CoC and management. Identifying optimal mechanisms tailored to forensic needs will strengthen these conceptual models as they transition to implementation (Table 4).

Table 4. Consensus Mechanisms

Consensus Mechanism	Reference
Practical Byzantine Fault Tolerance (PBFT)	[9, 44]
Proof-of-Authority (PoA)	[57]
Proof of Work (PoW)	[60–62, 66]
Raft	[12]
Zero-Knowledge Proof (ZKP)	[63]
Unspecified	[8, 10, 11, 30, 33, 55, 56, 59, 64, 65, 67]

Storage Architectures Utilised: While blockchain technology has been proposed as a potential solution for storing evidence metadata and tracking chain of custody, the majority of research has not addressed the method for the actual storage of the evidence. The digital evidence management's storage architecture is a critical area needing more focus and presents a clear opportunity for future research. The chain of custody is intrinsically linked to this storage architecture, and its comprehensiveness can only be asserted when this connection is established.

Digital forensics processes play a crucial role in managing digital evidence. Standard procedures for collection, analysis, and preservation of digital evidence are paramount to ensure its authenticity and admissibility. Strict adherence to forensic best practices is essential, as any deviation could potentially undermine the admissibility and credibility of the evidence (Table 5).

Table 5. Storage Architectures

Storage Architecture	Reference	Paper year of publication
Filecoin	[44]	2021
Google Storage Codeline	[63]	2023
IPFS	[61, 62]	2021, 2022
Undisclosed Decentralised system	[57]	2021
Unspecified	[8–12, 30, 33, 55, 56, 59, 60, 64–67]	N/A

3.8 Open-Ended Issues

Blockchain technology is a relatively new field, and literature and research on blockchain-based chains of custody are still in their early stages, with gaps and room for future work. The papers evaluated above utilised various blockchain solutions available at the time to create a path for future research into digital evidence chain of custody and blockchain.

Digital forensics relies on the integrity of digital evidence, which is safeguarded by the method of chain of custody. The complexity and volume of digital evidence have further exacerbated the challenges of chain of custody management.

The surveyed papers propose various blockchain architectures and protocols to log custody transactions, verify integrity, and ensure provenance of digital evidence [10, 30, 33]. Key functionalities include cryptographic hashing for tamper-proofing, timestamping events, and enabling decentralised access control and verification. Both public and private blockchain configurations have been considered.

However, a clear approach for evidentiary file storage, either on-chain or off-chain, is not consistently defined. A few studies hint at using the InterPlanetary File System (IPFS) for distributed storage [61, 62] without offering in-depth implementation specifics. The choice of storage mechanisms directly affects scalability, privacy, and associated costs.

A few studies have provided more specifics on storage. For instance, Burri, et al. [59] propose storing hashed metadata on-chain while keeping the data files off-chain. Tian, et al. [34] describe a dual-chain architecture with a public chain storing hashes and permissions and a private chain holding the evidence. However, even in these cases, the exact storage systems and infrastructure are ambiguous.

Future studies should explore user perceptions and acceptance of blockchain-based digital evidence management systems and strive to establish a standardised regulatory framework and best practices in compliance with existing law. A thorough understanding of constraints and potential solutions for storage interoperability, privacy, system scalability, and performance are essential. Addressing these challenges successfully could significantly improve the usefulness of blockchain technology in managing digital evidence.

4 Conclusion

This research emphasises the crucial role of chain of custody in preserving the integrity of digital evidence in digital forensics. Current systems face challenges due to the high volume of digital evidence, insider threats, and security vulnerabilities.

This study's bibliometric analysis indicates that blockchain technology may offer a promising solution. The systematic review further highlights its potential for creating an auditable, and transparent ledger system for managing digital evidence. However, further research is needed to address the challenges and limitations of blockchain-based chain of custody, including the development of practical and scalable solutions for blockchain interoperability with existing storage architectures.

Additionally, more research is required to ensure that the storage architecture holding evidence is properly integrated into the blockchain-based chain of custody, covering the entire lifecycle of evidence.

References

1. Business-Wire: UK's Cleveland Police Selects NICE Investigate for Digital Evidence Management Process Transformation in the Cloud. https://www.businesswire.com/news/home/20201014005424/en/UK%E2%80%99s-Cleveland-Police-Selects-NICE-Investigate-for-Digital-Evidence-Management-Process-Transformation-in-the-Cloud. Accessed

2. Rao, S., Fernandes, S., Raorane, S., Syed, S.: A novel approach for digital evidence management using blockchain (2020)
3. Granja, F.M., Rafael, G.D.R.: The preservation of digital evidence and its admissibility in the court. Int. J. Electron. Secur. Digit. Forensics 9(1), 1–18 (2017)
4. Sadiku, M.N.O., Shadare, A.E., Musa, S.M.: Digital chain of custody. Int. J. Adv. Res. Comput. Sci. Softw. Eng. 7(7), 117 (2017)
5. Ali, M., Ismail, A., Elgohary, H., Darwish, S., Mesbah, S.: A procedure for tracing chain of custody in digital image forensics: a paradigm based on grey hash and blockchain. Symmetry 14(2) (2022)
6. Losavio, M.M., et al.: The juridical spheres for digital forensics and electronic evidence in the insecure electronic world. Wiley Interdisc. Rev. Forensic Sci. 1(5), e1337 (2019)
7. Prayudi, Y., Ashari, A., Priyambodo, T.K.: The framework to support the digital evidence handling. J. Cases Inf. Technol. 22(3) (2020)
8. Tsai, F.-C.: The application of blockchain of custody in criminal investigation process. Procedia Comput. Sci. 192, 2779–2788 (2021)
9. Bonomi, S., Casini, M., Ciccotelli, C.: B-CoC: a blockchain-based chain of custody for evidences management in digital forensics (2018)
10. Yan, W., Shen, J., Cao, Z., Dong, X.: Blockchain based digital evidence chain of custody. Presented at the Proceedings of the 2020 The 2nd International Conference on Blockchain Technology (2020)
11. Al-Khateeb, H., Epiphaniou, G., Daly, H.: Blockchain for modern digital forensics: the chain-of-custody as a distributed ledger. In: Jahankhani, H., Kendzierskyj, S., Jamal, A., Epiphaniou, G., Al-Khateeb, H. (eds.) Blockchain and Clinical Trial. ASTSA, pp. 149–168. Springer, Cham (2019). https://doi.org/10.1007/978-3-030-11289-9_7
12. Ahmad, L., Khanji, S., Iqbal, F., Kamoun, F.: Blockchain-based chain of custody: towards real-time tamper-proof evidence management. In: Proceedings of the 15th International Conference on Availability, Reliability and Security (2020)
13. Sheth, H., Dattani, J.: Overview of blockchain technology. Asian J. Convergence Technol. (AJCT) (2019). ISSN-2350-1146
14. Iqbal, W., Qadir, J., Tyson, G., Mian, A.N., Hassan, S.-U., Crowcroft, J.: A bibliometric analysis of publications in computer networking research. Scientometrics 119, 1121–1155 (2019)
15. Khanra, S., Dhir, A., Mäntymäki, M.: Big data analytics and enterprises: a bibliometric synthesis of the literature. Enterp. Inf. Syst. 14(6), 737–768 (2020)
16. Tandon, A., Kaur, P., Mäntymäki, M., Dhir, A.: Blockchain applications in management: a bibliometric analysis and literature review. Technol. Forecast. Soc. Change 166 (2021)
17. Lawal, I.A., Klink, M., Ndungu, P., Moodley, B.: Brief bibliometric analysis of "ionic liquid" applications and its review as a substitute for common adsorbent modifier for the adsorption of organic pollutants. Environ. Res. 175, 34–51 (2019)
18. Xue, X., Wang, L., Yang, R.J.: Exploring the science of resilience: critical review and bibliometric analysis. Nat. Hazards 90, 477–510 (2018)
19. Tran, B.X., et al.: The current research landscape of the application of artificial intelligence in managing cerebrovascular and heart diseases: a bibliometric and content analysis. Int. J. Environ. Res. Public Health 16(15) (2019)
20. Zeng, S., Ni, X., Yuan, Y., Wang, F.-Y.: A bibliometric analysis of blockchain research, pp. 102–107. IEEE (2018)
21. Dabbagh, M., Sookhak, M., Safa, N.S.: The evolution of blockchain: a bibliometric study. IEEE Access 7, 19212–19221 (2019)
22. Ante, L.: Smart contracts on the blockchain–a bibliometric analysis and review. Telematics Inform. 57, 101519 (2021)

23. Bertoglio, R., Corbo, C., Renga, F.M., Matteucci, M.: The digital agricultural revolution: a bibliometric analysis literature review. IEEE Access **9** (2021)
24. Guo, Y.-M., Huang, Z.-L., Guo, J., Li, H., Guo, X.-R., Nkeli, M.J.: Bibliometric analysis on smart cities research. Sustainability **11**(13) (2019)
25. Swgde, I.: Digital evidence: standards and principles. Forensic science. Digital Evidence: Standards and Principles. Forensic Science Communications, A—pill (2000). https://www.swgde.org/home
26. Horsman, G.: ACPO principles for digital evidence: time for an update? Forensic Sci. Int. Rep. **2** (2020)
27. Berghs, S., Morrison, G.S., Goemans-Dorny, C.: Electronic evidence: challenges and opportunities for law enforcement. In: Biasiotti, M.A., Mifsud Bonnici, J.P., Cannataci, J., Turchi, F. (eds.) Handling and Exchanging Electronic Evidence Across Europe. LGTS, vol. 39, pp. 75–123. Springer, Cham (2018). https://doi.org/10.1007/978-3-319-74872-6_6
28. Biasiotti, M.A.: A proposed electronic evidence exchange across the European Union. Digit. Evid. Elec. Signature L. Rev. **14**, 1 (2017)
29. Shah, M., Saleem, S., Zulqarnain, R.: Protecting digital evidence integrity and preserving chain of custody. J. Digit. Forensics Secur. Law (2017)
30. Chopade, M., Khan, S., Shaikh, U., Pawar, R.: Digital forensics: maintaining chain of custody using blockchain, pp. 744–747. IEEE (2019)
31. Cosic, J., Baca, M.: A framework to (Im) Prove "Chain of Custody" in digital investigation process. In: Central European Conference on Information and Intelligent Systems 2010, p. 435. Faculty of Organization and Informatics Varazdin (2010)
32. Prayudi, Y., Ashari, A., Priyambodo, T.K.: Digital evidence cabinets: a proposed framework for handling digital chain of custody. Int. J. Comput. Appl. **107**(9) (2014)
33. Lone, A.H., Mir, R.N.: Forensic-chain: blockchain based digital forensics chain of custody with PoC in Hyperledger composer. Digit. Investig. **28**, 44–55 (2019)
34. Tian, Z., Li, M., Qiu, M., Sun, Y., Su, S.: Block-DEF: a secure digital evidence framework using blockchain. Inf. Sci. **491**, 151–165 (2019)
35. Kumar, R., Tripathi, R.: Implementation of distributed file storage and access framework using IPFS and blockchain. In: Fifth International Conference on Image Information Processing (ICIIP), pp. 246–251. IEEE (2019)
36. Yaga, D., Mell, P., Roby, N., Scarfone, K.: Blockchain technology overview (NISTIR-8202), NIST: National Institute of Standards and Technology (2018)
37. Ramadoss, R.: Blockchain technology: an overview. IEEE Potentials **41**(6), 6–12 (2022)
38. Comert, O.: Blockchain revolution: how the technology behind bitcoin and other cryptocurrencies is changing the world (2020)
39. Mingxiao, D., Xiaofeng, M., Zhe, Z., Xiangwei, W., Qijun, C.: A review on consensus algorithm of blockchain (2017)
40. Guo, R., Shi, H., Zhao, Q., Zheng, D.: Secure attribute-based signature scheme with multiple authorities for blockchain in electronic health records systems. IEEE Access **6** (2018)
41. Christidis, K., Devetsikiotis, M.: Blockchains and smart contracts for the internet of things. IEEE Access **4** (2016)
42. Hewa, T., Ylianttila, M., Liyanage, M.: Survey on blockchain based smart contracts: applications, opportunities and challenges. J. Netw. Comput. Appl. **177** (2021)
43. Zheng, Z., Xie, S., Dai, H., Chen, X., Wang, H.: An overview of blockchain technology: architecture, consensus, and future trends (2017)
44. Khan, A.A., Uddin, M., Shaikh, A.A., Laghari, A.A., Rajput, A.E.: MF-ledger: blockchain hyperledger sawtooth-enabled novel and secure multimedia chain of custody forensic investigation architecture. IEEE Access **9** (2021)
45. Ismail, S., Reza, H., Zadeh, H.K., Vasefi, F.: A blockchain-based IoT security solution using multichain (2023)

46. Martino, W.: The first scalable, high performance private blockchain. Revision v1. 0 (2016)
47. Alruwaili, F.F.: CustodyBlock: a distributed chain of custody evidence framework. Information (2021)
48. Reedy, P.: Interpol review of digital evidence 2016–2019. Forensic Sci. Int. Synerg. **2** (2020)
49. Arshad, H., Jantan, A.B., Abiodun, O.I.: Digital forensics: review of issues in scientific validation of digital evidence. J. Inf. Process. Syst. (2018)
50. Watney, M.M.: Cross-border law enforcement: Gathering of stored electronic evidence. J. Inf. Warfare (2016)
51. Mougayar, W.: The Business Blockchain: Promise, Practice, and Application of the Next Internet Technology. Wiley (2016)
52. Baldi, A.M., Celestrini, J.R., Andreão, R.V., Mota, V.F.S., Santos, C.A.S.: A blockchain approach for eHealth situation-aware data processing (2022)
53. Caro, M.P., Ali, M.S., Vecchio, M., Giaffreda, R.: Blockchain-based traceability in Agri-Food supply chain management: a practical implementation. Presented at the 2018 IoT Vertical and Topical Summit on Agriculture - Tuscany (IOT Tuscany) (2018)
54. Chakrabarti, A., Chaudhuri, A.K.: Blockchain and its scope in retail. Int. Res. J. Eng. Technol. (2017)
55. Xiong, Y., Du, J.: Electronic evidence preservation model based on blockchain. Presented at the Proceedings of the 3rd International Conference on Cryptography, Security and Privacy - ICCSP 2019 (2019)
56. Lone, A.H., Mir, R.N.: Forensic-chain: Ethereum blockchain based digital forensics chain of custody. Sci. Pract. Cyber Secur. J. (2018)
57. Li, M., Lal, C., Conti, M., Hu, D.: LEChain: a blockchain-based lawful evidence management scheme for digital forensics. Futur. Gener. Comput. Syst. **115**, 406–420 (2021)
58. Zhang, S., Li, L., Chang, L., Gu, T., Liu, H.: A ciphertext-policy attribute-based encryption based on multi-valued decision diagram. In: Intelligent Information Processing IX: 10th IFIP TC 12 International Conference, IIP (2018)
59. Burri, X., Casey, E., Bollé, T., Jaquet-Chiffelle, D.-O.: Chronological independently verifiable electronic chain of custody ledger using blockchain technology. Forensic Sci. Int. Digit. Investig. **33** (2020)
60. Jaquet-Chiffelle, D.-O., Casey, E., Bourquenoud, J.: Tamperproof timestamped provenance ledger using blockchain technology. Forensic Sci. Int. Digit. Invest. **33** (2020)
61. Khan, A.A., Shaikh, A.A., Laghari, A.A.: IoT with multimedia investigation: a secure process of digital forensics chain-of-custody using blockchain hyperledger sawtooth. Arab. J. Sci. Eng., 1–16 (2022)
62. Durga, S., Daniel, E., Deepakanmani, S., Neeba, T.M., Ravi, V.: Blockchain-based privacy preservation technique for digital forensics records. In: Artificial Intelligence and Blockchain in Digital Forensics, pp. 211–229. River Publishers (2023)
63. Santamaría, P., Tobarra, L., Pastor-Vargas, R., Robles-Gómez, A.: Smart contracts for managing the chain-of-custody of digital evidence: a practical case of study. Smart Cities **6**(2), 709–727 (2023)
64. Rajasekar, V., Sathya, K., Velliangiri, S., Karthikeyan, P.: Blockchain-based identity management systems in digital forensics. In: Artificial Intelligence and Blockchain in Digital Forensics, pp. 241–259. River Publishers (2023)
65. López-Aguilar, P., Solanas, A.: An effective approach to the cross-border exchange of digital evidence using blockchain. In: Saponara, S., De Gloria, A. (eds.) Applications in Electronics Pervading Industry, Environment and Society. LNEE, vol. 866, pp. 132–138. Springer, Cham (2022). https://doi.org/10.1007/978-3-030-95498-7_19

66. Chougule, H., Dhadiwal, S., Lokhande, M., Naikade, R., Patil, R.: Digital evidence management system for cybercrime investigation using proxy re-encryption and blockchain. Procedia Comput. Sci. **215**, 71–77 (2022)
67. Akhtar, M.S., Feng, T.: Using blockchain to ensure the integrity of digital forensic evidence in an IoT environment. EAI Endorsed Trans. Creative Technol. **9**(31), e2 (2022)

Main Track–Short Paper and PhD Track

Forest Fire Prediction Using Multi-Source Deep Learning

Abdul Mutakabbir[1]([✉]), Chung-Horng Lung[1], Samuel A. Ajila[1],
Marzia Zaman[2], Kshirasagar Naik[3], Richard Purcell[4], and Srinivas Sampalli[4]

[1] Department of Systems and Computer Engineering, Carleton University, Ottawa,
ON, Canada
mutakabbir@cmail.carleton.ca, {chlung,ajila}@sce.carleton.ca
[2] Research and Development, Cistel Technology, Ottawa, ON, Canada
marzia@cistel.com
[3] Department of Electrical and Computer Engineering, University of Waterloo,
Waterloo, ON, Canada
snaik@uwaterloo.ca
[4] Faculty of Computer Science, Dalhousie University, Halifax, NS, Canada
richard.purcell@dal.ca, srini@cs.dal.ca

Abstract. Forest fire prediction is an important aspect of combating
forest fires. This research focuses on the effectiveness of multi-source
data (lightning, hydrometric and weather) in the probability prediction
of forest fires using deep learning. The results showed that the weather
model had the best predictive power (average $F1Score = 0.955$). The
lightning model had an average $F1Score = 0.924$, while the hydrometric
model had an average $F1Score = 0.690$. The single-source models were
then merged to see the impact of the multi-source data. The multi-source
model had an average $F1Score = 0.929$, whereas the average $F1Score$
for the previous three single-source model was 0.856. The results showed
that the multi-source model performed similarly to the best-performing
single-source model (weather) with a 60% reduction in training data. The
multi-source model had a negligible impact from the poor-performing
single-source model (hydrometric).

Keywords: Deep Learning · Multi-Modal · Multi-Source Data · Big
Data · Big Data Analysis · Binary Classification · Forest Fires

1 Introduction

Forestry contributed 2.3 billion dollars in revenue to the Canadian economy in
2022 and accounted for 205,365 direct jobs [2]. So, it is essential to protect forests.
Deforestation is governed and controlled by governing bodies, but forest fires
cannot be governed and are difficult to control. They can only be mitigated. For
this reason, it is important to have tools that can predict their occurrence. Forest
Fires can be broadly classified as anthropogenic and natural. Anthropogenic
factors are quickly detected and reported as they are caused by humans. Hence,

© ICST Institute for Computer Sciences, Social Informatics and Telecommunications Engineering 2024
Published by Springer Nature Switzerland AG 2024. All Rights Reserved
Z. Tan et al. (Eds.): BDTA 2023, LNICST 555, pp. 135–146, 2024.
https://doi.org/10.1007/978-3-031-52265-9_9

they can be more easily controlled and subdued. On the other hand, naturally occurring forest fires are hard to combat as they can go unnoticed for long periods causing greater destruction. For this reason, the research focuses only on naturally occurring forest fires.

Naturally occurring forest fires are often ignited by lightning [5]. Although lightning might be the cause of ignition, other factors can also impact the occurrence of forest fires [6] such as drought, weather, wind, etc. For this reason, it is essential to have multiple sources of data. A single source of data may not be effective in correctly predicting forest fires, hence multi-source approach was investigated in this research. In multi-modal learning, multiple sources and/or types of data are used, but only one model exists which makes the prediction. The terms multi-source and multi-modal learning are used interchangeably in this paper.

This paper is an extension of the research on the applicability of the Spatio-Temporal Agnostic Sampling (STAS) framework [10]. In this research, the applicability of multi-source data in forest fire prediction is studied. In the initial research, it was found that the historical feature data had an impact on the models' performance for the single-source weather data. With the introduction of multi-source data in this research, it was found that the models' performance was not impacted by the historical feature data. This research aims to investigate a multi-modal approach to predicting forest fires. A single source or type of data is not sufficient to build general models on forest fires, as they are impacted by multiple factors. It was noticed that the models could predict the probability of forest fires by taking in time series information from different sources of data. The models learned the variation in time series information to predict the severity and probability of forest fires. From the proposed research presented in this paper, it is clear that a multi-source approach using lightning, weather, and hydrometric features was successful in making predictions about forest fires.

The rest of the paper is divided as follows: in Sect. 2, we take up a Literature Review in related areas. In Sect. 3, Datasets used in the research are presented while Sect. 4 discusses the Methodology applied. Section 5 deals with Experimentation and Results followed by the Conclusion in Sect. 6.

2 Literature Review

A review of related literature shows extensive research on forest fires and lightning. There is also sizable work separately on water level, fires, and deep learning. However, there is hardly any research on multi-modal deep learning for forest fire prediction. This paper is an attempt to address this research gap. Due to space limitations, this paper does not address some points in detail. These points are discussed in the previous work [10].

Holle [4] reviewed global lightning impacts and suggested that people living closer to lightning-prone areas are increasingly affected by forest fires caused by lightning. Kochtubajda and Burrows [7] discussed such lightning-caused fires. Data for their study period (1998 to 2018) were obtained from Canadian Lightning Detection Network (CLDN). These provide a good source of background information on lightning detection and lightning-caused forest fires.

The Canadian Forest Fire Weather Index system is the main source of data for hydroponics. Hydrometric sensors facilitate real-time monitoring of groundwater levels. Research on water level and forest fires, duff moisture code, hydroponics and hydrometrics was carried out by [9,13] among others. In [13], the authors stated that the vulnerability of the study area was based on the hydrological condition. They found that when the groundwater level was less, there was more probability of fire. It was found that the highest risk of fire was in the month of March. Earlier research on hydroponics [18] also presented the increased risk of fire with decreased groundwater levels.

In [17], the authors proposed that the outputs from their study could be used for calibrating and validating the hydrological and climate models. Sanjaya et al. [12] proposed the use of satellite data or weather data in place of the Fire Danger Rating System (FDRS) which is implemented in Canada. They proposed Advanced-FDRS as a new algorithm to develop a fire warning system. In their study, Sun et al. [15] stated that forest fire spread behaviour depends on both dynamic factors and static factors. The dynamic factors include moisture content in vegetation and air. The static factors are the vegetation type in a particular region and the terrain slope. Research on water level and fire is limited. Though research on hydroponics and hydrometrics is vast, it is mainly focused on irrigation and drought. A consideration of drought as a possible factor of forest fire and the role of water both as fuel moisture content and groundwater level in forest fire research is limited.

In a recent study, Akkus et al. [1] defined multi-modal deep learning as the method of combining different channels of information simultaneously. They presented an overview of the different methods used in multi-modal deep learning to overcome the challenges of unstructured data and combining inputs of individual modals. Gao et al. [3] stated that multi-modal data consist of several modalities containing descriptions of things of interest with each modality-independent distribution. Correlations between modalities may also be understood through multi-modal approaches. In [11,14], the authors also presented a review and survey of multi-modal deep learning.

The authors in [8] described Random Multi-modal Deep Learning (RMDL) and showed how it could improve classification by including a variety of data as input. In their proposed RMDL approach, they used Deep Neural Network (DNN), CNN and RNN DL architectures. In a recent research, Vikram and Sinha [16] proposed a multi-modal framework for the detection of forest fires. They used two types of sensors, i.e., one for sensing the temperature, relative humidity, and drought condition of the forest zone. The other sensor was used to simultaneously capture images of the forest zone. However, this is not a very effective method, because the forest has to be divided into many small zones to capture images. Further, a large number of sensors would need to be installed. Their proposed framework is not suitable for large forests.

3 Datasets

This section describes the data used in the research. Four sources of data were used: 1) Fire, 2) Hydrometrics, 3) Lightning, and 4) Weather. Hydrometrics, lightning, and weather are the three single-source datasets used in this research, while the fire data is used to classify this data between fire and non-fire events. All the sources of data contain information for only Canada. The fire and weather datasets are discussed in detail in [10].

The hydrometrics dataset is used because drought plays a major role in forest fires [5]. It was acquired from Environment Canada (EC). It is a collection of different tables, of which, daily flow and daily level are of importance to this research. Spatio-Temporal Agnostic Sampling (STAS) [10] was applied to both features in the hydrometric dataset, as was done for weather data in [10].

The lightning dataset is a proprietary dataset and was obtained from EC. It is not publicly available. The dataset contains a number of features, of which, only two features, event strength and multiplicity are of importance. The event strength gives the strength of a lightning strike, while the multiplicity specifies how many flashes occurred for a single event of lightning. Spatial and temporal information was also recorded to perform aggregation on the data. The lightning data were aggregated to smaller regions, as there are no stations associated with this dataset. Minimum, maximum, and average values were extracted for both event strength and multiplicity. Additionally, the sum of multiplicity was also considered. The final dataset for lightning had 7 features. The aggregated values for the lightning dataset then underwent STAS preprocessing [10] where spatial and temporal information is discarded.

Hydrometric, lightning, and weather datasets are recorded in different time-frames. Hydrometric information was available between the years 1860 to 2022, while lightning information was available only between 2011 to 2022 and weather information was available between 1998 to 2017. When training the single-source models, the entire timeframe of each source was considered for training. While training the multi-source model (multi-modal model) the timeframe between 2011 to 2018 was considered as it intersected all three datasets. A summary of the above-mentioned dataset is provided in Table 1.

Table 1. Datasets Summary

Source	Data Available Timeframe		No. of Features
	Start Year	End Year	
Fire	1917	2020	-NA-
Hydrometric	1860	2022	2
Lightning	2011	2022	7
Weather	1998	2018	31

4   Methodology

As stated earlier, this research is an extension of the previous research conducted in [10]. The preprocessing for data from all three sources of data followed the STAS instructions. Since it was known from previous research [10] that the number of nearest stations (K) hyperparameter did not play an impact on the models' performance, K was not considered in this research. The other two hyperparameters for STAS, the number of past days (N) and the number of past months for non-fire events (M) are considered in this research. N determines the amount of historical information that will exist in the dataset for both fire and non-fire events. M specifies how many months in the past we are looking at since the time of a fire event to extract the non-fire points. For example, consider $N = 7$ (one week of historical information) and $M = 3$ (looking back 3 months to extract non-fire points). If a fire event occurred on February 28, 2023, then the fire event for the dataset will consider features from February 28, 2023, backward up until February 21, 2023, since we are looking at a week of historical information. Similarly, the non-fire event for the dataset is extracted from November 28, 2022, backward up until November 21, 2022, since M was chosen to be 3 months in the past for non-fire events.

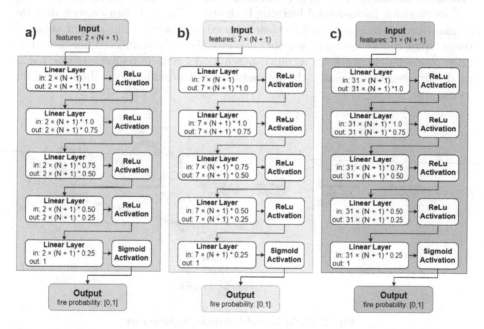

Fig. 1. Single-Source Deep Learning Binary Classification Model Architectures: a) Hydrometrics Model, b) Lightning Model, and c) Weather Model

The models need to output the probability of fire, given a set of features. A binary classification model was chosen for this task. Since the aim was to study the effects of multi-source data on the performance of the models, deep learning models were chosen as they provide the flexibility of merging different single-sourced models. The single-source deep learning models for hydrometrics, lightning, and weather were built similarly to the weather models as described in [10]. A pictorial representation of the three single-source deep learning binary classification models is shown in Fig. 1. All three single-source models output values are in the range [0–1]. 0 indicates fire will not occur while 1 indicates fire will occur. The final activation in these models is Sigmoid to ensure the values are in the range [0–1]. The three different single-source models are colored differently throughout this paper to distinguish them. The hydrometrics model is colored blue, the lightning model is colored yellow, and finally, the weather model is colored purple.

The multi-source deep learning models are built by fusing the single-source models. When fusing the single-source models, a weighted average approach is not used. The output layer in all the single-source models is dropped and is then joined to a fully connected network with a final activation of Sigmoid. During the training, the fully connected network determines the weights associated with the input provided by each of the single-source models. Since the final layer is dropped in the single-source models, they will be referred to as networks instead of models in the case of multi-source models. A high-level overview of the architecture for multi-modal learning is shown in Fig. 2. It can be seen that the single-source data is provided to their respective networks. The output values of these single-source networks are then fed into the fully connected network. This fully connected network for a multi-source model will, hereafter, be referred to as the fire network. Finally, the fire network will provide the probability of fire as output.

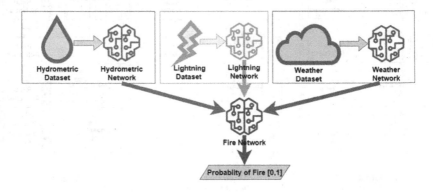

Fig. 2. Multi-Modal Learning Architecture

A deeper representation of the multi-source models can be seen in Fig. 3. It can be seen that the final layer for all the single-source models shown in Fig. 1 is discarded for the multi-source network in Fig. 3. The output of the final hidden layer in all the single-source networks is then passed on to the fire network as input. The fire model then outputs the probability of fire between [0–1]. The number of inputs for all single-source networks is different. It can be calculated using Eq. 1 with the following description:

$$NIF = SFC \times (N + 1) \tag{1}$$

NIF represents the number of input features for the network, while SFC represents the feature count of the source. SFC is multiplied by $(N + 1)$ because the day the fire occurs is also considered a part of the historical information. The input is then fed to their respective source networks. The hidden layer size in each network drops by 25% and there are a total of 3 hidden layers and 1 input layer [10]. The final hidden layer neurons (FLC) can be calculated using Eq. 2 with the following description:

$$FLC = SFC \times (N + 1) \times 0.25 \tag{2}$$

The value of FLC is rounded up to the nearest integer. Then the number of input features for the fire network (NIF_f) can be calculated using Eq. 3, derived as follows:

$$NIF_f = \sum_{single-source} FLC$$

$$NIF_f = (\sum_{single-source} SFC) \times (N + 1) \times 0.25 \tag{3}$$

The sum of SFC for the proposed approach in this research is 40 $(2 + 7 + 31)$, therefore, $NIF_f = 40 \times (N+1) \times 0.25$. The layer size in the fire network also drops incrementally by 25% for each layer. The final output layer has an activation of Sigmoid to have an output value between [0–1].

For this research, $F1Score$ was used as a metric to evaluate the models. $F1Score$ provides the harmonic mean of precision and recall, therefore, the impact of both precision and recall can be seen in the model. Ideally, an $F1Score \geq 0.9$ is considered to be excellent. If the score is between 0.8 and 0.9, it is considered to be good. A score between 0.7 and 0.8 is considered to be acceptable. Scores less than 0.7 are considered to be bad.

5   Experimentation and Results

The single-source models shown in Fig. 1 were first trained on their respective datasets for the entire timeframe. The hyperparameters were the same as the ones used in the previous research [10]. The $F1Score$ was recorded for all the single-source models for the varying values of the hyperparameters N and M. Table 2 shows the model metrics of both the single-source models and multi-source models. The first two columns are the hyperparameters N and M, respectively. The remaining columns are for different model types (single-source and multi-source). Two columns are grouped for each model type. The first column in the group specifies the number of input features for the model and the second specifies the $F1Score$ for the model. It can be seen that the weather models are the best-performing single-source models followed by the lightning models. The hydrometrics models are the worst-performing models.

For the multi-source, first, the dataset needed to be built. Since all single-source data are in different timeframes, a timeframe that was common to all three was chosen. It can be seen from Table 1 that the common years are 2011 and 2018. Therefore, a timeframe from 2011 to 2018 was chosen. This reduced the dataset size significantly. Then the data from all three single-sources were collected for the timeframe 2011 to 2018. The data from all the single-sources were merged by location and time to form the multi-source dataset. This dataset was then randomly split into test (20%) and train (80%).

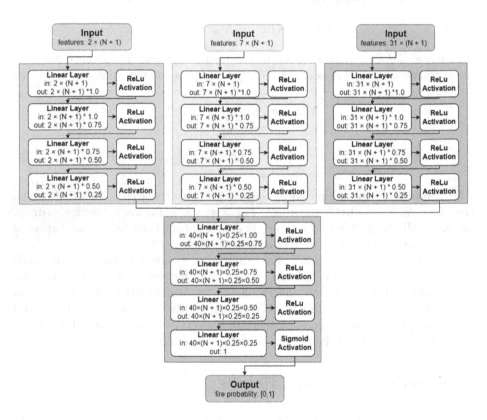

Fig. 3. Multi-Source Deep Learning Binary Classification Model Architectures

The multi-source model was built for each combination of hyperparameters (N and M) described in the previous research [10]. For all the pre-trained single-source models, for a given combination of hyperparameters, their output layer was discarded. The resulting models are called single-source networks (as seen in Fig. 2). The final hidden layers from all single-source networks were then

connected to a fully connected fire network as shown in Fig. 3. This formed the
multi-source model. The weights for the single-source network were frozen in the
multi-source model. The only trainable weights were the weights from the fully
connected fire network. The multi-source model then underwent training similar
to the single-source models for all the combinations of hyperparameters defined
in [10]. The results of the multi-source models for different hyperparameter combinations are presented in Table 2. A description of how to read the table was
provided earlier. A comparison of multi-source model performance with N and
M is shown using the box plot in Fig. 5. It can be seen that in the multi-source
models, N has an insignificant impact on model performance, whereas M has a
major impact on the models' performance.

Table 2. Model Metrics Preprocessed using STAS

| N | M | Single-Source Model | | | | | | Multi-Source Model | |
| | | Hydrometrics Model | | Lightning Model | | Weather Model | | | |
		No. of Input Features	F1 Score	No. of Input Features	F1 Score	No. of Input Features	F1 Score	No. of Input Features	F1 Score
7	3	16	0.687	56	0.913	248	0.962	320	0.958
14	3	30	0.647	105	0.932	468	0.975	600	0.951
30	3	62	0.674	217	0.949	961	0.986	1240	0.962
7	5	16	0.692	56	0.977	248	0.991	320	0.993
14	5	30	0.691	105	0.984	468	0.994	600	0.988
30	5	62	0.674	217	0.988	961	0.995	1240	0.988
7	6	16	0.685	56	0.977	248	0.995	320	0.996
14	6	30	0.683	105	0.986	468	0.997	600	0.995
30	6	62	0.684	217	0.989	961	0.998	1240	0.994
7	7	16	0.681	56	0.976	248	0.994	320	0.989
14	7	30	0.764	105	0.979	468	0.997	600	0.989
30	7	62	0.742	217	0.985	961	0.997	1240	0.989
7	9	16	0.683	56	0.906	248	0.976	320	0.964
14	9	30	0.636	105	0.927	468	0.983	600	0.965
30	9	62	0.809	217	0.940	961	0.991	1240	0.973
7	12	16	0.662	56	0.709	248	0.760	320	0.682
14	12	30	0.663	105	0.732	468	0.801	500	0.666
30	12	62	0.664	217	0.788	961	0.813	1240	0.659

A comparison of the single-source models with the multi-source model is
shown in Fig. 5. The comparison is presented with box plots for the multi-source
model with all three of the single-source models. One key thing to note for this
comparison is that the dataset size for the multi-source model was 0.4 times
the single-source weather data, 0.72 times the single-source lightning dataset,

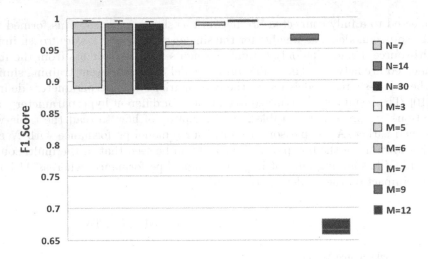

Fig. 4. Impact of N and M on Multi-Source Models' Performance

and 0.08 times the hydrometric dataset. It can be seen that the multi-source model shown in red in Fig. 5 was not impacted by having poorly performing networks exist in it (hydrometric). The multi-source model did as well as the best-performing single-source model (weather) shown in purple in Fig. 5. On average the $F1Score$ for the multi-source models was less than 1% lower when compared with the best single-source weather model, while the sizes of the training data for the multi-source model was 72% of the size of training data for single-source weather models.

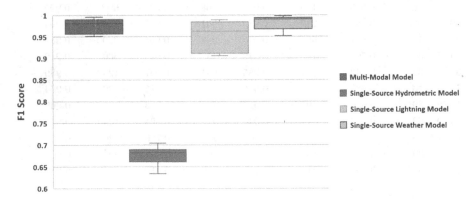

Fig. 5. $F1Score$ Comparison of Multi-Source Model and Single-Source Models

6 Conclusion

This paper proposed a multi-source deep learning approach to forest fire predictions. To the best of our knowledge, there is no research on forest fire prediction using multi-source data. Three different data sources (hydrometric, lightning, and weather) were used to investigate and predict the probability of forest fires. The single-source models in this research were trained on a larger timeframe (hydrometric over 103 years, lightning over 10 years, and weather over 20 years). The proposed multi-source model was trained on a shorter timeframe of 8 years to ensure that all the sources of data are in the same timeframe. Based on the experimental results, the proposed approach seemed viable for forest fire predictions. Even with less training data, the $F1Score$ of the multi-source model was high. It was also seen that the multi-source model was not impacted by the low-performing single-source networks in the model. On average the $F1Scores$ of the multi-source model were only 1% lower than the $F1Scores$ of the best-performing single-source model (weather). It was also seen that the multi-source model's performance is independent of N. In future, it is proposed to compare this research with an increased timeframe of data and study the impact of federated learning. It is also proposed to compare the impact of multi-source data on severity (area burned) shown in our previous research [10].

Acknowledgements. This research was funded by NSERC Canada, and supported by Research Computing Services at Carleton University. The authors thank Fatemeh and Parveen for their support.

References

1. Akkus, C., et al.: Multimodal deep learning. arXiv:2301.04856 (2023)
2. Canada, N.R.: The State of Canada's Forests: Annual Report 2022. Natural Resources, Canada (2022)
3. Gao, J., et al.: A survey on deep learning for multimodal data fusion. Neural Comput. **32**, 829–864 (2020)
4. Holle, R.L.: Some aspects of global lightning impacts. In: International Conference on Lightning Protection (2014)
5. Johnson, E.A., Miyanishi, K.: Forest Fires: Behavior and Ecological Effects. Academic Press Inc, San Diego (2001)
6. Johnson, J.M., Khoshgoftaar, T.M.: Deep learning and data sampling with imbalanced big data. In: IEEE 20th International Conference on Information Reuse and Integration for Data Science, IRI, pp. 175–183 (2019)
7. Kochtubajda, B., Burrows, W.R.: Cloud-to-ground lightning in Canada: 20 years of CLDN data. Atmos. Ocean **58**, 316–332 (2020)
8. Kowsari, K., et al.: RMDL: random multimodel deep learning for classification. In: International Conference on Information Systems and Data Mining (2018)
9. Mapari, R.G., et al.: An IoT based automated hydroponics farming and real time crop monitoring. In: 2nd International Conference on Intelligent Technologies (CONIT) (2022)

10. Mutakabbir, A., et al.: Spatio-temporal agnostic deep learning modeling of forest fire prediction using weather data. In: 2023 IEEE 47th Annual Computers, Software, and Applications Conference (COMPSAC), pp. 346–351 (2023). https://doi.org/10.1109/COMPSAC57700.2023.00054

11. Ramachandram, D., Taylor, G.W.: Deep multimodal learning: a survey on recent advances and trends. Signal Process. Mag. **34**, 96–108 (2017)

12. Sanjaya, H., et al.: Indonesia fire danger rating system (Ina-FDRS), a new algorithm for the fire prevention in Indonesia. In: IEEE Asia-Pacific Conference on Geoscience, Electronics and Remote Sensing Technology (AGERS) (2019)

13. Silviana, S., Saharjo, B., Sutikno, S.: Fire risk analysis based on groundwater level... IOP Conf. Ser. Mater. Sci. Eng. **796**, 012041 (2020)

14. Summaira, J., et al.: Recent advances and trends in multimodal deep learning: a review. arXiv:2105.11087v1 (2021)

15. Sun, T., et al.: Mountains forest fire spread simulator based on geo-cellular automation combined with Wang Zhengfei velocity model. IEEE J. Sel. Top. Appl. Earth Observ. Rem. Sens. **6**, 1971–1987 (2013)

16. Vikram, R., Sinha, D.: A multimodal framework for forest fire detection and monitoring. Multimed. Tools Appl. **82**, 9819–9842 (2023)

17. Wang, S., Li, J., Russell, H.A.: Methods for estimating surface water storage changes and their evaluations. J. Hydrometeorol. **24**, 445–461 (2023)

18. Young, R., Giese, R.: Introduction to Forest Fire. Wiley, Oxford (1991)

Research on Preprocessing Process for Improved Image Generation Based on Contrast Enhancement

Tae-su Wang, Minyoung Kim, Cubahiro Roland, and Jongwook Jang$^{(\boxtimes)}$

Dong-eui University, Busan 47340, Republic of Korea
`tswang@office.deu.ac.kr, jwjang@deu.ac.kr`

Abstract. Lighting conditions in daytime environments can reduce the object recognition rate by causing blurring, over-exposure, and shadows that mask important information about the object's shape and size. These phenomena also decrease the quality of image data, with outdoor quality being significantly lower than indoor quality. As deep learning-based object recognition algorithms heavily rely on image quality, a preprocessing process is required to improve the quality of learning image data and achieve high performance. To address this, the paper proposes a contrast-enhanced image generation preprocessing process that can improve image quality and mitigate the effects of poor lighting conditions.

Keywords: Contrast enhancement · CLAHE · SSIM · PSNR · LoFTR

1 Introduction

Light is one of the biggest factors that reduces the object recognition rate in an image, making it difficult to recognize the object's original objects. In particular, if the lighting conditions are bright or rough in daytime environments, the object can be blurred or over-exposed, making it difficult to distinguish the features of the object. In addition, shadows due to increased contrast from light may mask important information about the shape and size of the object. These phenomena reduce the quality of image data, and the quality is significantly lower outdoors than indoors. Deep learning-based object recognition algorithms, which mainly use images as learning data, are highly dependent on the quality of learning data, requiring a preprocessing process to improve the quality of learning image data and obtain high data quality for high performance [1–3].

This paper proposes a contrast-enhanced image generation preprocessing process to improve problems caused by lighting conditions in daytime environments and improve quality.

2 Proposed Preprocessing Process

The preprocessing process proposed in this paper can be largely divided into optimal value extraction, image generation, and quality verification stages.

Z. Tan et al. (Eds.): BDTA 2023, LNICST 555, pp. 147–155, 2024.
https://doi.org/10.1007/978-3-031-52265-9_10

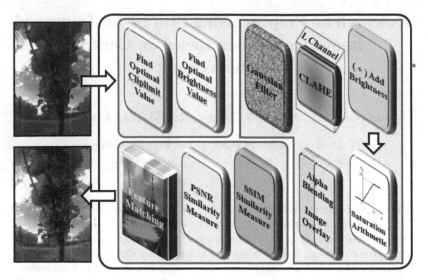

Fig. 1. Preprocessing Process

Figure 1 shows the image of the proposed preprocessing process.

Since the illumination or shadow area of the object in the image data varies depending on location, time, and environmental factors, it is necessary to find the optimal value when applying the contrast improvement technique.

Figure 2 is an object image according to a change in the position of a light source. It can be seen that the illumination and shadow areas of the object are different as the position of the sun, which is a light source, changes due to changes in time factors. In this paper, CLAHE(Contrast Limited Adaptive Histogram Equation) was used as a contrast enhancement technique [4].

Fig. 2. Image of an object according to a change in position of the light source

The CLAHE algorithm, also called contrast-limited adaptive histogram equalization, is an algorithm that evenly flattens the histogram distribution level for the brightness of an image and consequently increases the contrast of the image. It has the effect of making it easier to discriminate image information with low contrast. In this paper, the createCLAHE function of the OpenCV library was used.

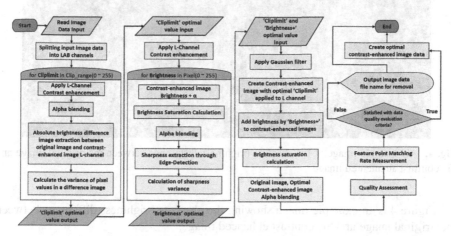

Fig. 3. Preprocessing process flowchart

Figure 3 is a flowchart of the proposal preprocessing process. It can be seen that the image improved through flowchar is created through two values (Cliplimit, Brightness) and undergoes a verification process through quality evaluation.

2.1 Extract Optimal Values

In the optimal value extraction step, the parameter 'cliplimit' is obtained with the optimal value for the contrast limit boundary value and the additional brightness to be applied to improve the shadow area. The cliplimit optimal value can calculate the absolute brightness difference between the original image and the simple CLAHE applied image, calculate the variance of the pixel value in the difference image, and specify the maximum value among the variance values repeated for the cllimit parameter range.

In the CLAHE algorithm, as the value of the parameter 'cliplimit' increases, more aggressive contrast enhancement occurs, and noise and artifacts may be excessively amplified. On the other hand, lower values may not improve contrast enough. The absolute difference in brightness between the two images indicates how much the pixel values have changed after the contrast enhancement. The variance calculation process is a measure of how spread out the pixel values are from the average value, with high variance values indicating a significant range of pixel values and low variance values indicating that the pixel values are close together. So, the value that produces the highest variance for cliplimit represents the optimal value because it represents the best balance between avoiding noise and overamplification.

Fig. 4. An example image of the absolute brightness difference between the original image and the contrast augmented image

Figure 4 is an example image showing the absolute brightness difference between the original image and the contrast enhanced image.

The optimal value for additional brightness is first edge-detection for contrast-enhanced images with cliplimit optimal values applied to calculate the variance for sharpness. The maximum value among the variance values when repeated for the pixel range 0 to 255 may be designated as an optimal value for additional brightness.

Edge Detection highlights areas of an image that have large changes or abrupt transitions in intensity between objects or areas. Because the variance for sharpness indicates how widely the sharpness values are spread throughout the image, a higher variance for sharpness is optimal because it captures both strong and subtle edges with varying levels of edge enhancement.

Figure 5 is an example image showing sharpness through edge detection.

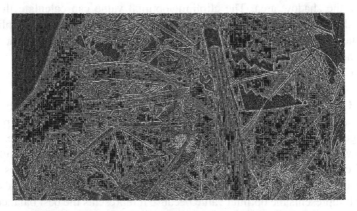

Fig. 5. Illustrative image of sharpness with edge detection

2.2 Generation an Image

When the optimal value is obtained, the following image generation process is performed. First, when the original image of the daytime environment is received, the non-uniform pixel value is adjusted evenly and Gaussian blur is processed to alleviate noise [5]. Next, a contrast improvement technique for the L (Luminosity) channel of the Lab channel is applied using the cliplimit optimal value. After increasing the brightness of the contrast-enhanced image by the optimal value, a saturation arithmetic for the contrast-enhanced image is applied. The reason for applying saturation-operation is to maintain image quality by preventing the brightness or color value of image data from changing too much [6]. Images to which saturation-operation is applied apply alpha blending with the original image to overlay the image.

Alpha blending refers to a display method that mixes the background RGB value and the RGB value above it by assigning a new value called "Alpha" to the computer's color expression value "RGB" for visual and effect when another image is overlaid on the image. Alpha blending is applied because in the case of images with simple contrast enhancement techniques, pixels are often damaged to improve contrast, resulting in noise areas, which reduce data quality [7].

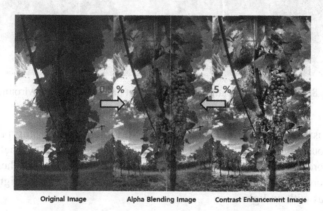

Original Image   Alpha Blending Image   Contrast Enhancement Image

Fig. 6. Original & Alpha Blending & Contrast Enhancement Images

Figure 6 shows the original, alpha blending, and contrast enhanced images. In this paper, we applied alpha blending to the original image and the contrast improved image by specifying it as a 0.5 ratio.

Fig. 7. Result of applying preprocessing process to various daytime environment images

Fig. 8. Result of application of pretreatment process in night environment

Figure 7 is the result before and after applying the preprocessing process of this paper to various daytime environment images, and Fig. 8 is the result before and after applying the preprocessing process in the night environment. Although there is a certain degree of improvement in the night environment, it can be seen that significant noise occurs in areas without light.

2.3 Verifying the Quality of the Generated Image

In the quality verification stage, the quality of image data generated is measured through PSNR(Peak Signal-to-Noise Ratio), SSIM(Structural Simplicity Index Measure), and Feature Point Matching comparison between the original image and the generated image. PSNR represents the power of noise for the maximum power that a signal can have with the maximum signal-to-noise ratio. It is mainly used when evaluating image loss information on the front axis of image or video loss and uses decibels (db) units [8]. The formula for PSNR is as follows.

$$PSNR = 10\log\frac{S^2}{MSE} \tag{1}$$

MSE (Mean Square Error) is a mean square error that is averaged over the square of the error, and s is the maximum value of the pixel [9]. The higher the PSNR level, the lower the loss than the original image.

SSIM refers to a structural similarity index and is a method designed for evaluating human visual image quality differences, not numerical errors. The similarity of the two images is compared using three factors: luminance, contrast, and structural difference between pixel values [10]. The formula for SSIM is as follows.

$$
\begin{aligned}
SIM\,(x, y) &= l(x, y)^\alpha \cdot c(x, y)^\beta \cdot s(x, y)^\gamma \\
&= \frac{(2\mu_x\mu_y + C_1)(2\sigma_{xy} + C_2)}{\left(\mu_x^2 + \mu_y^2 + C_1\right)\left(\sigma_x^2 + \sigma_y^2 + C_2\right)}
\end{aligned}
\tag{2}
$$

The numerical value of SSIM is between 0 and 1, and the closer it is to 1, the higher the similarity.

Feature point matching is to find similar points by comparing feature point descriptors extracted from two images, and this paper presents two methods. The first method is to detect feature points using the ORB(Oriented FAST and Rotated BRIEF) algorithm and to obtain feature point matching rates by applying the MAGSAC(Marginizing Sample Consensus) method to calculate the transformation matrix approximation for the matching point [11, 12].

The second method is to match feature points using LoFTR (Detector-Free Local Feature Matching with Transformers) [13]. Traditional local feature matching methods rely on detecting key points in an image, but this can be a tricky and computationally expensive task, especially when dealing with low-texture or repetitive areas. LoFTR, on the other hand, is a novel approach to local feature matching in computer vision using a transducer-based architecture that does not rely on explicit keypoint detection. LoFTR encodes image patch pairs into feature vectors and predicts correspondence between them, which is trained end-to-end on large datasets and achieves state-of-the-art performance on benchmark datasets. LoFTR is an innovative local feature matching solution that is particularly useful for matching images with low-textured or repetitive regions, can reduce computational costs, and can improve the accuracy of the matching process.

Figure 9 is an example image of feature point matching for two methods.

$$
Accuracy = 100 \times \frac{Count(Correct\ Matching\ Points)}{Count(All\ Matching\ Points)}
\tag{3}
$$

When correctly matched feature points are divided by the number of matched feature points, accuracy for feature point matching can be obtained.

For 30 images (Size: 720 * 1280), an experiment was conducted to compare the performance of the process applying the two methods. The first method (using MAGSAC) took 1 min and 8 s, and the average feature matching rate was 94.5%. The second method (using LoFTR) took 4 min and 10 s, and the average feature matching rate was 99.78%.

Fig. 9. Feature matching example image

3 Conclusion

In this paper, we propose an optimized contrast enhancement image generation pre-processing process in the daytime environment to improve the problems caused by lighting conditions. The preprocessing process can be divided into three stages: optimal value extraction, image generation, and quality verification. The process first obtains the optimal value of the contrast limit boundary value and the additional brightness for shadow area improvement. Then, using Gaussian-blur processing and cliplimit optimal values for input images, contrast enhancement techniques for L channels are applied, and saturation-operation is applied, and alpha-blending with the original image is applied to create an improved image. Finally, the quality of the generated image may be verified through PSNR, SSIM, and feature point matching.

When speed is more important in the feature point matching process, it is better to use the method using ORB and MAGSAC, and when high performance is required, it is better to use LoFTR. The preprocessing process proposed in this paper can be applied to various environments, not just the daytime environment, but the improvement is low for areas with little light.

In future research, we plan to conduct a comparative study on the improvement method for areas with little light during the computation process and the performance comparison of the deep learning object recognition model on the existing image dataset and the image dataset generated through the process of this paper.

Acknowledgement. This research was supported by the MSIT (Ministry of Science and ICT), Korea, under the Grand Information Technology Research Center support program (IITP-2023–2016-0-00318) supervised by the IITP (Institute for Information & communications Technology Planning & Evaluation).

References

1. Shah, J.H., et al.: Robust face recognition technique under varying illumination. J. Appl. Res. Technol. **13**(1), 97–105 (2015). https://doi.org/10.1016/S1665-6423(15)30008-0

2. Tang, H., Zhu, H., Fei, L., Wang, T., Cao, Y., Xie, C.: Low-illumination image enhancement based on deep learning techniques: a brief review. Photonics **10**(2), 198–222 (2023). https://doi.org/10.3390/photonics10020198
3. Bi, X., Li, M., Zha, F., Guo, W., Wang, P.: A non-uniform illumination image enhancement method based on fusion of events and frames. Optik **272**, 170329 (2023). https://doi.org/10.1016/j.ijleo.2022.170329
4. Zuiderveld, K.: Contrast limited adaptive histogram equalization. Graphics Gems IV, pp. 474–485 (1994)
5. Gedraite, E.S., Hadad, M.: Investigation on the effect of a Gaussian Blur in image filtering and segmentation. In: Proceedings ELMAR-2011, pp. 393–396 (2011)
6. Park, G.-H., Cho, H.-H., Yunand, J.-H., Choi, M.-R.: Image enhancement method by saturation and contrast improvement. In: 7th International Meeting on Information Display, pp. 1139–1142. The Korean Infomation Display Society (2007)
7. Opencv Homepage-imageArithmetic. https://opencv-python.readthedocs.io/en/latest/doc/07.imageArithmetic/imageArithmetic.html
8. Horé, A., Ziou, D.: Image Quality metrics: PSNR vs. SSIM. In: 20th International Conference on Pattern Recognition, pp. 2366–2369. IEEE Computer Society, Istanbul, (2010). https://doi.org/10.1109/ICPR.2010.579
9. Probabilitycourse Homepage-MSE (Mean Squared Error). https://www.probabilitycourse.com/chapter9/9_1_5_mean_squared_error_MSE.php.
10. Lo, S. -W.: SSIM for video representing and matching. In: 6th IEEE/International Conference on Advanced Infocomm Technology (ICAIT), pp. 65–66. IEEE, Hsinchu (2013). https://doi.org/10.1109/ICAIT.2013.6621495
11. Wang, X., Zou, J., Shi, D.: An improved ORB image feature matching algorithm based on SURF. In: 3rd International Conference on Robotics and Automation Engineering (ICRAE), pp. 218–222. IEEE, Guangzhou (2018). DOI: https://doi.org/10.1109/ICRAE.2018.8586755
12. Barath, D., Matas, J., Noskova, J.: MAGSAC: Marginalizing Sample Consensus. In: IEEE/CVF Conference on Computer Vision and Pattern Recognition (CVPR), pp. 10189–10197. IEEE, USA (2019)
13. Sun, J., Shen, Z., Wang, Y., Bao, H., Zhou, X.: LoFTR: detector-free local feature matching with transformers. In: IEEE/CVF Conference on Computer Vision and Pattern Recognition (CVPR), pp. 8918–8927. IEEE, USA (2021). https://doi.org/10.48550/arXiv.2104.00680

An Auditable Framework for Evidence Sharing and Management Using Smart Lockers and Distributed Technologies: Law Enforcement Use Case

Belinda I. Onyeashie[✉], Petra Leimich, Sean McKeown, and Gordon Russell

Edinburgh Napier University, Edinburgh, Scotland
belinda.onyeashie@napier.ac.uk

Abstract. This paper presents a decentralised framework for sharing and managing evidence that uses smart lockers, blockchain technology, and the InterPlanetary File System (IPFS). The system incorporates Hyperledger Fabric blockchain for immutability and tamper-proof record keeping and employs cryptographic measures to protect the confidentiality of shared and stored evidence. IPFS is employed for secure and efficient storage of digital evidence, while smart lockers provide a solution for managing physical-digital evidence All actions performed on IPFS or smart lockers are recorded on the blockchain, guaranteeing a comprehensive and auditable chain of custody report at the end of an investigation. The goal of this framework is to improve the security, integrity, and accessibility of all digital evidence types, thereby enhancing the efficiency and reliability of investigative processes.

Keywords: Blockchain · Smart Locker · Hyperledger · IPFS · Smart Contracts · Encryption

1 Introduction

The advent of big data has brought about significant transformations in the landscape of evidence management. The exponential growth in data volume and variety has posed challenges for traditional evidence management systems. The sheer scale and diversity of data sources, including structured and unstructured data, demand innovative approaches to effectively handle and process evidence [1]. Moreover, the integration of diverse evidence data for comprehensive analysis requires scalable and auditable evidence management systems [2]. Traditional centralised systems, with their inherent limitations in scalability and auditability, struggle to meet these demands [3]. Consequently, there is a pressing need to adapt evidence management practices to accommodate the characteristics of big data.

To address these challenges, there is an increasing demand for evidence management systems that can ensure the authenticity, reliability, and accessibility of digital

Z. Tan et al. (Eds.): BDTA 2023, LNICST 555, pp. 156–167, 2024.
https://doi.org/10.1007/978-3-031-52265-9_11

evidence [2]. These systems must be capable of securely storing and managing digital evidence while preserving its integrity and authenticity [4]. Furthermore, they must provide mechanisms to ensure that the privacy and security of the data are upheld [2]. Traditional centralised approaches have demonstrated limitations in guaranteeing data integrity, transparency, and privacy [3]. The process relies on multiple paper forms documents and signature logs that are hard to trace and may be susceptible to errors and issues related to legibility [5]. These challenges necessitate the development of decentralised frameworks that can address these shortcomings and provide robust solutions for evidence storage, sharing and management in the context of the ever-growing volume and complexity of data.

Research on blockchain-based chain of custody for digital evidence management has revealed several gaps. While some studies have examined the use of blockchain for this purpose, most have not adequately addressed the lifecycle of evidence or considered the storage and management requirements of different digital evidence formats.

In this paper, a decentralised framework is proposed for evidence sharing and management using smart lockers and decentralised technologies. Our framework leverages the security and immutability of blockchain to ensure the integrity of evidence, while allowing for efficient and transparent recording and sharing of evidence trails through the use of smart lockers and decentralised technologies. This approach addresses the challenges posed by big data, and evidence management enabling secure and efficient evidence storage, sharing, and management.

The subsequent sections of this paper delve into the current challenges with evidence management process, theoretical foundations, architectural design, implementation details, a brief feasibility highlights and potential future directions of the proposed decentralised evidence sharing and management framework.

1.1 Challenges of Current Evidence Management Processes

Law enforcement agencies are accumulating massive volumes of digital evidence from body-worn cameras, surveillance systems, social media investigations, and other digital sources. Managing these rapidly expanding big data poses major challenges for evidence integrity and usability [1]. The widespread use of mobile devices such as cell phones and digital cameras has made them prevalent at nearly every arrest and crime scene [6]. As a result, these devices often contain valuable information relevant to criminal activities and necessitate physical seizure and transportation for subsequent analysis [1, 7]. When cyber-physical evidence is seized, it is customarily stored in a secure facility pending analysis and examination [5]. However, this approach and existing digital evidence storage systems have significant limitations some of which are highlighted below:

Centralised Storage Rooms

1. Lack of oversight and reliance on participants to follow protocol leaves room for error or intentional mishandling of evidence [8].
2. Paper logs of access are vulnerable to inaccuracy, loss, or manipulation [5].
3. No system-enforced access restrictions or environmental monitoring [5, 9].

Analog Tracking

1. Paper evidence logs can be forged, omitted, or lost, breaking the chain of custody [5].
2. No immutable record of all interactions with evidence [10].
3. Difficult to coordinate evidence access and transfers between facilities [5, 9].

Limited Security

1. Storage rooms are often secured by normal locks and keys, allowing potential insider threats [5, 9]
2. No transparent systemised tracking of who accessed evidence or when [10].
3. Evidence can be tampered with or degraded without detection [7].

Law enforcement must prioritise the integrity, security, and privacy of evidence [7]. A robust architecture is required to effectively harness big data in policing and to guarantee the reliability of evidence. A shift towards decentralised evidence management could improve security, accessibility, and management at the big data scale [1]. Potential solutions include technologies such as blockchain, distributed storage, advanced access controls, and standardised metadata for efficient digital evidence management [11] (Wang et al., 2021).

2   Relevant Technologies

This section will discuss the relevant technologies that are essential to the proposed framework for evidence sharing and management. These technologies provide the foundation for our decentralised approach, enabling a complete lifecycle of digital evidence management. The key features and suitability of these technologies will be explored and their relevance to the problem statement discussed in Sect. 1.

Existing approaches to digital evidence storage and management, such as centralised databases, have evolved to address the complexities of handling large amounts of evidence. However, these traditional methods suffer from potential single points of failure from centralised data centre, vulnerability to unauthorised access, and data tampering risks [10]. While blockchain has been proposed as a solution to monitor evidence trails, current approaches do not fully encompass the entire lifecycle of evidence [12]. Most approaches [13–16] only cater to specific types of evidence and do not consider the management of physical-digital evidence seized during investigation. This oversight can lead to challenges in tracing potential tampering or data loss during evidence acquisition.

An evidence management system is incomplete if the storage architecture for evidence is not clearly defined. The system should cover the entire lifecycle of evidence, which includes acquisition of data from source, preservation, analysis, storage, and presentation in court [5]. However, in the current research on this topic, there is inconsistency in the methods employed for storing digital evidence, and often, the specific non-blockchain evidence storage architecture utilised is not explicitly disclosed. Additionally, managing the chain of custody and ensuring data integrity in a dynamic and collaborative investigative environment remains challenging.

The remainder of this section will discuss technologies which each address an element required to render a functioning cyber-physical evidence management system:

i) Blockchain, providing an auditable ledger of user access and data manipulation.
ii) Storage technologies for large scale evidence storage and sharing; and
iii) Encryption principles which facilitate appropriate user access and control.

2.1 Blockchain and Its Feasibility for Evidence Storage

Blockchain technology has emerged as a potential solution to complement big data by offering improved auditability, enhanced data integrity, real-time data analytics capabilities, and improved overall quality of big data [17]. However, storing sensitive data directly on the blockchain is not a recommended practice in the context of digital evidence management [12]. While blockchain technology offers several advantages such as immutability, decentralisation, and transparency, it is not designed to handle large volumes of sensitive data efficiently and securely.

Blockchain networks consist of multiple nodes that replicate and store the entire transaction history, including all data stored on the blockchain. As the volume of data increases, the storage requirements for each node become significantly larger, which can hinder the performance and scalability of the blockchain network [18]. Storing sensitive data directly on the blockchain would exacerbate this scalability challenge, making it impractical for managing large amounts of digital evidence.

Another concern is data privacy and confidentiality [2]. Blockchain networks are inherently transparent, meaning that all transactions and data stored on the blockchain are visible to all participants. While the data itself is secured through cryptographic algorithms, the metadata associated with transactions, including timestamps and transaction hashes, can still reveal sensitive information. Storing sensitive data on the blockchain would compromise the privacy and confidentiality of that data [2], which is a critical consideration when dealing with digital evidence. Instead, the blockchain is primarily used to record the chain of custody, which is a document that records the sequential trail of evidence as it passes through different departments and participants at each stage of an investigation [5]. The chain of custody records data on the method, time, place, and participant who handled the data during its acquisition, processing, storage, and eventual use in investigations. This ensures that the information presented has not been tampered with and is genuine before it is admitted into evidence, thus ensuring the integrity and traceability of digital evidence [2, 12]. However, with the traditional approach of manually handling chain of custody on paper, the chain of custody may be susceptible to human error or erasure, making it difficult to evidence integrity [12]. The blockchain, with its decentralised and immutable features, may be the ideal technological framework for this purpose as a log of all evidence activity can be stored and generated from the blockchain to prove or disprove a case [2, 12]. Consequently, while the blockchain serves as a medium to log the chain of custody, the actual sensitive evidence data can be stored on a scalable and efficient system designed for managing and storing diverse cyber-physical evidence data.

2.2 Evidence Storage Architectures

Digital evidence storage architecture consists of technology, software, and methods for storing and managing digital evidence. The storage of digital evidence needs to be designed with the investigators' time and ability to work without being hindered by their location in mind [9]. Various architectures for storing digital evidence have been developed and are classified as either centralised, decentralised, or hybrid.

In a centralised storage system, all digital evidence is held in a single location, which is often a server or collection of servers [10]. This method is easy to handle because all the evidence is stored in one area and can be accessed by authorised staff from any location. However, because all evidence is maintained in a single area, centralised storage systems may be susceptible to security breaches [12].

Evidence stored in a centralised location can be fraught with challenges including security breaches, modification and issue in the reliance on manual evidence intake processes, which can be time-consuming and prone to errors or legibility issues [9]. However, centralised evidence storage cannot be completely eliminated as evidence such as mobile phones, laptops etc. when seized may require a temporary storage location before analyses. Additionally, automating, and digitising evidence access can therefore bolster the chain of custody, such as with smart lockers with automatically evidence access to the items within.

Smart lockers in a centralised location can help to mitigate these issues by providing automated documentation which can protects evidence integrity. Bowes [19] highlights the adoption of smart lockers by law enforcement agencies aiming to modernise their evidence management practices. These smart lockers create a digital record that includes when evidence is deposited and by whom, as well as when it is retrieved by an evidence custodian [19]. This reduces the risk in short-term evidence management and complies with digital forensic procedures for evidence management before it is uploaded to the distributed storage system after analysis.

Distributed file storage systems have gained popularity for data storage and management [20]. The distributed peer-to-peer function of these systems provides a useful alternative to centralised file storage, addressing issues related to data sharing and availability in the event of system failure. Figure 1 shows the characterisation of storage types, including popular software defined storage systems such as Ceph, GlusterFS, IPFS, and HDFS. Le, et al. [21] summarised the features and drawbacks of these file systems and evaluated IPFS in terms of performance and security. Building on positive research findings from evaluations of IPFS performance and its interoperability with blockchain to safely scale and manage big data, this paper proposes utilising IPFS for this framework.

2.3 IPFS

IPFS is a distributed file system that provides a decentralised approach to storing and sharing data. It ensures data integrity through a content-addressable file system, where files are identified by their content rather than their location [21, 22]. Each file is assigned a unique cryptographic hash, which serves as its identifier.

In traditional centralised storage systems, the integrity of data can be compromised if a single point of failure occurs. In contrast, IPFS is designed to facilitate efficient

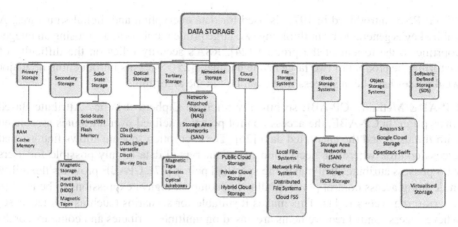

Fig. 1. Characterisation of storage types

and decentralised data storage, with files distributed across multiple nodes in the network [22]. The content-addressable nature of IPFS enables seamless data sharing and collaboration. Additionally, IPFS is designed to handle large-scale data storage and retrieval [22], with its distributed architecture allowing for the addition of new nodes to accommodate increasing volumes of digital evidence. This scalability is critical in big data management, where the volume and variety of digital evidence sources can be substantial.

2.4 Encryption Methods (Evidence Security and Access Control)

The use of blockchain and distributed storage systems alone is not sufficient for managing sensitive confidential data as evidence. These systems must be incorporated into a comprehensive evidence management system that encompasses the entire lifecycle of evidence. The storage and sharing of digital evidence in investigations pose challenges related to the need for encryption and secure sharing methods among multiple participants [15]. These challenges as outline above include concerns about the authenticity, integrity, privacy, and security of the evidence, as well as difficulties associated with digital forensic processes [2]. Encryption algorithms are essential for ensuring security and confidentiality of evidence during data sharing in investigations., investigators can ensure access is limited to authorised participants by encrypting data. This is important for digital evidence as it can be easily copied or tampered with if not secured.

There are several encryption algorithms that can be used for file sharing. Symmetric and asymmetric encryption algorithms are fundamental types of encryptions used to secure data [23]. Symmetric encryption uses the same key for encryption and decryption. Examples include AES, DES, and TripleDES. Asymmetric encryption uses a pair of keys: one for encryption and one for decryption. Examples include RSA, DSA, CP-ABE and ECC. The public key encrypts data, while the private key decrypts it [24]. Asymmetric encryption is often used for secure communication over the internet, such as in SSL/TLS protocols [23].

RSA: RSA, introduced in 1977, is used for data encryption and digital signatures. A public key is generated by multiplying two large prime numbers and choosing an integer coprime to the totient of the product [24]. RSA's security relies on the difficulty of factoring the product of two large prime numbers [25]. Since its introduction, no major weaknesses have been successfully exploited in the algorithm.

CP-ABE Method: CP-ABE specifically refers to Ciphertext-Policy Attribute-Based Encryption. In CP-ABE, the access control policy is defined over attributes associated with the users and the encrypted data [26]. The encryption scheme allows fine grained access control, where the decryption of the encrypted data is only possible for users who possess attributes that match the specified policy [27]. CPABE provides flexibility in defining access control policies, allowing complex logical expressions to be used in determining access rights. This makes it suitable for scenarios (such as this use case) where access control requirements are based on multiple attributes and complex conditions. It enables secure and efficient sharing of encrypted data while maintaining control over who can access the decrypted information. The access control strategy in CP-ABE is encrypted into the ciphertext. This feature makes it suitable for data sharing use cases.

3   System Overview

The process of managing digital evidence comes with considerable challenges, primarily legal preservation of data and facilitating investigative access. However, a system that integrates blockchain smart lockers with the InterPlanetary File System (IPFS) presents substantial advantages, particularly for maintaining the chain of custody and fostering collaboration [22]. When authorities seize physical devices such as laptops or phones, a blockchain ledger immutably records their storage in tamper-resistant smart lockers. This procedure cryptographically validates the chains of custody and securely stores the evidence in controlled environments.

Once authorised, investigators extract digital evidence from source devices and securely save it on IPFS. In the process, smart contracts record these actions on the blockchain, thereby promoting accountability. Smart contracts [11] function as the rule's engine, enabling tamper-resistant automation of evidence sharing and auditing.

Furthermore, the decentralised nature of the IPFS network eliminates central points of failure and allows authorised participants to access and analyse evidence concurrently and in a permissioned manner [22]. IPFS integrates with blockchain ecosystems to connect off-chain evidence files with on-chain evidence metadata. This approach facilitates efficient collaboration across agencies while retaining control over the data [22]. Robust access logs and encryption mechanisms ensure enhanced security. The combined architecture maintains immutable custody records, negates insider threats, and enables large-scale controlled evidence sharing and storage. This integration simplifies digital evidence management while upholding evidentiary standards.

3.1 System Requirements

Based on the gaps identified in literature and in practice, the system will prioritise the secure management and preservation of digital evidence throughout its entire lifecycle. The system aims to manage all kinds of digital evidence including cyber-physical evidence. This includes implementing measures to protect against unauthorised access, tampering, or deletion, and employing encryption techniques to safeguard confidentiality. Access controls will ensure that only authorised individuals can view or share evidence.

The proposed system aims to achieve secure storage of all evidence types, allowing for seamless sharing among participants regardless of their location. Relevant metadata, such as timestamps, file properties, geolocation data, or device information, will be recorded and organised on a permissioned blockchain. A permissioned blockchain as the name implies, is invitation-only [18]. This is to ensure the integrity of the network and that only trusted participants may have access to the system data.

The system will support collaboration among participants involved in an investigation, providing features for secure communication, sharing of evidence, and collaborative analysis. Case management functionalities will enable investigators to organise and track the progress of assigned cases, assign tasks, and generate reports.

Maintaining a reliable chain of custody is crucial in digital investigations. The system will track the movement of digital evidence from the time of collection to its use in investigation, automatically logging actions taken on the system. The system will support the generation of a comprehensive, non-repudiated, and auditable chain of custody log, allowing participants to extract relevant information and present it in a manner that is admissible in court.

3.2 System Design and Case Study

The proposed decentralised evidence sharing, and management framework integrates smart lockers, permissioned blockchain technology, and the InterPlanetary File System (IPFS) to address the challenges of traditional centralised approaches. Smart lockers provide secure storage for physical devices containing digital evidence, while a permissioned Hyperledger blockchain establishes a trust framework and maintains an immutable ledger of transactions. IPFS enables decentralised and efficient storage of evidence files, and smart contracts automate evidence management processes.

The system includes participants such as law enforcement agencies, investigators, courts, and lawyers, with an investigation administrator or controller maintaining evidence and granting access privileges. The blockchain maintains an access control list for both the smart locker and IPFS, and there is a requirement for multiple physical partipants to cross verify physical interactions with the smart locker. The permissioned blockchain provides a secure and transparent way to manage access to the smart locker and IPFS, with different access levels granted to participating nodes.

The proposed framework is divided into four main phases: Participant Registration and Authentication, Evidence encryption and storage, Evidence retrieval, Chain of Custody report generation.

Participant Registration and Authentication Phase: The Investigator Administrator (IA) serves as the system controller; they are usually responsible for initialising and registering the participants. The IA is usually an entity that has been confirmed to have no conflicts of interest with the investigation.

This phase involves the IA generating a public key and primary secret key using the CP-ABE algorithm. Each participant is assigned a private key that corresponds to their specific attribute set. These attributes define the access policies or permissions granted to each participant. The IA receives the participant's public key and encrypts their private key using RSA encryption, then securely distributes the encrypted private keys to their respective participants.

The proposed encryption method ensures the privacy and security of digital evidence before it is uploaded to the distributed storage system. First, the investigator administrator encrypts the digital evidence then, the encrypted digital evidence is uploaded or stored to either the distributed storage system or the smart locker depending on the evidence type. The encrypted digital evidence (hash value) is obtained and stored to the blockchain (Fig. 2).

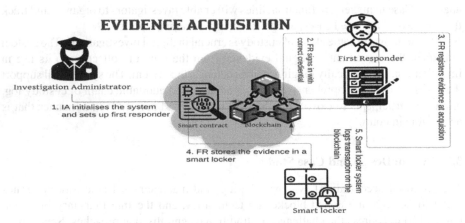

Fig. 2. Evidence acquisition and storage to blockchain based-smart locker.

Evidence Encryption and Storage Phase: The evidence encryption and storage phase are initialised in two ways. If the evidence acquired is unstructured that is, in its raw unprocessed form e.g., laptop, mobile phones etc. containing evidence, then it will need to first be registered on the blockchain, then stored in the smart locker for the appropriate department/ participant to retrieve for analysis. Otherwise, if the evidence is already digitised, then it can be encrypted and stored directly to the distributed storage system. The smart locker is blockchain based and is part of the main system. Every action taken on the smart locker is automatically recorded on the blockchain (Fig. 3).

Evidence Retrieval Phase: An evidence requester such as digital investigator, etc., can obtain the encrypted evidence hash value, evidence data and other data like chain of custody log only when they meet certain conditions. When a participant receives the encrypted digital evidence from the IA, obtained from IPFS using its content identifier

EVIDENCE ENCRYPTION AND UPLOAD

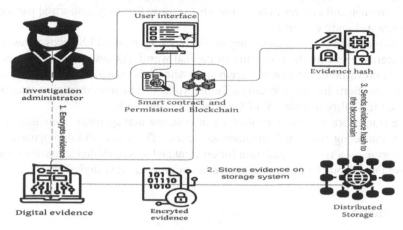

Fig. 3. Evidence encryption and upload

(CID). They then use their CP-ABE private key to decrypt the evidence, and if their attribute set satisfies the predefined access criteria, they can successfully access the evidence's contents.

Participants private keys will be sent through a secure off-blockchain communication channel to improve scalability and avoid system overhead. A participant does not need to receive a new encrypted private key every time they request evidence, as their private key is associated with their attribute set and can be used to decrypt any ciphertext with an access policy satisfied by their attributes. Once the participant has received and decrypted their encrypted private key from the IA using their RSA private key, they can use their CP-ABE private key to decrypt any authorised encrypted evidence. If their attribute set changes or their old private key is compromised, the IA will generate a new CP-ABE private key for the participant, encrypt it using the participant's public key, and securely transmit it to them.

Chain of Custody Report Generation: The log of every action taken on the smart locker and distributed storage recorded on the blockchain, creating an immutable and transparent audit trail of system activity. When requested, maybe by the court, the IA can generate comprehensive reports of the evidence trail throughout the investigation. The court can also be granted access by the IA to verify the chain of custody.

4 Conclusions

The Decentralised Evidence Sharing and Management Framework presented in this paper offers a secure and comprehensive solution for cyber-physical evidence in investigative processes. The integration of these components (Permissioned blockchain, IPFS and smart locker) ensures data immutability, secure storage of evidence and enables the recording of every action taken during an investigation, establishing a transparent and accurate chain of custody report. Additionally, cryptographic techniques protect sensitive information and enforce access controls to ensure that only authorised participants can access and share evidence.

Implementing emerging technologies like blockchain and IPFS necessitates resolving concerns regarding their viability in the real world. As law enforcement agencies seek to improve their evidence management systems, it is logical to assess the feasibility of transition efforts before proceeding. Future works will include an implementation and a detailed feasibility assessment of the proposed framework.

The framework addresses challenges in evidence management, including storage, sharing, tampering risks, and unauthorised access. The successful deployment of this system promises a robust foundation for efficient and secure evidence management and improve the reliability of digital evidence in our progressively digital era.

References

1. D'Anna, T., et al.: The chain of custody in the era of modern forensics: from the classic procedures for gathering evidence to the new challenges related to digital data. Healthcare 11(5), 634 (2023). https://doi.org/10.3390/healthcare11050634
2. Li, M., Lal, C., Conti, M., Hu, D.: LEChain: a blockchain-based lawful evidence management scheme for digital forensics. Futur. Gener. Comput. Syst. 115, 406–420 (2021)
3. Soltani, S., Seno, S.A.H.: A survey on digital evidence collection and analysis. In: 7th International Conference on Computer and Knowledge Engineering (ICCKE), Mashhad, Iran, (2017)
4. Khan, A.A., Shaikh, A.A., Laghari, A.A.: IoT with multimedia investigation: A secure process of digital forensics chain-of-custody using blockchain hyperledger sawtooth. Arab. J. Sci. Eng. 48, 10173–10188 (2022)
5. Sisodia, U.: Chain of custody: scaling the investigation to the event. In: Singh, J., Sharma, N.R. (eds.) Crime Scene Management within Forensic Science, pp. 407–418. Springer, Singapore (2022). https://doi.org/10.1007/978-981-16-6683-4_16
6. Okmi, M., Por, L.Y., Ang, T.F., Al-Hussein, W., Ku, C.S.: A systematic review of mobile phone data in crime applications: a coherent taxonomy based on data types and analysis perspectives, challenges, and future research directions. Sensors 23(9), 4350 (2023)
7. Moussa, A.F.: Electronic evidence and its authenticity in forensic evidence. Egypt. J. Forensic Sci. 11(1), 1–10 (2021). https://doi.org/10.1186/s41935-021-00234-6
8. Singh, A., Ikuesan, R.A., Venter, H.: Secure storage model for digital forensic readiness. IEEE Access 10, 19469–19480 (2022). https://doi.org/10.1109/ACCESS.2022.3151403
9. Prayudi, Y., Ashari, A., Priyambodo, T.K.: The framework to support the digital evidence handling: a case study of procedures for the management of evidence in Indonesia. J. Cases Inf. Technol. 22(3), 51–71 (2020). https://doi.org/10.4018/JCIT.2020070104
10. Rao, S., Fernandes, S., Raorane, S., Syed, S.: A novel approach for digital evidence management using blockchain. In: Proceedings of the International Conference on Recent Advances in Computational Techniques (IC-RACT) (2020)
11. Wang, S., Ouyang, L., Yuan, Y., Ni, X., Han, X., Wang, F.-Y.: Blockchain-enabled smart contracts: architecture, applications, and future trends. IEEE Trans. Syst. Man Cybern. Syst. 49(11), 2266–2277 (2019)
12. Tian, Z., Li, M., Qiu, M., Sun, Y., Su, S.: Block-DEF: a secure digital evidence framework using blockchain. Inf. Sci. 491, 151–165 (2019)

13. Biswas, R., Biswas, S.: Blockchain based digital forensics: a fundamental perspective. Artificial Intelligence and Blockchain in Digital Forensics: River Publishers (2023)
14. Khan, A.A., Uddin, M., Shaikh, A.A., Laghari, A.A., Rajput, A.E.: MF-ledger: blockchain hyperledger sawtooth-enabled novel and secure multimedia chain of custody forensic investigation architecture. IEEE Access **9**, 103637–103650 (2021)
15. Chougule, H., Dhadiwal, S., Lokhande, M., Naikade, R., Patil, R.: Digital evidence management system for cybercrime investigation using proxy re-encryption and blockchain. Procedia Comput. Sci. **215**, 71–77 (2022)
16. Chopade, M., Khan, S., Shaikh, U., Pawar, R.: Digital forensics: maintaining chain of custody using blockchain. In: 2019 Third International Conference on I-SMAC (IoT in Social, Mobile, Analytics and Cloud) (I-SMAC) (2019)
17. Deepa, N., et al.: A survey on blockchain for big data: approaches, opportunities, and future directions. Future Gener. Comput. Syst. **131**, 209–226 (2022)
18. Ramadoss, R.: Blockchain technology: an overview. IEEE Potentials **41**(6), 6–12 (2022)
19. Bowes, P.: Irrefutable evidence: modern technology transforms short-term storage (2023). https://www.pitneybowes.com/us/blog/how-smart-lockers-improve-evidence-management.html. Accessed 07 May 2023
20. Faruq, A.M., Andri, S.M., Yudi, P.: Clustering storage method for digital evidence storage using software defined storage. IOP Conference Series Materials Science and Engineering **722**, 012063 (2020)
21. Le, V., Moazeni, R., Moh, M.: Improving security and performance of distributed IPFS-based web applications with blockchain. In: Abdullah, N., Manickam, S., Anbar, M. (eds.) ACeS 2021. CCIS, vol. 1487, pp. 114–127. Springer, Singapore (2021). https://doi.org/10.1007/978-981-16-8059-5_8
22. Jamulkar, S., Chandrakar, P., Ali, R., Agrawal, A., Tiwari, K.: Evidence management system using blockchain and distributed file system (ipfs). In: Misra, R., Shyamasundar, R.K., Chaturvedi, A., Omer, R. (eds.) Machine Learning and Big Data Analytics (Proceedings of International Conference on Machine Learning and Big Data Analytics (ICMLBDA) 2021), pp. 337–359. Springer International Publishing, Cham (2022). https://doi.org/10.1007/978-3-030-82469-3_30
23. Smid, M.E.: Development of the advanced encryption standard. J. Res. Nat. Inst. Stand. Technol. **126** (2021).
24. Nisha, S., Farik, M.: RSA public key cryptography algorithm–a review. Int. J. Sci. Technol. Res. **6**(7), 187–191 (2017)
25. Hamza, A., Kumar, B.: A review paper on DES, AES, RSA encryption standards. In: 2020 9th International Conference System Modeling and Advancement in Research Trends (SMART). IEEE (2020)
26. Zhang, S., Li, L., Chang, L., Tianlong, G., Liu, H.: A ciphertext-policy attribute-based encryption based on Multi-valued decision diagram. In: Shi, Z., Mercier-Laurent, E., Li, J. (eds.) Intelligent Information Processing IX: 10th IFIP TC 12 International Conference, IIP 2018, Nanning, China, October 19-22, 2018, Proceedings, pp. 303–310. Springer International Publishing, Cham (2018). https://doi.org/10.1007/978-3-030-00828-4_30
27. Sethi, K., Pradhan, A., Bera, P.: Practical traceable multi-authority CP-ABE with outsourcing decryption and access policy updation. J. Inf. Secur. Appl. **51**, 102435 (2020). https://doi.org/10.1016/j.jisa.2019.102435

SECSOC Workshop

A Review of the Non-Fungible Tokens (NFT): Challenges and Opportunities

Mwrwan Abubakar[1]([✉]), Nilupulee A. Gunathilake[1], William J. Buchanan[1], and Brian O'Reilly[2]

[1] Blockpass Identity Lab (BIL), School of Computing, Engineering and the Built Environment, Edinburgh Napier University, Edinburgh, UK
{m.abubakar,n.gunathilake,b.buchanan}@napier.ac.uk
[2] TreeGreen Ltd. trading as EGG Lighting, Glasgow, UK
brian@egglighting.com

Abstract. Non-Fungible Token (NFT) is an emerging blockchain-based technology. These tokens can represent digital assets, as it has proof of ownership built in. NFTs have the potential to hugely influence both the decentralised markets that exist now and the commercial possibilities that will arise in the future. While there is a wealth of information about NFTs accessible, NFTs are still in an early stage, and some potential obstacles need to be properly addressed. Therefore, in this study, we aim to present a comprehensive review of NFTs and an in-depth study of their underlying fundamental technologies, the current state of their technology roadmap and the potential they present. The paper focuses on the most significant obstacles that must be overcome to use NFT technology from the points of view of security, confidentiality, ownership, administration and property ownership. By doing so, we want to bring attention to these concerns since they have been noticed. Additionally, we go over some of the solutions that can be put into action to avoid some of the challenges that may appear.

Keywords: Blockchain · Non-Fungible Token (NFT) · Cryptography

1 Introduction

Before blockchain-based technology was widely used, the processes for validating digital asset ownership commodities and, consequently, the means of securing them were vulnerable to manipulation, resulting in substantial losses. This is because fast technology breakthroughs and their expansion come in tandem with greater security problems, especially those related to legitimacy [1]. On the other hand, the development of blockchain and distributed ledger technologies led to the creation of a new kind of token known as Non-Fungible Token (NFT) [2]. These tokens indicate digital assets and have integrated evidence of ownership.

This research is Partially funded by the Scottish Funding Council under SFC Innovation Voucher Scheme Agreement.

Z. Tan et al. (Eds.): BDTA 2023, LNICST 555, pp. 171–190, 2024.
https://doi.org/10.1007/978-3-031-52265-9_12

The fact that each token has a new quality that makes it one of a kind and distinguishable from others has strengthened the safety of resources and enhanced the concept of unique ownership. Figure 1 shows differences among fungible, semi-fungible and non-fungible tokens. As more and more uses for NFTs are discovered, interest in this cutting-edge technology grows and attracts a wider audience. By incorporating a digital certificate of the owner into each token, the non-fungibility and uniqueness of NFTs make it possible to easily determine an asset's owner [3]. While this does not completely solve the issue of validity and counterfeit money, it dramatically reduces its severity and makes it much easier to identify.

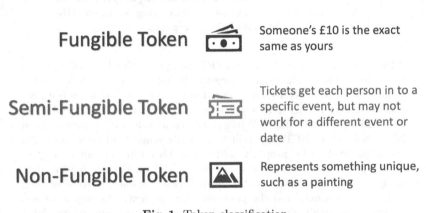

Fig. 1. Token classification

In addition, it solves the issue of consumers being misled into purchasing counterfeit items, such as tickets or artwork. This is a problem that has been affecting businesses for years. It is simple for purchasers to track down the proprietors of the products that are up for sale, which ensures that they are making a legal investment. Moreover, the emergence of NFTs is opening up new possibilities for creative firms, which have struggled to build online marketplaces in an age controlled by internet-based corporations owing to the absence of exclusive ownership. The introduction of NFTs alleviated this difficulty. By associating a single piece of one-of-a-kind data with a single digital asset on a blockchain, NFTs provide enhanced mechanisms for confirming the authenticity and legality of asset ownership. Customers of NFTs are capitalising on the benefits of NFTs to boost the efficiency and safety of selling their own unique works, therefore increasing their potential for financial gain [3].

Although NFT is a relatively new technology, there is a significant amount of enthusiasm behind it in the scientific community. NFT is not restricted to digital assets, and many other use cases have surfaced recently. According to the study in [4] data collected over the day, shows that the NFT market sees an average trading volume of \$4,592,146,914.50, while the cryptocurrency industry as whole notices a volume of \$341,017,000.00. In such a short time, NFT-related solutions have contributed 1.3% of the whole Bitcoin market's liquidity. Unique digital artefacts can bring in thousands of times more money for early investors. As of May 2021, the market for NFT-related products and services had expanded significantly from May 2020. More specifically, there were a total of 25,729 sales, and those sales generated \$34,530,649,86 in U.S. currency. Some have even labelled NFT "the future of digital assets" because of its sudden surge in popularity. In addition to the data presented above, many people have also expressed curiosity about other types of NFTs. They take part in gaming and trading involving NFTs with equal fervour. More than 10,000 collectable punks (6,039 men and 3,840 women) were created thanks to CryptoPunks [5], one of the earliest NFTs developed on Ethereum, which also contributed to the broad adoption of the ERC-721 standard. By making the process of breeding virtual pets into a game in 2017, CryptoKitties [5] informally drew attention to NFTs and introduced them to the market.

1.1 Problem Statement

As a result of the many beneficial results that have arisen from this merging, NFT technology has attracted an extraordinary amount of interest from the scientific and industrial community. Although NFT technologies show promise, they are still in their development, and several possible obstacles must be properly addressed. For example, concerns about users' privacy and security are among the most significant threats posed by the many applications for NFTs already in existence. Since all transactions take place online, any details of such deals are open to abuse by anybody with access to the internet [6]. However, with technologies such as Zero-Knowledge Proof (ZKP), these issues can be solved. ZKP is a cryptographic system that enables one party to demonstrate specified qualities to another without releasing those attributes [7]. One example would be demonstrating the subject's age without giving the real age.

In addition, users' growing interest in cryptocurrencies such as bitcoin and Ethereum has given rise to a variety of new platforms, one of which is web wallets. Even though blockchain technology is the backbone of web wallets, accounts can still be compromised by hackers using means such as phishing, malware, or Distributed Denial of Service (DDoS) attacks. For this reason, it is suggested that collectors and traders who retain significant quantities of NFTs utilise more than simply an online wallet to store their assets. The most reliable methods of keeping your bitcoin secure in the long run are hardware wallets like Trezor [8] that guarantee the encryption keys never leave the device. Increasing the number of people using these wallets might lessen the likelihood of security breaches and hacking attempts. Binance and Coinbase are two types of non-browser wallets. These services have advanced security teams and support Two-Factor Authentication (2FA) [8].

1.2 Our Contribution

Although a wealth of information regarding NFTs is readily available, the NFT technologies are in a very early stage and some potential obstacles need to be properly addressed. Throw this study we provided a comprehensive review of NFT and their underlying foundational technologies, with the intention of enhancing understanding and awareness of this emerging technological innovation. Our main contribution to this paper can be summarised as follow:

- Provided in-depth study of NFTs and their fundamental components, the current state of their technological roadmap, and the potential they present.
- Analysis of the business cases for tokenization and discussed various markets for purchasing and selling NFTs in various industries.
- Analysis of the most significant obstacles that must be overcome to use NFT technology and outline the existing technical and business risks involved in the tokenization process and discussed some solutions that are now available.
- Finally, provided an investigation into the possible security concerns, and suggested some defensive measures that are necessary to solve these concerns.

The remainder of this paper is organised as follows. We first started with a background overview of blockchain technology in Sect. 2. Then in Sect. 3, we provided an in-depth study of the NFT and its fundamental components, protocols and standards, discussed various markets of the NFTs, and discussed its desired properties. In Sect. 4, we discussed the NFT challenges and summarised the most significant obstacles that need to be overcome. Section 5, presented a security analysis of the NFT technology and investigated the possible security concerns and suggested some defensive measures that are necessary to solve these concerns. Finally, we concluded the paper in Sect. 6.

2   Background Overview of Blockchain Technology

Blockchain is a decentralised digital ledger that preserves all of the transactions that take place across the blockchain network. Because it is distributed, it does not need a centralised authority to perform its functions. In 2008, [9] Nakamoto made the first suggestion that would become known as blockchain technology. Transaction process in blockchain is as in Fig. 2. The term 'blockchain' refers to a decentralised database that stores a list of data records and keeps these records connected and secure via cryptographic protocols. The Byzantine problem has been there for a long time, but blockchain technology has found a solution. This solution has been agreed upon by a broad network of players who cannot be trusted. Once the majority of the distributed nodes have validated the data being shared on the blockchain, the data becomes immutable. This is because any modifications made to the data that is being stored would render all future data invalid.

Nodes are an essential component of the blockchain system. They are used to represent customers' personal computers or other devices that have associated with the blockchain network. Nodes have been used to accomplish various activities, including mining, routing and acting as a wallet by holding a copy of the blockchain data. Additionally, the nodes' responsibility is to locate the peers

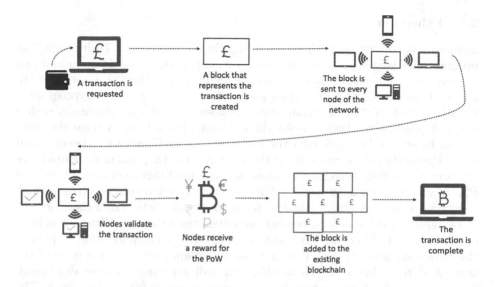

Fig. 2. Transcation process in blockchain

directly linked to the blockchain network. In addition to this, it is the responsibility of each node to establish and keep a relationship with its peers that have been found [9]. Every single node contributes to verifying transactions and spreading them further. Additionally, nodes function as a distributed network by keeping copies of the blockchain, which includes details about all the activities that have been preserved in the blockchain system, thereby displacing the need for centralised servers to store the transaction data in favour of a decentralised and distributed ledger. In conclusion, nodes have the potential to also act as miners, a role in which they might be rewarded with cryptocurrency for their efforts in verifying and confirming previous transactions carried out over the blockchain [9].

Cryptographic codes are used to permanently record blockchain transactions, and the network can verify the integrity of individual blocks. This idea guarantees that the blockchain will remain secure. Because of the one-of-a-kind nature of the hash values, it is possible to identify fraudulent activity since any changes made to a block in the chain instantly result in a new hash value. All transactions may be examined in full transparency thanks to the decentralised nature of the blockchain's structure [9]. However, the technology can be used in many scenarios and is the subject of study in various disciplines. As a result, the idea has piqued the interest of other efforts coming from various sectors, such as banking, public and welfare care, privacy and security smart contracts and the Internet of Things (IoT). Despite this, the financial sector is generally considered the most significant user. It seems that the reason for this is that it is often impossible to determine an item's actual owner.

2.1 Ethereum

Ethereum is a distributed ledger technology that incorporates a Turing-complete programming language. A configurable ownership model, transaction format and state transition mechanisms are all user-definable due to their abstract layer. To this end, decentralised applications are used, which are a set of cryptographic rules executed only when certain conditions are met [10]. Furthermore, such a network provides the backbone for the Ethereum blockchain's virtual currency, Ether. Ether can be considered the fuel that powers Ethereum's decentralised apps. Payments can be made using this currency to other accounts or machines performing a certain activity. Therefore, you can use Ether to make conventional P2P payments, launch decentralised applications, create tokens and create smart contracts. Ether can also be used to build smart contracts. The Ethereum network agrees on the state of a central computer (the Ethereum Virtual Machine, or EVM) in all Ethereum blockchain systems. Every computer that is part of the Ethereum network, also known as an Ethereum node, stores a copy of the current state of this particular machine. In addition, every member can broadcast a request for this machine to carry out any computation they want. The calculation is checked, validated and executed by other participants in the network whenever a request of this kind is broadcast. Because of this execution, the EVM will enter a new state, which will then be committed and broadcast over the whole network [10].

2.2 Smart Contract

Nick Szabo was the first person to use this terminology, 'smart contracts', which was coined in 1994 [11], before using the decentralised ledger to host them. This was proposed as an idea for a technology that could monitor and ensure compliance with the conditions of an agreement that had been negotiated online. Smart contracts have been used to facilitate the movement of Bitcoin from one user to another when specific requirements are met [9]. However, this is restricted to the realm of digital money. On the other hand, Ethereum treats the smart contract as an item in its own right, complete with a separate account and a unique address. In addition to facilitating communication between contracts, this account may also be used to store data, receive digital currency and make payments. Ethereum replaced the difficult language used by Bitcoin with a language known as solidity, which is a Turing complete language. This change was made so that developers could create their own smart contracts [10]. Smart contracts allow unknown parties and decentralised players to carry out fair trades without needing a trustworthy third party. In addition, they provide a uniform mechanism that can be used to construct apps for various business sectors. Every person involved can see the states that include the requirements and directions, guaranteeing that everyone can see how the rules are followed. To guarantee the sequence-dependent execution of their procedures, most NFT solutions [12] rely on blockchain platforms that are based on smart contracts.

3 Non-Fungible Token (NFT)

NFT is an abbreviation for 'Non-Fungible Tokens', which refers to digital assets reflective of physical and digital creative labour or Intellectual Property (IP). Some examples of NFT include gifs, music, games, digital art, video clips, and other media types. Because each token in an NFT system cannot be exchanged for another token, the term 'nonfungible' refers to the fact that each token is an independent entity that stands in for a particular thing. The NFTs are a component of blockchains in general and the Ethereum blockchain in particular. However, they are distinct from Ethereum cryptocurrencies, which are fungible, meaning that they may be traded for other assets of a similar kind. This is because NFT is an Ethereum smart contract-based coin. It was first suggested in Ethereum Improvement Proposals (EIP)-721 [13], and further work was carried out in EIP-1155 [14].

NFT is not the same as other cryptocurrencies similar to Bitcoin in terms of the features built into it. Bitcoin is a conventional coin, meaning that all of the coins are comparable and cannot be differentiated from one another. In comparison, NFT cannot be imitated and traded, making it an ideal choice for describing something or someone in a unique way. A developer may use NFTs on digital currencies to prove the presence of digital goods like movies, photos, artwork, theater tickets, and other tangible assets. These digital assets can take the shape of movies, images, art, etc. Applications in NFT can be recognised as indicated in Fig. 3. Additionally, the inventor can earn royalties whenever a successful deal occurs on any NFT marketplace or via peer-to-peer trading. Because of its full-history commodities, deep volatility, and simple compatibility, NFT can be an efficient mechanism for preserving IP. This is because NFT is a distributed ledger that many parties can use. In this section, we will investigate the possibilities presented by NFTs and talk about a few common areas that can profit from using NFTs [4].

3.1 Protecting Digital Collectibles

Digital assets may include everything from collectibles and wine to digital photos and movies, digital property investment, domain names, and even jewels and crypto passports. For our example today, let us go to the artistic world. Traditional artists are limited in where they may show their work. Due to inattention, the prices do not fairly reflect the value of the works. Unfortunately, platforms and advertisements have eaten into their profits from sharing their work online. NFTs are liable for creating digital copies of their work that incorporate credentials. Artists are not required to sign up for ownership of their work or material for distribution services. The financial benefits to them are substantial. Artists seldom stand to gain royalties on later sales of their works [15]. An NFT may be designed such that the artist receives a predetermined royalty payment whenever an NFT based on his digital work is sold, such as SuperRare [16], MakersPlace [17], VIV3 [18]. These platforms might be used to efficiently manage and secure digital artworks. Furthermore, numerous sites like Mintable [19] and Mintbase

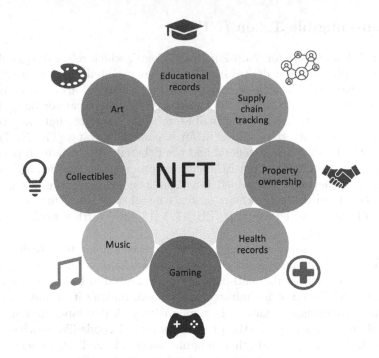

Fig. 3. NFT applications

[20] have made it easy for ordinary people to create their own NFT works by providing them with pre-made templates and other templates and tools to work from.

3.2   Boosting Gaming Industry

There are many unrealised possibilities for NFT in the gaming industry. Numerous past crypto-themed video games have been published, including CryptpoKitties [21], Cryptocats [22], CryptoPunks [23], Meebits [24], etc. A novel and engaging feature of these games is the 'breeding' system. Users have the option of taking care of their own pets and spending considerable time in the breeding of new springs. They may even buy rare or limited edition digital pets to flip for a profit. With the bonus, many investors are eager to get in on the action, which has boosted NFTs' appeal. The NFT serves many fascinating functions, like establishing a chain of titles for virtual things in games and encouraging the economic marking of ecological hotspots. Producers of games and players alike stand to gain from such endeavours. Game developers who are also NFT publishers of features, such as guns and skins may be eligible for royalties on every instance of their creations being resold on the international market. In this case, everyone becomes victorious. The gamers may obtain unique and personalised gaming gear. Because of this, a business model will emerge that is mutually beneficial for NFT players and developers. After that, the blockchain community further broadens NFTs to include many additional forms of digital assets.

3.3 Tokenised Stock

Tokenised stocks are essentially the same as shares of stock in an openly listed firm, such as those traded on the Nasdaq or the S&P 500. These indexes measure the performance of 500 of the largest publicly traded companies in the United States. On the other hand, tokenised equities are represented by digital tokens rather than traditional stock certificates. When an investor purchases a conventional stock on an exchange or during an Initial Public Offering (IPO), their shares will normally appear in their brokerage account shortly after the transaction is completed. The methodology for tokenised equities is the same, with one significant modification being required. Since the shares are based on a blockchain, they can be purchased and traded on a cryptocurrency exchange just like any other cryptocurrency. When generating a tokenised stock, the procedure often involves the participation of a custodian and an investing institution. The institution purchases the underlying stock, which is deposited with the custodian. Tokens are distributed over a blockchain and are denominated in shares held in reserve by the custodian. The value of the underlying shares is used to determine the price of each token. After that, the tokens might be posted on a crypto exchange, where they would function similarly to other cryptocurrencies in terms of being able to be purchased and exchanged. Those who own stock tokens are granted the same exposure to the underlying stock as if they held the shares themselves, including the right to receive dividend payments if appropriate. However, they do not hold any shares in the company. They own an asset that is a derivative backed by real company shares [25].

To raise cash, which is the primary objective of the majority of firms, tokenising equity is being done by many businesses for the same reason that they issue shares of stock. Instead of issuing extra shares or going public via the more conventional route of having an IPO, there might be significant benefits to be gained by releasing digital tokens to increase a company's capital [26]. Tokenised equity is putting the securities and exchange regularities in a position where it has no choice but to regulate cryptocurrencies like Bitcoin and others. However, the federal government has been somewhat slow to decide how or if they want to handle Bitcoin regulations and other cryptocurrencies. Tokens are considered securities since they have the same qualities and functions as stocks and are thus issued by firms in place of shares. This indicates they must register with the appropriate authorities and submit the required paperwork. Because of this, Security Token Offerings (STOs) came into existence. STOs are comparable to Initial Coin Offerings (ICOs), which are essentially the same as ICOs except for the additional stipulation that the company that issues the tokens admits that the token symbolises fairness and is, therefore, security [26].

3.4   Protocols

The development of an NFT calls for using an underlying distributed ledger to keep records and the execution of tradable transactions across a peer-to-peer network. In most of its coverage, this paper considers the distributed ledger to be a specialised database that holds NFT data. In particular, we are working on the assumption that the ledger has the qualities of fundamental security, integrity, and accessibility. In addition to this, two other responsibilities make up an NFT system. These are the NFT owner and the NFT buyer. The step-by-step procedure can be found below:

- **NFT digitisation**: The owner of an NFT makes sure that all of the details included in the lease, including the title and description, are correct. After that, he or she converts the raw data into the appropriate digital format using a computer.
- **NFT store**: An owner of NFTs often places raw information in a database that is not part of the blockchain. It is important to note that they are permitted to save the raw data inside of a blockchain, although this procedure requires a significant amount of gas.
- **NFT signing**: A transaction is signed by the NFT owner and sent to a smart contract along with a hash of the NFT data.
- **NFT mint and trade**: Once the smart contract has received the transactions with the NFT data, the minting and trading procedure may commence. The reasoning behind the Token Standards is the primary mechanism that supports NFTs.
- **NFT confirmation**: The minting process is considered finished after verifying that the transaction took place. With this method, NFTs will indefinitely connect to a specific blockchain address, which will prove their persistence.

Each block in a blockchain-based system has a certain amount of storage space available. When the storage space in one block is exceeded, more transactions will be added to a subsequent block connected to the initial data block [27]. In the end, all interconnected bricks have produced a history that covers a lengthy period of time and is unchangeable. The NFT system may be considered an application that uses blockchain technology. In order to activate the smart contract, a fresh transaction has to be sent each time an NFT is created or sold. Following the confirmation of the transaction, the information about the NFT and the ownership information is appended to a new block. This operation ensures that the history of the NFT is not altered and that ownership is maintained.

3.5   Standards

ERC-20. Tokens are increasingly being created using the ERC-20 [28] standard. It introduces the concept of fungible tokens that may be built atop Ethereum if certain requirements are fulfilled. Tokens are made interchangeable because of the standard (in terms of type and value). An arbitrary token will always have the same value as each and every other token. This has contributed to the mania around ICOs since 2015 and continues to do so today. This is how many public chains and several blockchain-based DApps get enough initial investment for their projects.

ERC-721. ERC-721 [29] introduces a new token standard that is not interchangeable with existing tokens. This token type is distinct from those already in circulation. To be more specific, each NFT has a contract address and a corresponding uint256 variable called tokenId that provide a globally unique identifier. Additionally, the tokenId could be entered into a system to generate random, one-of-a-kind identifiers, like zombie or cartoon figure images.

ERC-1155. To further increase the description of both fungible and non-fungible tokens, there is a specification described as ERC-1155 (multi-token standard) [14]. A graphical user interface is provided regardless of the number of tokens being represented. According to the previous norms, each tokenId in contact may only include a single token type. With ERC-20, for instance, any currency type may be used with a dedicated smart contract. The ERC-721 standard also centralises the distribution of NFTs in a single contract with standard parameters. ERC-1155, on the other hand, is an extension of the capabilities of tokenId, and each of its components may separately represent a distinct adjustable token type. Metadata, lock times, dates, supplies, and other individualised qualities may all be stored in this field. We have provided an image for your consideration to further illustrate the aforementioned structural distinctions between the two.

3.6 Desired Properties

NFT schemes are fundamentally decentralised applications, and as a result, they use the advantages and features provided by the public ledgers upon which they are built. The following is a summary of the most important characteristics:

- **Verifiability**: The NFT, together with the token information and ownership, may be independently confirmed by the public.
- **Transparent execution**: All transactions involving NFTs, from creation through exchange and purchase, are transparent.
- **Availability**: There is never an outage in the NFT system. On the other hand, all tokens and NFTs issued are always open for purchase and sale.
- **Tamper resistance**: Once a deal has been validated, the associated NFT metadata and trade records are unchangeable.
- **Usability**: The most recent ownership information is displayed simply and easily on each NFT.
- **Atomicity**: Trading NFTs can be done in a single transaction that is simultaneous, consistent, segregated, and permanent. The NFTs can share the same execution state.
- **Tradability**: Every non-fiat currency and the things that correspond to it may be traded and exchanged with complete freedom.

4   NFT Challenges

As with any developing technology, many hurdles must be cleared before the NFT, as mentioned above, applications may be developed. We address both the system-level concerns generated by blockchain-based platforms and human elements such as governance, legislation, and society as we explore some common obstacles from accessibility, safety, democratic accountability, and extensibility [6].

4.1   Usability Challenges

Testing a product or design for usability is evaluating how well it performs for the intended audience in terms of their time, effort, and overall happiness. Most NFT techniques are developed using Ethereum as their base layer. As a result, it should not surprise that the primary issues with Ethereum were inherited. In this article, we will explore two significant difficulties that directly affect the user's experience.

4.2   Slow Confirmation

The transactions related to NFTs are often sent to the smart contract to accomplish dependable and transparent administration (such as mining, selling, and exchange). Current NFT systems, on the other hand, are inextricably linked to the public blockchains on which they are based, which causes them to have poor efficiency. Bitcoin reaches merely 7 Transactions Per Second (TPS) [30] while Ethereum does only 30 TPS. This ultimately leads to the validation of NFTs taking an incredibly long time. In order to resolve this problem, either the topology of the blockchain has to be redesigned, the structure needs to be optimised [31], or the consensus procedures need to be improved [32].

4.3   High Gas-Prices

When it comes to the minting of NFTs at a big scale, which entails uploading the information to the blockchain network, high gas costs have become a serious concern for NFT markets. This is particularly true when gas prices are taken into consideration. Because smart processing contracts require computing resources and storage space, the fees associated with NFT-related transactions are always higher than those associated with simpler transfer operations. As of the time, this article was written, mining one NFT coin may cost up to $150 USD or more [33]. The expense of doing a simple NFT trade might range from $60 USD to $100 USD for each transaction. The widespread adoption of this technology is severely hampered by the high costs associated with its complicated operations and heavy congestion.

4.4   Data Inaccessibility

A cryptographic "hash" is used in the more popular NFT projects. To reduce the amount of gas needed, the identifier, which will serve in place of a copy of the file, will be tagged with the token before being added to the blockchain. Since the original file might be deleted or corrupted, this raises scepticism about the NFT among users. Many NFT projects have combined their infrastructure with a dedicated file-sharing platform such as IPFS [34]. If users know an IPFS address and are connected to the IPFS network, they may access the content in inquiry. This integration allows users to discover content more easily.

Nevertheless, these kinds of systems are unavoidable. When users "upload" their files to the server, When you transfer metadata to IPFS nodes, there is no assurance that the data will be duplicated across all nodes. The data might become inaccessible if a property is kept on IPFS and that node loses network connectivity. DECRYPT.IO and CHECKMYNFT.COM have identified and reported this problem. There is also the possibility that an NFT may refer to an incorrect file address. In such a situation, it would be difficult for a user to demonstrate that they are the rightful owner of the NFT. It is risky to build an NFT system around storage provided by an external system because of the potential for data loss [35].

4.5   Anonymity and Privacy

Currently, there is a lack of research on the security and confidentiality of NFTs. The Ethereum network, upon which most accounting entries of NFTs are conducted, provides only pseudo-anonymity rather than full invisibility or privacy. Users can hide some facets of their identity, despite the fact that the general public is informed of the links between their real names and their associated email addresses. Users' activity associated with the exposed address may be seen in any other case [36]. Due to the complexity of the cryptographic primitives and confidentiality requirements, existing privacy-preserving methods, such as ring signatures, encryption algorithm, zero-knowledge verification, and multi-party computation have been introduced as a solution for privacy issues in NFTs [37]. Reducing the high cost of computing is essential for implementing privacy-promised methods in blockchain-based systems as in other distributed ledgers. In addition, the information collected from users is the primary focus of any system. However, there is always a chance that the data (kept off-chain but related to tags on-chain) will become unconnected or misused.

4.6   Governance Consideration

NFTs, much like the scenarios that most cryptocurrencies find themselves in, are met with obstacles such as stringent management from the governance. On the other hand, figuring out how to appropriately manage this young technology and the market it corresponds to is another difficulty. Two concerns that are common on both sides are discussed below.

Legal Dilemmas. In many fields, including law and politics, NFTs confront obstacles. Potential danger zones include commodity markets, foreign exchange, Know Your Customer (KYC) information, and more. It is necessary to be thoroughly aware of the regulatory oversight and problems linked with the issue before moving further into the NFT tracks. Some countries, like China and India, may have strict regulations on the buying and selling of NFTs and cryptocurrencies. In order to successfully exchange, trade, sell, or purchase NFTs, one must first overcome the hurdles management provides. In accordance with the law, users are only permitted to engage in derivatives trading on regulated exchanges (like those for stocks and commodities), or they must trade tokens directly with another individual [38]. Many nations, such as Malta and France, are working on enacting appropriate regulations to control the market for digital assets and related services [39]. In other places, problems are handled using the laws already in place. They demand that purchasers adhere to conditions that are difficult to understand and are often even contradictory. This means that thorough research must be conducted before putting any real money into NFTs.

Property Taxation Concerns. According to the regulations now in place, goods associated with IP, such as books, artworks, and domain names, among other things are considered taxable. Contrarily, this does not include applicable to NFT-based transactions. Even while only a small number of countries, such as the US (via the Internal Revenue Service, or known as IRS), tax cryptocurrency as ownership, the vast majority of governments and regions throughout the world have not yet pondered doing so; this might lead to a surge in the amount of fraudulent financial activities disguised as NFT trading. Many governments worldwide have expressed an interest in determining consistent tax consequences for the distribution of NFTs [40]. In particular, tax liabilities arising from investment income on NFT investments must be the responsibility of the relevant individuals. It is also necessary to impose taxes on exchanges of NFT for NFT, NFT for IP, and Ether for NFT (or vice versa). Also, high-yield commodities, such as rare books and art, need a more lenient tax rate. Following such in-depth deliberation, it has been suggested that NFT-related transactions seek out the advice of a specialised tax department for additional help.

4.7   Intellectual Property (IP) Right

This includes information regarding IP to help compensate for the next major factor on the list of dangers and roadblocks posed by NFTs. It is essential to analyse a person's ownership rights regarding a particular NFT. Before completing a purchase, it is essential to ascertain whether or not the vendor holds the NFT in question. There have been documented cases of individuals photographing non-circulating tax receipts (NFTs) or minting replicas of NFTs. Therefore, when an NFT is acquired, the purchaser receives the rights to use it but not the rights to its IP. The terms and conditions necessary to acquire ownership of an NFT are stored in the metadata of the underlying smart contract [41].

It should come as no surprise that applications for NFT can provide significant income possibilities. They are, nevertheless, confronted with a great number of challenges. NFTs are experiencing a big market hype bubble due to the support they receive from notable public figures. The fact that the volume of trading in NFTs has increased more than once in only one year indicates that they have a lot of untapped potential. The exchange of NFTs, on the other hand, is not subject to any particular regulations or guidelines.

5 Security Analysis

The blockchain, storage, and web application that make up an NFT system are the three components that make up a combined technology known as an NFT system. It is difficult to do a security assessment on the NFT system because each component can become an attacking interface, which leaves the whole system very exposed to the attacker. As a result, we have chosen to implement the threat and risk assessment, which considers all elements of a system's security, including its authenticity, integrity, non-reliability, availability, and access control. We do an investigation into the possible security concerns, and we suggest a few of the defensive measures that are necessary to solve these concerns.

5.1 Cybersecurity

The development of the digital world and an increase in the volume of NFTs transactions have led to a major rise in the danger of cybercrime and fraudulent activity. Criminals with malicious intent can impersonate well-known NFT tokens and sell fake NFTs using their identities. Theft of copyright, piracy of popular NFTs, and the distribution of free NFTs are some of the other key dangers and difficulties that NFT tokens face in terms of cybersecurity and fraud. The recent instances of hackers stealing NFTs from users of Nifty Gateway are one of the most current illustrations of the cybersecurity risk associated with NFTs [36]. Although the development of technology makes it possible to conduct transactions involving digital assets with increased efficacy but also presents risks, most notably in the cyber security domain.

5.2 Spoofing

Spoofing is the capacity to pretend to be something else, such as another user or machine on the system. A hostile attacker might exploit identification flaws or steal a user's private key while minting or selling interactions with NFTs, allowing the attacker to unlawfully transfer ownership of the NFTs. Because of this, we strongly advise establishing a formal verification for the NFT smart contract and using a cold wallet to prevent private key information leaks.

5.3   Tampering

The term 'tampering' refers to the act of deliberately modifying NFT data, which is a violation of the system's integrity. Assume that the blockchain is a secure public transaction ledger and that the hash method is both preimage and second preimage resistant. Once a transaction has been validated, the metadata and possession of NFTs cannot be deliberately altered beyond that point. Nevertheless, the data held outside of the blockchain is susceptible to manipulation. When trading or exchanging NFT-related assets, we strongly advise our customers to give the original data in addition to the hash data to the NFT buyer. This is because the hash data is used to verify the authenticity of the original data [42].

5.4   Smart Contracts Security

From the perspective of the NFT environment, one of the most pressing challenges is creating and protecting smart contracts. Poly Network, a well-known protocol for Decentralised Finance (DeFi) that allows cross-chain interoperability, was recently the victim of an attack by hackers. The theft of almost $600 million worth of NFTs draws attention to severe problems in the security of smart contracts [43]. One of the primary factors that might result in weaknesses in smart contracts is the absence of certain security standards that have been validated throughout the industry. This issue pertains to the Solidity programming language. Because both the transactions and the code in a smart contract are immutable, the developers must make certain that both the code and each transaction are secure. On the other hand, there are no clearly established standard methods for constructing smart contracts that programmers should adhere to across all projects. Developers do not have access to the tools that would simplify the process of creating, testing, verifying, and auditing smart contracts. More significantly, developers do not have access to the tools that would allow them to work together.

5.5   Repudiation

The term "non-repudiation" refers to the scenario in which a statement's creator cannot refute it. Those involved in blockchain transactions cannot deny the transaction's legitimacy or their behaviour. A non-repudiation service aims to ensure the authenticity of transmitted data by amassing and delivering irrefutable proof of message delivery. Therefore, it is impossible to refute that one user sent NFT to another [44]. Cryptography, such as digital signatures, is used to accomplish nonrepudiation, which also includes services for authentication, auditing, and recording. Digital signatures in blockchain ensure that a party cannot subsequently dispute delivering information or repudiate the authenticity of its signature. A malicious attacker might intercept the hash data or cause it to bind with the attacker's address. Since a multi-signature contract requires confirmation from more than one party before it can legally bind, we think it can help alleviate some of the severity of the problem. In addition, the attackers can easily take advantage of the connection between the hash and the transaction. As a result, we advise that developers of NFTs employ privacy-preserving smart contracts rather than standard smart contracts to safeguard their users' personal information.

5.6 DoS

DoS attacks breach the availability of the NFT service and bring it to a halt, although unauthorised users may use it. To users' great relief, blockchain technology ensures that their transactions will always be highly available. Users authorised to do so may access the necessary information whenever required, and there will be no loss of data resources as a result of unintended mistakes. DoS attacks may also be launched against non-blockchain-based resources, such as centralised web apps or raw data, which can disrupt NFT operations. The decentralised autonomous organisation and parity wallet hacks of 2016 and 2017, respectively, demonstrated the critical flaws in Ethereum smart contracts. Ethereum's fundamental flaws were uncovered in the 2016 Decentralised Autonomous Organisation (DAO) and 2017 parity wallet hacks. The approach given in [45] employs two Artificial Intelligence (AI) techniques-Random Forest (RF) and XGBoost that grant complete independence to decision-making skills within the proposed security framework. Second, an interplanetary file system is proposed enabling data load balancing and distributed file storage of IoT data. They also suggested a distributed system based on cloud and fog computing for monitoring smart contracts for DDoS attacks. The detection system's efficacy is measured against a real-world IoT dataset called BoT-IoT. As smart contracts control the distribution of sales permits in the NFT system. Once again, a weak smart contract's design can cause NFTs to lose their desirable qualities. Another technique was described in [46] as a potential sort of attack that can be launched against the memory pools (mempools) of blockchain-based cryptocurrencies. This study examined the implications of such an assault on the Bitcoin mempool on the transaction fees paid by normal users. Additionally, the study offered methods to prevent such an assault. The countermeasures consist of fee-based as well as age-based designs that maximise the size of the mempool and assist in mitigating the consequences of DDoS attacks. Then, they simulated their designs and assessed their utility under various attack conditions. The findings can be applied to other blockchain-based apps that cache network events using memory pools.

6 Conclusion

This study provided a comprehensive review of NFTs and an in-depth study of their underlying fundamental technologies, illustrated their technical framework, and unique characteristics, and analysed the business cases, and the possible roadblocks that may arise. The paper started with a background on blockchain technology and its decentralised structures, the Ethereum blockchain and discussed the role of smart contracts in the development of tokenization. In addition, the paper provided an in-depth study of the NFT and its fundamental components, protocols and standards, discussed various markets of the NFTs, and discussed its desired properties. However, the ever-increasing prevalence of the usage of NFTs is accompanied by many obstacles. So, therefore, the paper outlined the existing technical and business risks involved in the tokenization process, discussed the NFT challenges and summarised the most significant obstacles that need to be overcome, such as the absence of industry-wide security standards for smart contracts, the lack of clarity about intellectual property rights, the potential for fraud as a result of artist impersonation, transparency that breaches the user's security and privacy, and the severe negative impacts on the environment caused by the high amount of energy consumption. The paper goes further and presented a security analysis of the NFT technology and investigated the possible security concerns and suggested some defensive measures that are necessary to solve these concerns. Finally, we hope that the findings of this study provide a point of reference and motivation for future research efforts in this domain.

References

1. Catalini, C., Gans, J.S.: Some simple economics of the blockchain. Commun. ACM **63**(7), 80–90 (2020)
2. Steinwold, A.: The History of Non-Fungible Tokens (NFTs) (2019). Retrieved from Medium: https://medium.com/@Andrew.Steinwold/the-history-of-non-fungible-tokens-nftsf362ca57ae10
3. Raman, R., Raj, B.E.: The world of NFTs (non-fungible tokens): the future of blockchain and asset ownership. In: Enabling Blockchain Technology for Secure Networking and Communications, pp. 89–108. IGI Global (2021)
4. Wang, Q., Li, R., Wang, Q., Chen, S.: Non-fungible token (NFT): overview, evaluation, opportunities and challenges. arXiv preprint arXiv:2105.07447 (2021)
5. Plachimowicz, E., Wójcik, P.: What makes Punks worthy? Valuation of Non-Fungible Tokens based on the CryptoPunks collection using the hedonic pricing method. No. 2022–27 (2022)
6. Rehman, W., e Zainab, H., Imran, J., Bawany, N.Z.: NFTs: applications and challenges. In: 2021 22nd International Arab Conference on Information Technology (ACIT), pp. 1–7. IEEE (2021)
7. Hasan, J.: Overview and Applications of Zero Knowledge Proof (ZKP). Nanjing University of Posts and Telecommunications, Nanjing (2019)
8. Khan, A.G., et al.: Security of cryptocurrency using hardware wallet and QR code. In: 2019 International Conference on Innovative Computing (ICIC). IEEE (2019)
9. Nakamoto, S., Bitcoin, A.: A peer-to-peer electronic cash system (2008). Bitcoin https://bitcoin.org/bitcoin.pdf4.2
10. Buterin, V.: A next-generation smart contract and decentralized application platform 2014 (2019). https://github.com/ethereum/wiki/wiki/White-Paper
11. Szabo, N.: Smart Contracts (1994). https://www.fon.hum.uva.nl/rob/Courses/InformationInSpeech/CDROM/Literature/LOTwinterschool2006/szabo.best.vwh.net/smart.contracts.html

12. Arora, A., Kanisk, K.S.: Smart Contracts and NFTs: non-fungible tokens as a core component of blockchain to be used as collectibles. In: Khanna, K., Estrela, V.V., Rodrigues, J.J.P.C. (eds.) Cyber Security and Digital Forensics. LNDECT, vol. 73, pp. 401–422. Springer, Singapore (2022). https://doi.org/10.1007/978-981-16-3961-6_34

13. Entriken, W., Shirley, D., Evans, J., Sachs, N.: EIP-721: ERC-721 non-fungible token standard. Ethereum Improvement Proposals 721 (2018)

14. Radomski, W., Cooke, A., Castonguay, P., Therien, J., Binet, E., Sandford, R.: EIP 1155: ERC-1155 multi token standard. Ethereum, Standard (2018)

15. Ali, M., Bagui, S.: Introduction to NFTs: the future of digital collectibles. Int. J. Adv. Comput. Sci. Appl. **12**(10), 50–56 (2021)

16. Tran, K.C.: What is SuperRare? 26 March 2020. https://decrypt.co/resources/what-is-superrare-3-minute-guide-explained-art-collectible

17. Makersplace: Rare, Authentic & Curated Digital Art. https://makersplace.com/

18. VIV3: WELCOME TO VIV3 - Explore the Marketspace. https://viv3.com/

19. Mintable: MoonPay — MINTABLE - Revolutionizing WEB3 Payments. https://mintable.app/

20. Mintbase: What can I do with Mintbase? https://docs.mintbase.io/

21. CryptoKitties: CryptoKitties. https://www.cryptokitties.co/

22. CryptoCat NFT: CRYPTOCATS, Collectible 8-bit Cats on Ethereum Blockchain. https://cryptocats.thetwentysix.io/

23. CryptoPunks V1. https://v1punks.io/. Accessed 02 Mar 2023

24. Larva Labs: What are the Meebits? https://meebits.app/. Accessed 02 Mar 2023

25. Bhandarkar, V.V., Bhandarkar, A.A., Shiva, A.: Digital stocks using blockchain technology the possible future of stocks? Int. J. Manage. (IJM) **10**(3) (2019)

26. Roth, J., Schär, F., Schöpfer, A.: The Tokenization of assets: using blockchains for equity crowdfunding. In: Theories of Change: Change Leadership Tools, Models and Applications for Investing in Sustainable Development, pp. 329–350 (2021)

27. Antonopoulos, A.M.: Mastering Bitcoin: Unlocking Digital Cryptocurrencies. O'Reilly Media, Inc., Sebastopol (2014)

28. Vogelsteller, F., Buterin, V.: ERC-20 token standard (2015). https://github.com/ethereum/EIPs/blob/master/EIPS/eip-20-token-standard.md (2018)

29. Entriken, W., Shirley, D., Evans, J., Sachs, N.: ERC-721 non-fungible token standard (2018). Ethereum Foundation-https://eips.ethereum.org/EIPS/eip-721

30. Croman, K., et al.: On scaling decentralized blockchains. In: Clark, J., Meiklejohn, S., Ryan, P.Y.A., Wallach, D., Brenner, M., Rohloff, K. (eds.) FC 2016. LNCS, vol. 9604, pp. 106–125. Springer, Heidelberg (2016). https://doi.org/10.1007/978-3-662-53357-4_8

31. Abubakar, M., Jarocheh, Z., Al-Dubai, A., Liu, X.: A survey on the integration of blockchain and IoT: challenges and opportunities. In: Jiang, R., et al. (eds.) Big Data Privacy and Security in Smart Cities. Advanced Sciences and Technologies for Security Applications, pp. 197–221. Springer, Cham (2022). https://doi.org/10.1007/978-3-031-04424-3_11

32. Abubakar, M., Jaroucheh, Z., Al-Dubai, A., Buchanan, B.: PoNW: a secure and scalable proof-of-notarized-work based consensus mechanism. In: Proceedings of the 2020 4th International Conference on Vision, Image and Signal Processing, pp. 1–8 (2020)

33. Baldwin, A.: How Much Does It Cost to Mint an NFT? The Answer (2022). https://www.cryptopolitan.com/how-much-does-nft-minting-cost/

34. Ossa, P.: Evaluating decentralized storage services for storing NFT related data (2021)

35. Ali, O., Momin, M., Shrestha, A., Das, R., Alhajj, F., Dwivedi, Y.K.: A review of the key challenges of non-fungible tokens. Technol. Forecast. Soc. Chang. **187**, 122248 (2023)
36. Das, D., Bose, P., Ruaro, N., Kruegel, C., Vigna, G.: Understanding security issues in the NFT ecosystem. In: Proceedings of the 2022 ACM SIGSAC Conference on Computer and Communications Security, pp. 667–681 (2022)
37. Salleras, X., Rovira, S., Daza, V.: FORT: right-proving and attribute-blinding self-sovereign authentication. Mathematics **10**(4), 617 (2022)
38. Uribe, D., Waters, G.: Privacy laws, genomic data and non-fungible tokens. J. Br. Blockchain Assoc. (2020)
39. Blemus, S.: Law and blockchain: a legal perspective on current regulatory trends worldwide. Revue Trimestrielle de Droit Financier (Corporate Finance and Capital Markets Law Review) RTDF 4–2017 (2017)
40. Nguyen, A.Q.: The mysteries of NFT taxation and the problem of crypto asset tax evasion. SMU Sci. Technol. Law Rev. **25**(2), 323 (2022)
41. Okonkwo, I.E.: NFT, copyright and intellectual property commercialization. Int. J. Law Inf. Technol. **29**(4), 296–304 (2021)
42. Kshetri, N.: Scams, frauds, and crimes in the nonfungible token market. Computer **55**(4), 60–64 (2022)
43. Wright, T.: Hackers stole at least $600 M in Poly exploit across three chains (2021)
44. Hasan, H.R., et al.: Incorporating registration, reputation, and incentivization into the NFT ecosystem. IEEE Access **10**, 76416–76433 (2022)
45. Kumar, R., Kumar, P., Tripathi, R., Gupta, G.P., Garg, S., Hassan, M.M.: A distributed intrusion detection system to detect DDoS attacks in blockchain-enabled IoT network. J. Parallel Distrib. Comput. **164**, 55–68 (2022)
46. Saad, M., Njilla, L., Kamhoua, C., Kim, J., Nyang, D., Mohaisen, A.: Mempool optimization for defending against DDoS attacks in PoW-based blockchain systems. In: 2019 IEEE International Conference on Blockchain and Cryptocurrency (ICBC), pp. 285–292. IEEE (2019)

Author Index

© ICST Institute for Computer Sciences, Social Informatics and Telecommunications Engineering 2024
Published by Springer Nature Switzerland AG 2024. All Rights Reserved
Z. Tan et al. (Eds.): BDTA 2023, LNICST 555, pp. 191–192, 2024.
https://doi.org/10.1007/978-3-031-52265-9

Printed in the United States
by Baker & Taylor Publisher Services